Reading and Note Taking Study Guide

WORLD
HISTORY

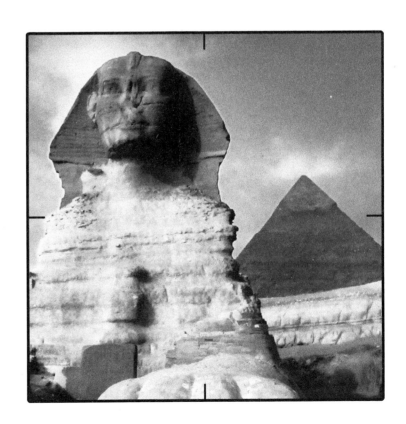

PEARSON

Boston, Massachusetts • Chandler, Arizona • Glenview, Illinois • New York, New York

Acknowledgments

Grateful acknowledgment is made to the following for copyrighted material:

Images:
Cover: GlowImages/Alamy

ISBN-13: 978-0-32-888045-4

ISBN-10:   0-32-888045-0

10   18

Contents

World History

Reading and Note Taking Study Guide

Topic 9
Civilizations of Asia (500–1650)

Topic 10
The Renaissance and Reformation
(1300–1650)

Topic 11
New Global Connections (1415–1796)

Topic 12
Absolutism and Revolution (1550–1850)

Topic 13
The Industrial Revolution (1750–1914)

Topic 14
Nationalism and the Spread of
Democracy (1790–1914)

Topic 15
The Age of Imperialism (1800–1914)

How to Use the *Reading and Note Taking Study Guide*

The **Reading and Note Taking Study Guide** will help you better understand the content of Pearson *World History*. It will also help you develop your note taking, reading, and vocabulary skills. Each study guide consists of three components. The first component focuses on developing a graphic organizer for the material covered by each topic that will help you take notes as you read.

Name _____ Class _____ Date _____

TOPIC 18

Note Taking Study Guide
WORLD WAR II (1930–1945)

Focus Question: How did the Allies turn away from appeasement, respond to Axis aggression, and win World War II?

As you read the Lesson Summaries on the following pages, complete the graphic organizer below to understand why the Allies changed their policy of appeasement to Axis aggression to a policy of fighting back and how they won World War II.

World War II

Allied appeasement	Axis aggression	Allied response
•	•	•
•	•	•
•	•	•
•	•	•
	•	

The **Focus Question** gives you a tool to focus your reading.

Each **Note Taking Study Guide** has a graphic organizer. Completing the graphic organizer will help you comprehend the material and retain important details. Use your completed graphic organizer to review and to prepare for assessments.

The second component highlights the central themes, issues, and concepts of each lesson in the topic.

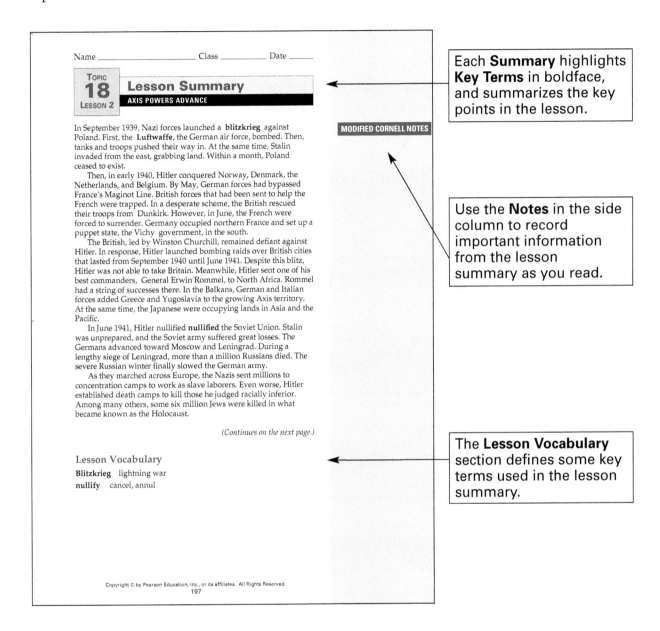

Name _____ Class _____ Date _____

TOPIC **18**
LESSON 2

Lesson Summary
AXIS POWERS ADVANCE

In September 1939, Nazi forces launched a **blitzkrieg** against Poland. First, the **Luftwaffe**, the German air force, bombed. Then, tanks and troops pushed their way in. At the same time, Stalin invaded from the east, grabbing land. Within a month, Poland ceased to exist.

Then, in early 1940, Hitler conquered Norway, Denmark, the Netherlands, and Belgium. By May, German forces had bypassed France's Maginot Line. British forces that had been sent to help the French were trapped. In a desperate scheme, the British rescued their troops from Dunkirk. However, in June, the French were forced to surrender. Germany occupied northern France and set up a puppet state, the Vichy government, in the south.

The British, led by Winston Churchill, remained defiant against Hitler. In response, Hitler launched bombing raids over British cities that lasted from September 1940 until June 1941. Despite this blitz, Hitler was not able to take Britain. Meanwhile, Hitler sent one of his best commanders, General Erwin Rommel, to North Africa. Rommel had a string of successes there. In the Balkans, German and Italian forces added Greece and Yugoslavia to the growing Axis territory. At the same time, the Japanese were occupying lands in Asia and the Pacific.

In June 1941, Hitler nullified **nullified** the Soviet Union. Stalin was unprepared, and the Soviet army suffered great losses. The Germans advanced toward Moscow and Leningrad. During a lengthy siege of Leningrad, more than a million Russians died. The severe Russian winter finally slowed the German army.

As they marched across Europe, the Nazis sent millions to concentration camps to work as slave laborers. Even worse, Hitler established death camps to kill those he judged racially inferior. Among many others, some six million Jews were killed in what became known as the Holocaust.

(Continues on the next page.)

Lesson Vocabulary
Blitzkrieg lightning war
nullify cancel, annul

MODIFIED CORNELL NOTES

197

Each **Summary** highlights **Key Terms** in boldface, and summarizes the key points in the lesson.

Use the **Notes** in the side column to record important information from the lesson summary as you read.

The **Lesson Vocabulary** section defines some key terms used in the lesson summary.

The third component consists of review questions that assess your understanding of each lesson in the topic.

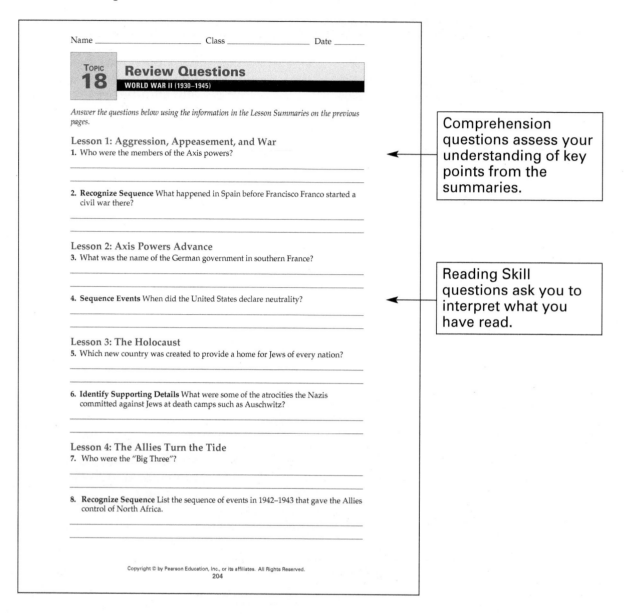

Name _____ Class _____ Date _____

TOPIC
18 **Review Questions**
WORLD WAR II (1930–1945)

Answer the questions below using the information in the Lesson Summaries on the previous pages.

Lesson 1: Aggression, Appeasement, and War
1. Who were the members of the Axis powers?

_____
_____

2. **Recognize Sequence** What happened in Spain before Francisco Franco started a civil war there?

_____
_____

Lesson 2: Axis Powers Advance
3. What was the name of the German government in southern France?

_____
_____

4. **Sequence Events** When did the United States declare neutrality?

_____
_____

Lesson 3: The Holocaust
5. Which new country was created to provide a home for Jews of every nation?

_____
_____

6. **Identify Supporting Details** What were some of the atrocities the Nazis committed against Jews at death camps such as Auschwitz?

_____
_____

Lesson 4: The Allies Turn the Tide
7. Who were the "Big Three"?

_____
_____

8. **Recognize Sequence** List the sequence of events in 1942–1943 that gave the Allies control of North Africa.

_____
_____

204

Comprehension questions assess your understanding of key points from the summaries.

Reading Skill questions ask you to interpret what you have read.

TOPIC 1	Note Taking Study Guide
	ORIGINS OF CIVILIZATION (PREHISTORY – 300 B.C.)

Focus Question: What led to the development of agriculture and the ancient river valley civilizations?

As you read the Lesson Summaries on the following pages, complete the graphic organizer below to help you identify the causes and effects of the development of agriculture on ancient river valley civilizations.

CAUSES

-
-

EFFECTS

-
-

TOPIC 1 LESSON 1

Lesson Summary
LEARNING ABOUT OUR PAST

The long period before the invention of writing is called **prehistory**. Then about 5,000 years ago, humans invented writing and recorded history began.

Historians learn details of the past from **artifacts,** such as clothing, coins, and artwork. However, most rely on written evidence, such as letters or tax records. Historians must also evaluate evidence to determine if it is reliable. Then they interpret it to explain why an event, such as a war, happened. Historians help us understand what happens today and what may happen in the future.

Anthropology is the study of the development of people and their societies. Some anthropologists study human bones to understand how physical traits have changed. Others study **cultures** from the past and present. **Archaeology**, a specialized branch of anthropology, is the study of past cultures through material remains, including buildings and artifacts. In the past, archaeologists might just have chosen a likely site and started digging to try to find ancient artifacts. Today, they work with experts in many fields, such as geology and biology. They also use modern innovations, such as computers and aerial photography. A technique for measuring radioactivity helps these scholars determine the age of objects.

(Continues on the next page.)

Lesson Vocabulary

prehistory   the long period of time before people invented writing

historians   scholars who study and write about the historical past

artifact   object made by humans

anthropology   the field of study related to the origins and development of people and their societies

culture   the way of life of a society, which includes its beliefs, values, and practices

archaeology   the study of past people and cultures through their material remains

Name_____ Class_____ Date_____

MODIFIED CORNELL NOTES

Before the 1950s, anthropologists knew little about early humans and their ancestors. Anthropologists Mary and Louis Leakey searched for clues in East Africa at Olduvai Gorge. There they found many ancient stone tools. The tools showed that whoever had made them had developed the skills and tools, or **technology**, to survive. Early human relatives, or hominids, must have made them. Then, in 1959, after two decades of searching, Mary Leakey found the skull of an early hominid. In 1974, anthropologist Donald Johanson found pieces of a hominid skeleton in Ethiopia. "Lucy" was at least 3 million years old. Discoveries like these helped establish that a number of different groups of hominids, such as *Homo habilis and Homo erectus*, lived over the course of several million years. Two groups of Homo sapiens arose. One group—the Neanderthals—disappeared between 50,000 and 30,000 years ago. Early modern humans were then the only hominids on Earth.

Lesson Vocabulary

technology the skills and tools people use to meet their basic needs and wants

Name_____ Class_____ Date_____

MODIFIED CORNELL NOTES

Scholars have divided prehistory into eras called the Old Stone Age, or Paleolithic Period, and the New Stone Age, or Neolithic Period. During both, people made stone tools. However, during the New Stone Age, people began to develop new skills and technologies that led to dramatic changes.

Early modern humans lived toward the end of the Paleolithic Period. They were **nomads** who moved around in small groups, hunting and gathering food. These people made simple tools and weapons, built fires for cooking, and used animal skins for clothing. They also developed spoken language, which helped them cooperate during the hunt. Some people also began to bury their dead. This suggests belief in a spiritual world or life after death. Cave paintings around the world depict animals and humans. Many scholars think that our ancestors believed the world was full of spirits and forces that might reside in animals, objects, or dreams. Such beliefs are known as **animism**.

The New Stone Age began about 12,000 years ago (or about 10,000 B.C.), when nomadic people made a great breakthrough—they learned to farm. By producing their own food, people no longer needed to roam in search of it. As a result, early farmers settled the first permanent villages. This transition from nomadic life to settled farming brought about such dramatic changes in people's way of life that it is often called the Neolithic Revolution. No greater change in human history took place until the Industrial Revolution of the late 1700s. These early farmers were the first to **domesticate** plants and animals.

Archaeologists have unearthed the remains of some early Neolithic villages, including Çatalhüyük in modern-day Turkey, and Jericho, which exists today in the West Bank. In these settled communities, people accumulated personal property. A council of male elders or elite warriors made the important decisions for all the villagers. To farm successfully, people developed new technologies, such as ways to protect their crops, calendars, and the use of animals for plowing. However, not all technologies were invented everywhere at the same time.

Lesson Vocabulary

nomad   person who moves from place to place to find food

animism   the belief that the world was full of spirits and forces that might reside in animals, objects, or dreams

domesticate   to raise in a controlled way

TOPIC 1
LESSON 3

Lesson Summary
CIVILIZATION BEGINS

The earliest civilizations developed near major rivers. Rivers provided water, transportation, and food. Floodwaters made the soil fertile. In such rich conditions, farmers produced **surpluses**, which allowed them to store food and feed growing populations. As populations grew, villages expanded into cities. Away from these cities, people lived in farming villages or as nomadic herders on grasslands, or **steppes**. Unlike these **traditional economies**, however, in the new cities some people had jobs other than farming.

The rise of cities is the main feature of **civilization**. In addition to this, historians distinguish other basic features of most early civilizations. They include organized governments, complex religions, job specialization, social classes, arts and architecture, public works, and writing.

In these early civilizations, central governments led by chiefs or elders coordinated large-scale projects such as farming or public works, established laws, and organized defense. Most people were **polytheistic**, believing in many gods. Usually, the gods were associated with natural forces such as the sun or rivers. Also, for the first time, individuals began to specialize in certain jobs. Some became **artisans**. In many civilizations, people's jobs determined their social rank. Priests and nobles usually occupied the top level. Wealthy merchants and artisans were next. Below them were peasants, the majority of people who farmed the surrounding land. In many civilizations, slaves occupied the lowest social level. Art and architecture developed, reflecting the beliefs and values of the civilization. Skilled workers built large, ornate palaces and temples decorated with paintings and statues. Many civilizations also developed writing from **pictographs**. As writing grew more complex, only specially trained people called **scribes** could read and write.

(Continues on the next page.)

Lesson Vocabulary

surplus   more than is necessary

steppe   dry grassland

traditional economy   an economy that relies on habit, custom, or ritual and tends not to change over time

civilization   a complex, highly organized social order

polytheistic   the belief in many gods

artisan   skilled craftsperson

pictograph   simple drawing that looks like the objects it represents

scribe   specially trained person who could read and write

MODIFIED CORNELL NOTES

TOPIC 1 LESSON 3

Lesson Summary
CIVILIZATION BEGINS (continued)

Over time, early civilizations changed. Famine, drought, or other disasters sometimes led people to migrate. Migration, as well as trade and warfare, led to **cultural diffusion**. Trade introduced people to new goods or better methods of making them. In warfare, victorious armies forced their ways of life on conquered peoples while they incorporated aspects of the new cultures into their own. Rulers acquired more territory. This brought about the development of **city-states** and, later, the rise of the first **empires**.

Lesson Vocabulary

cultural diffusion   the spread of ideas, customs, and technologies from one people to another

city-state   a political unit that included a city and its surrounding lands and villages

empire   a group of states or territories controlled by one ruler

Name_____ Class_____ Date_____

Answer the questions below using the information in the Lesson Summaries on the previous pages.

Lesson 1: Learning About Our Past

1. What evidence do historians study to learn about the past?

_____

_____

2. What have stone tools taught anthropologists about early humans?

_____

_____

Lesson 2: The Neolithic Revolution

3. What religious beliefs did early modern humans develop during the Old Stone Age?

_____

_____

4. **Compare and Contrast** How was civilization different in the Old Stone Age as compared to the New Stone Age?

_____

_____

Lesson 3: Civilization Begins

5. What roles did central governments have in early civilizations?

_____

_____

6. **Draw Conclusions** Why did early civilizations develop near major rivers?

_____

_____

TOPIC 2

Note Taking Study Guide

THE ANCIENT MIDDLE EAST AND EGYPT (3200 B.C.–500 B.C.)

Focus Question: How did geography influence the location of river valley civilizations?

As you read the Lesson Summaries on the following pages, complete the graphic organizer below to help you identify the geographic features that influenced the location and development of river valley civilizations.

Geographic Features	Effect

Name_____ Class_____ Date_____

Lesson Summary
A CIVILIZATION EMERGES IN SUMER

Around 3300 B.C., Sumer, the world's first civilization, arose in southeastern Mesopotamia. Mesopotamia lay within the Fertile Crescent, between the Tigris and Euphrates rivers. The region's geography affected its people. Frequent flooding forced Sumerians to work together to protect homes and control water for irrigating farms. Although the region had rich soil, it lacked natural resources. Yet Sumerians built some of the world's first great cities using bricks from readily available clay and water. Sumerians also became traders along the rivers.

Eventually, Sumer had 12 city-states, which often battled over control of land and water. So people turned to war leaders for protection. Over time, this changed when war leadership evolved into hereditary monarchy, in which a king or queen exercises central power. Sumerian society had a social rank, or **hierarchy**, including an upper class (rulers, priests, officials), a small middle class (lesser priests, scribes, merchants, artisans), and a vast lower class (peasant farmers). Like most ancient peoples, Sumerians practiced polytheism, the worship of many gods. In **ziggurats**, stepped platforms topped by a temple, priests led religious ceremonies.

Perhaps the Sumerians' greatest achievement was the invention of writing. Beginning as simple pictographs, by 3200 B.C. writing had developed into wedge-like symbols, called **cuneiform**. Cuneiform could be used to record complex information. People now had access to knowledge beyond what they could remember. Eventually, conquering Akkadian, Babylonian, and Assyrian armies swept across the region.

However, Sumerians left a lasting legacy. Besides creating a writing system, they developed basic astronomy and early mathematics. They created a number system based on six, setting up 60-minute hours and 360-degree circles. We still use this system today. Akkadians, Babylonians, and Assyrians carried Sumerian learning across the Middle East. They adopted cuneiform for their own use. Babylonians recorded the Sumerian oral poem, *The Epic of Gilgamesh*, in cuneiform, thus preserving it. They also expanded on Sumerian learning to develop basic algebra and geometry, to create accurate calendars, and to predict eclipses. Later, the Greeks and Romans built on Sumerian knowledge; then they went on to influence all of Western civilization.

Lesson Vocabulary

hierarchy   system of ranking groups

ziggurat   in ancient Mesopotamia, a large, stepped platform thought to have been topped by a temple dedicated to the city-state's chief god or goddess

cuneiform   in the ancient Middle East, a system of writing that used wedge-shaped marks

TOPIC 2 LESSON 2

Lesson Summary

EMPIRES IN MESOPOTAMIA

MODIFIED CORNELL NOTES

Many groups rose to power in ancient Mesopotamia and made long-lasting cultural contributions. Some invaders simply destroyed; others created vast empires. The first invader, in 2300 B.C., was the Akkadian leader, Sargon. He conquered Sumer and formed the world's first empire. In 1790 B.C., Hammurabi, king of Babylon, unified Mesopotamia. He made the first important attempt to **codify**, or arrange and record, all laws of a state. Hammurabi's Code was carved on public pillars for all to see. It included **civil laws**, which covered private matters, like contracts, taxes, marriage, and divorce, and **criminal laws**, which covered offenses against others, like robbery and murder.

Other conquerors brought new learning to Mesopotamia. Hittites extracted iron from ore to forge strong weapons. Although their empire collapsed around 1200 B.C., ironsmithing spread to Asia, Africa, and Europe, launching the Iron Age. Next, Assyrians, though warlike, created a well-ordered society and founded one of the world's first libraries.

Later, the ruthless Babylonian king Nebuchadnezzar controlled the region. He rebuilt and restored the city of Babylon to greatness. His empire eventually stretched from the Persian Gulf to the Mediterranean Sea. However, it fell to Persia in 539 B.C. The Persian empire was enormous. It reached from present-day Turkey to India. Emperor Darius I formed provinces ruled by local governors and a **bureaucracy**, or system of government through departments and subdivisions administered by officials who follow set rules. He also encouraged unity by building roads across the empire and establishing a single Persian coinage. This helped people move from a **barter economy** toward a **money economy**. Another unifying force came from the Persian prophet Zoroaster, who taught belief in a single god and ideas of heaven, hell, and final judgment day. When both Christianity and Islam emerged, or arose, in the Middle East, these new religions stressed similar beliefs.

(Continues on the next page.)

Lesson Vocabulary

codify   to arrange or set down in writing

civil law   branch of law that deals with private rights and matters

criminal law   a branch of law that deals with offenses against others

bureaucracy   system of government through departments and subdivisions administered by officials who follow set rules

barter economy   an economic system in which one set of goods or services is exchanged for another

money economy   an economic system in which goods and services are paid for through the exchange of a token of agreed value

TOPIC 2 / LESSON 2

Lesson Summary

EMPIRES IN MESOPOTAMIA (continued)

Not all achievements came from conquerors, however. The Phoenicians were skilled sea traders from the eastern Mediterranean coast. They formed colonies around the Mediterranean. A **colony** is a settlement ruled by people from another land. The Phoenicians spread Middle Eastern culture over a large area. However, perhaps their greatest achievement was the creation of an **alphabet**. The Greeks expanded on this letter system, leading to the alphabet we use today.

Lesson Vocabulary

colony a territory settled and ruled by people from another land

alphabet writing system in which each symbol represents a single basic sound

Name_____ Class_____ Date_____

TOPIC 2
LESSON 3

Lesson Summary

THE HEBREWS AND THE ORIGINS OF JUDAISM

MODIFIED CORNELL NOTES

About 4,000 years ago, the ancient Israelites developed Judaism, one of today's major religions. Unlike neighboring peoples, Israelites were **monotheistic**, believing in only one god. They believed every event reflected God's plan. So, they recorded events and laws in the Torah. It is the most sacred text of the Israelites, or Jews, and includes the first five books of the Hebrew Bible.

According to the Torah, about 2000 B.C., Abraham, and his family migrated to a region called Canaan. Abraham is considered the father of the Israelites. The Israelites believed that God made a **covenant**, or binding agreement, with Abraham. This covenant promised a special relationship with God and a homeland in Canaan. However, famine forced the Israelites into Egypt, where they became slaves. Much later, Moses led their exodus, or departure, from Egypt back to Canaan.

There, they established the kingdom of Israel around 1000 B.C. Under the second king, David, the feuding 12 tribes of Israel were united into one kingdom. Then, David's son Solomon undertook the task of turning Jerusalem into an impressive capital city. He completed a massive temple and increased Israel's influence in the region. However, after his death, the kingdom split and eventually fell to the Assyrians and Babylonians.

Israelite society was **patriarchal**, meaning that men held the greatest authority. Also, from early times, law was central to Judaism. The Torah contains laws on such subjects as cleanliness, food preparation, and crime. Also in the Torah is a special set of laws called the Ten Commandments. These laws stress moral conduct and religious duty, such as keeping the Sabbath, a holy day of rest and worship. Often in Jewish history, **prophets**, or spiritual leaders, arose. They urged social justice and taught strong codes of **ethics**, or moral standards of behavior.

(Continues on the next page.)

Lesson Vocabulary

monotheistic   believing in one god

covenant   a promise and an agreement

patriarchal   relating to a society in which men hold the greatest legal and moral authority

prophet   spiritual leader who interprets God's will

ethics   moral standards of behavior

Name_____ Class_____ Date_____

MODIFIED CORNELL NOTES

For a 500-year period that began with the Babylonian Captivity, many Jews left or were exiled from Israel. This spreading out of Jews around the world is called the **Diaspora**. Still, they maintained their identity in close-knit communities, following religious laws and traditions. This helped them to survive centuries of persecution.

Judaism has been an important religion. From that culture and faith, both Christianity and Islam emerged, creating an ethical legacy we call the Judeo-Christian tradition.

Lesson Vocabulary

Diaspora   the spreading out of Jews beyond their historic homeland

Name_____ Class_____ Date_____

Lesson Summary
EGYPTIAN CIVILIZATION

MODIFIED CORNELL NOTES

Fertile land along the Nile brought early peoples to Egypt, and over time, a powerful Egyptian civilization arose. Farming flourished in the rich soil deposits from annual river floods.

Egypt was made up of two regions. Upper Egypt began at the Nile's first **cataract**, or waterfall, in the south. Lower Egypt covered the Nile's **delta**, the triangular marshland where it emptied into the Mediterranean. About 3100 B.C., King Menes united both regions. Though leadership passed from one **dynasty**, or ruling family, to another, Egypt generally remained united.

During the Old Kingdom, **pharaohs**, or Egyptian kings, organized a strong central government and established a bureaucracy with different jobs and authority levels. A **vizier**, or chief minister, was the pharaoh's chief of government business.

The Middle Kingdom saw unpredictable flooding and rebellion, but also growth in farmland and trade. Powerful Egyptian leaders ushered in an age of expansion in the New Kingdom. One of these leaders was Hatshepsut, the first female pharaoh. Her stepson, Thutmose III, a great military leader, stretched Egypt's borders to their greatest extent. Much later, Ramses II pushed north into Syria.

Ancient Egyptians made lasting contributions to civilization in many fields. Their religion, written language, art, science, and literature have fascinated people for thousands of years.

During the Old Kingdom, the chief god was the sun god, Re. By the Middle Kingdom, Egyptians called the supreme god Amon-Re. Most Egyptians related to the god Osiris, who ruled the dead. They also worshiped the goddess Isis, who promised life after death. People believed the afterlife was much like life on Earth, so they buried people's possessions with them. The Egyptians also learned to preserve bodies by **mummification**, or embalming and wrapping in cloth, so that the soul could return to the body.

(Continues on the next page.)

Lesson Vocabulary

cataract waterfall

delta triangular area of marshland formed by deposits of silt at the mouth of some rivers

dynasty ruling family

pharaoh title of the rulers of ancient Egypt

vizier chief minister who supervised the business of government in ancient Egypt

mummification the preservation of dead bodies by embalming them and wrapping them in cloth

TOPIC 2 LESSON 4 — Lesson Summary

EGYPTIAN CIVILIZATION (continued)

Ancient Egyptians made advances in learning. Their first writing system, **hieroglyphics**, used symbols. Symbols were originally carved in stone. They also developed material to write on, made from **papyrus** plants.

Egyptian civilization eventually declined; yet its written records survived. No one understood them until the early 1800s, when a French scholar, Jean Champollion, **deciphered**, or figured out meanings for, the carvings on the Rosetta Stone.

Egyptians also made advances in medicine, astronomy, and mathematics. Egyptian artwork and literature has endured for thousands of years.

Lesson Vocabulary

hieroglyphics a system of writing in which pictures called hieroglyphs represent objects, concepts, or sounds

papyrus plant used to make a paper-like writing material in ancient Egypt

decipher to figure out the meaning of

Name_____ Class_____ Date_____

<table>
<tr><td>TOPIC
2</td><td>**Review Questions**
THE ANCIENT MIDDLE EAST AND EGYPT (3200 B.C.–500 B.C.)</td></tr>
</table>

Answer the questions below using the information in the Lesson Summaries on the previous pages.

Lesson 1: A Civilization Emerges in Sumer

1. What major contributions to learning were made by Sumerians?

_____

_____

2. Cause and Effect How did Sumer's geography affect its development?

_____

_____

Lesson 2: Empires in Mesopotamia

3. Who was Sargon?

_____

_____

4. Summarize How did Darius I encourage unity?

_____

_____

Lesson 3: The Hebrews and the Origins of Judaism

5. What is the Torah?

_____

_____

6. What was the Diaspora?

_____

_____

Lesson 4: Egyptian Civilization

7. How did Egypt benefit from the Nile River?

_____

_____

8. Summarize What did Egyptians do to prepare for the afterlife?

_____

_____

Note Taking Study Guide
ANCIENT INDIA AND CHINA (2600 B.C.–A.D. 550)

Focus Question: What ideas and institutions developed in ancient India and China?

As you read the Lesson Summaries on the following pages, complete the graphic organizer below to help you identify, and describe the ideas and institutions that influenced the development of the ancient Indian and Chinese civilizations.

Indian Civilization	Chinese Civilization

TOPIC 3 LESSON 1	**Lesson Summary**
	EARLY CIVILIZATION IN SOUTH ASIA

MODIFIED CORNELL NOTES

The Indian **subcontinent** is a large landmass that juts out from Asia. It is divided into three zones: the Gangetic Plain, with rivers that support farming; the Deccan **plateau**, a raised area of level land too dry for farming; and the coastal plains, which receive plenty of rain. **Monsoons**, or seasonal winds, bring dry air from the northeast in winter and rains from the southwest in summer.

Civilization began on the subcontinent around 2600 B.C. in the Indus River valley. Archaeologists believe organized governments helped plan cities such as Harappa and Mohenjo-Daro. They were built with wide streets, strong building materials, and complex plumbing systems. Most people farmed, although some traded goods by ship with Sumer. People worshiped many gods and regarded certain animals as sacred, perhaps influencing later Indian beliefs such as the **veneration** of cattle. The civilization declined by about 1900 B.C., possibly as a result of environmental damage, a major flood, or an earthquake.

By 1500 B.C., nomadic herders had migrated into India from the north. They married local people, and **acculturation**, or the blending of cultures, took place. Their descendants, known as Aryans, learned to farm and built a civilization after 1000 B.C. There were many kingdoms, and Aryan warriors elected leaders called **rajahs**. Their society was divided into five groups. At the top were priests, followed by warriors, farmers and merchants, and workers and servants. At the bottom were dalits, who had to do work that others would not.

(Continues on the next page.)

Lesson Vocabulary

subcontinent large landmass that juts out from a continent

plateau raised area of level land

monsoon seasonal wind that regularly blows from a certain direction for part of the year

veneration special regard

acculturation the blending of two or more cultures

rajah in ancient India, the elected warrior chief of an Aryan tribe

Lesson Summary

EARLY CIVILIZATION IN SOUTH ASIA (continued)

People worshiped gods and goddesses who embodied natural forces, such as the sky and sun. Indra, the god of war, was the chief deity and used thunderbolts as weapons. Priests wrote sacred teachings in the **Vedas**, a collection of hymns and religious instructions. Epic poems were part of the culture. They described Aryan warfare, important religious beliefs, and valued behavior. Over time, Aryan beliefs changed. There was a move toward the concept of **brahman**, a single spiritual power beyond the gods of the Vedas and existing in all things. **Mystics** also sought direct communion with divine forces.

Lesson Vocabulary

Vedas a collection of prayers, hymns, and other religious teachings developed in ancient India beginning around 1500 B.C.

brahman in the belief system established in Aryan India, the single spiritual power that resides in all things

mystic person who devotes his or her life to seeking direct communication with divine forces

Name_____ Class_____ Date_____

MODIFIED CORNELL NOTES

Two major religions, Hinduism and Buddhism, emerged in ancient India. Although Hinduism grew out of the overlapping religious ideas of diverse groups, all Hindus share basic beliefs. One force, the brahman, is the basis of everything. People have an essential self, or **atman**. Their goal is to achieve **moksha**, or union with brahman.

Because most cannot achieve it in one life, **reincarnation** allows people to continue working toward moksha through several lifetimes. **Karma** affects a person's fate in the next life, and people who act correctly are reborn closer to brahman. By following **dharma**, or personal religious and moral duties, people can escape the cycle of death and rebirth. One part of dharma is **ahimsa**, or nonviolence, toward all people and things.

Hinduism was connected to a system of **castes**, or social groups. This system included strict rules for every part of life. People in higher castes were believed to be more spiritually pure; the lowest caste was considered untouchable. Despite its inequalities, the caste system ensured a stable social order by giving people a sense of identity. Each caste had a role in Indian society.

Siddhartha Gautama was born a Hindu prince in 563 B.C. When Gautama became aware of human suffering, he left his home to search for answers. Eventually, he believed he understood the cause and cure for suffering. He became known as the Buddha, or "the Enlightened One."

(Continues on the next page.)

Lesson Vocabulary

atman   in Hindu belief, a person's essential self

moksha   in Hindu belief, the ultimate goal of existence, which is to achieve union with brahman

reincarnation   in Hindu belief, the rebirth of the soul in another bodily form

karma   in Hindu belief, all the actions that affect a person's fate in the next life

dharma   in Hindu belief, a person's religious and moral duties

ahimsa   Hindu belief in nonviolence and reverence for all life

caste   in traditional Indian society, an unchangeable social group into which a person is born

Lesson Summary
THE ORIGINS OF HINDUISM AND BUDDHISM (continued)

MODIFIED CORNELL NOTES

The Buddha taught the Four Noble Truths, which explain life as suffering and give ways to overcome it. The fourth truth is to follow the Eightfold Path. The Eightfold Path includes "right aspirations" and directs people in achieving the goals of a moral life and enlightenment. Buddhists strive to achieve **nirvana**, or union with the universe and release from the cycle of death and rebirth.

Buddhism and Hinduism share many beliefs. However, Buddhism teaches people to seek enlightenment personally, rather than through priests or gods. It also rejects the caste system and teaches that everyone can reach nirvana.

Buddhism spread throughout Asia but gradually broke into two **sects**, or subgroups, with differing beliefs. Buddhism remained very popular in Asia but declined in India. Hinduism there absorbed some Buddhist ideas.

Lesson Vocabulary

nirvana   in Buddhist belief, union with the universe and release from the cycle of rebirth

sect   a subgroup of a major religious group

TOPIC 3
LESSON 3

Lesson Summary
POWERFUL EMPIRES EMERGE IN INDIA

MODIFIED CORNELL NOTES

Chandragupta Maurya founded the first Indian empire in 321 B.C. The Mauryan empire's capital had schools, libraries, and palaces. The government built roads and harbors, collected taxes, and managed businesses. A secret police force reported on crime and **dissent**, or ideas opposed to those of the government.

Chandragupta's grandson, Asoka, continued to expand the empire. Asoka began ruling in 268 B.C. He became a Buddhist and ruled by moral example. He sent **missionaries** to spread Buddhism throughout Asia. To help his people, Asoka built hospitals and roads. However, the empire declined after his death and ended around 185 B.C.

Rival princes then held power for about 500 years. Each kingdom had its own government and capital. Dravidians in the Deccan spoke different languages and had different traditions from peoples of northern India.

The Gupta dynasty united India from A.D. 320 to about 540. During this time, India enjoyed a period of great cultural achievement called a **golden age**. Prosperity contributed to a flowering of the arts and learning. Universities attracted students from many parts of Asia. Advances in mathematics included the system of numerals that we use today, the concept of zero, and the **decimal system**. Villages had more power than they had under the Mauryas.

Eventually, nomadic people from Central Asia overran Gupta India. For most Indians, everyday life revolved around the rules and duties associated with caste, family, and village. Villages produced most of the food and goods they needed. People regularly interacted with others from nearby villages while attending weddings, visiting relatives, or going to markets. Parents, children, and their offspring shared a common dwelling as a **joint family**. The father or oldest male served as head of the household. Children were trained to do the duties of their caste. Arranging good marriages was important and some families provided a **dowry**, or payment to the bridegroom.

Lesson Vocabulary

dissent   ideas that oppose those of the government

missionaries   people sent to do religious work in a territory or foreign country

golden age   period of great cultural achievement

decimal system   system of numbers based on 10

joint family   family organization in which several generations share a common dwelling

dowry   in some societies, payment a bride's family makes to the bridegroom and his family; payment a woman brings to a marriage

Name_____ Class_____ Date_____

MODIFIED CORNELL NOTES

The earliest civilization in China grew along the Huang River. This river carries **loess**, or fine windblown yellow soil, which raises the water level. People suffered from the river's frequent floods. The need to control the water likely led to the rise of government.

The Shang dynasty began about 1766 B.C. Kings ruled along with princes. The princes were probably the heads of **clans**, or groups of families claiming a common ancestor. Shang warriors used leather armor, bronze weapons, and horse-drawn chariots. They may have learned of chariots as they interacted with other Asian peoples.

The Zhou people overthrew the Shang in 1122 B.C. They promoted the Mandate of Heaven, or the divine right to rule. This idea later expanded to explain the **dynastic cycle**, or the rise and fall of dynasties. If rulers became corrupt, heaven would withdraw support and dynasties would fail. The Zhou established **feudalism**, where lords governed their own land but owed military service and support to a ruler. In the 600s B.C., iron tools made farming more productive, and the population increased. The Zhou dynasty ended when fighting feudal lords could not be controlled.

During the Shang dynasty, the Chinese prayed to many gods and nature spirits. During the Zhou dynasty, two great thinkers emerged: Confucius and Laozi. Confucius developed a **philosophy**, or system of ideas, that greatly influenced Chinese civilization. Confucius was concerned with social order and good government. He emphasized five key relationships between people. **Filial piety**, or respect for parents, was everyone's highest duty.

Laozi founded Daoism about the same time. It emphasized that people should live in harmony with nature. They should look beyond everyday cares and focus on the Dao, or "the way."

(Continues on the next page.)

Lesson Vocabulary

loess fine windblown yellow soil

clan group of families with a common ancestor

dynastic cycle rise and fall of Chinese dynasties according to the Mandate of Heaven

feudalism loosely organized system of government in which local lords governed their own lands but owed military service and other support to a greater lord

philosophy system of ideas

filial piety respect for parents

TOPIC 3

LESSON 4

Lesson Summary

ANCIENT CIVILIZATION IN CHINA (continued)

MODIFIED CORNELL NOTES

One great achievement of early China was silk-making. The Chinese kept the technique a secret for many years. They also developed a system of writing at least 4,000 years ago. Questions were written on **oracle bones**. After heating the bones, priests interpreted the answers. Later, a writing system evolved that included thousands of **characters**, or written symbols. The Chinese then turned writing into an art called **calligraphy**.

Lesson Vocabulary

oracle bones   in Shang China, animal bone or turtle shell used by priests to predict the future

characters   written symbols in writing systems such as that of the Chinese

calligraphy   the art of producing beautiful handwriting

TOPIC 3 LESSON 5

Lesson Summary
STRONG RULERS UNITE CHINA

The Qin Dynasty began in 221 B.C. when the leader of the Qin conquered the Zhou and proclaimed himself Shi Huangdi, or First Emperor. He centralized his power by adhering to Legalism, a philosophy that said that strength, not goodness, was a ruler's greatest virtue. He tortured and killed any who opposed his rule. Shi Huangdi replaced feudal states with military districts headed by loyal officials. To promote unity, he standardized weights and measures, coins, and Chinese writing. Under his orders, thousands of workers connected shorter walls to form the one Great Wall against invaders from the north.

The Han Dynasty began in 202 B.C. The most famous Han emperor, Wudi, ruled from 141 B.C. to 87 B.C. Instead of Legalism, Wudi made Confucianism the official belief system of the state. He improved transportation, controlled prices, and created a government **monopoly** on iron and salt. His policy of **expansionism** increased amount of the land under Chinese rule. He also opened a network of trade routes, later called the Silk Road.

Han rulers chose Confucian scholars as government officials, or **civil servants**. Young men could advance in government through skill, rather than family influence. They might be tested on their knowledge of the Five Classics, a collection of histories, poems, and handbooks compiled from the works of Confucius and others.

The Han dynasty was a golden age for Chinese culture. Han scientists wrote texts on chemistry, zoology, and botany. The Han invented the seismograph, the suspension bridge, the rudder, and paper from wood pulp. Medical treatment included **acupuncture** to relieve pain or treat illness. Artisans created products from jade, ceramics, bronze, and silk. Poets and historians wrote about the grandeur of Han cities.

As the Han dynasty aged, emperors could no longer control **warlords**, or local military rulers. Peasants rebelled. The last emperor was overthrown in A.D. 220, after 400 years of Han rule.

Buddhism had spread from India to China by about A.D. 100. It became increasingly popular during the times of crisis that followed the fall of the Han, and by A.D. 400 it had spread throughout China.

Lesson Vocabulary

monopoly   complete control of a product or business by one person or a group

expansionism   policy of increasing the amount of territory a government holds

civil servants   government officials

acupuncture   medical treatment, originated in ancient China, in which needles are inserted into the skin at specific points to relieve pain or treat various illnesses

warlord   local military ruler

Name_____ Class_____ Date_____

Answer the questions below using the information in the Lesson Summaries on the previous pages.

Lesson 1: Early Civilization in South Asia

1. Why do archaeologists think organized governments planned Harappa and Mohenjo-Daro?

_____

_____

2. What are the Vedas?

_____

_____

Lesson 2: The Origins of Hinduism and Buddhism

3. How does reincarnation relate to moksha?

_____

_____

4. Compare and Contrast How does Buddhism differ from Hinduism?

_____

_____

Lesson 3: Powerful Empires Emerge in India

5. Cause and Effect How did Buddhism influence Asoka's rule?

_____

_____

6. Summarize What were some of the advances of the Gupta dynasty?

_____

_____

Lesson 4: Ancient Civilization in China

7. What was the focus of Confucius's teachings?

_____

_____

8. Cause and Effect What impact did iron tools have on China?

_____

_____

TOPIC 3 | **Review Questions**

ANCIENT INDIA AND CHINA (2600 B.C.–A.D. 550) (continued)

Lesson 5: Strong Rulers Unite China

9. How did Legalism influence the rule of Shi Huangdi?

_____

_____

10. **Summarize** What were some of the changes that occurred in China during the reign of Wudi?

_____

_____

Note Taking Study Guide
THE AMERICAS (PREHISTORY–A.D. 1570)

Focus Question: What ideas in astronomy, mathematics, and architectural engineering developed in the Maya, Aztec, and Inca civilizations?

As you read the Lesson Summaries on the following pages, complete the graphic organizer to help identify the ideas related to astronomy, mathematics, and engineering that developed in the Maya, Inca, and Aztec civilizations.

Ideas in astronomy, mathematics, and architectural engineering
Maya
Inca
Aztec

Name_____ Class_____ Date_____

MODIFIED CORNELL NOTES

People first came to the Americas from Asia between 60,000 B.C. and 18,000 B.C. They may have walked across a land bridge or come by boat. In Mesoamerica, a cultural region including Mexico and Central America, people grew **maize** and other crops. They raised animals and settled into villages by about 1500 B.C. As populations grew, some of the villages developed into the early, great cities of the Americas.

The earliest American civilization, that of the Olmec, developed along the Gulf Coast of Mexico. That civilization lasted from about 1500 B.C. to 400 B.C. A class of priests and nobles led it. Later Mesoamerican peoples, including the Maya and Aztec, adopted elements of Olmec culture, such as carved stone, hieroglyphs, and the calendar.

Around 300 B.C., the Maya were building large cities in present-day Guatemala. By the time the Maya golden age began, about A.D. 250, Maya civilization included large, independent city-states throughout southern Mexico and Central America. The Maya were not united politically as an empire. Instead, cities maintained contact through trade and, sometimes, warfare. Maya cities included temples, palaces, and **stelae**, which were tall stone monuments decorated with carvings. Scribes carved each stela with historical information, such as the names of rulers and dates. They also wrote about astronomy and religion in books made of bark paper. However, around A.D. 900, the Maya abandoned most of their cities, possibly because of frequent warfare or over-farming.

Aztec civilization began in the Valley of Mexico. The Aztec founded Tenochtitlán, their capital city, in A.D. 1325. Because it was located on an island in a lake, they found ingenious ways to create more farmland. They built **chinampas**, which were artificial islands made from mud and reeds.

Unlike the Maya, the Aztec built an empire. They also fought wars continuously. War brought wealth and power. As their empire grew, the Aztec used **tribute**, or payment from conquered peoples, to make Tenochtitlán magnificent. They also sacrificed war prisoners to the sun god. Among the gods they worshiped were powerful gods from an earlier culture centered at the city of Teotihuacán. Although the city fell, its culture influenced later peoples of Mesoamerica.

Lesson Vocabulary

maize   corn

stelae   in the ancient world, tall, commemorative monuments that were often decorated

chinampa   in the Aztec empire, an artificial island used to cultivate crops and made of mud piled atop reed mats that were anchored to the lake bed with willow trees

tribute   payment that conquered peoples may be forced to pay their conquerors

TOPIC 4 / LESSON 2 — Lesson Summary
THE WORLD OF THE INCAS

MODIFIED CORNELL NOTES

The first cultures of South America developed in the Andean region. The earliest was the Chavín culture, named for the ruins at Chavín de Huantar in Peru. Around 900 B.C., the people built a huge temple complex. Chavín's arts and religion influenced later peoples of Peru. Later, between A.D. 100 and 700, the Moche people lived along the north coast of Peru. They improved farming techniques, built roads, and used relay runners to carry messages. They also used **adobe** to build the largest adobe structure in the Americas. Skilled artisans worked in textiles, gold, woodcarving, and ceramics.

The Nazca people lived between 500 B.C. and A.D. 500. They are known for the geoglyphs they etched in the desert of southern Peru. East of the Nazca, the city of Huari controlled mountains and coastal areas in Peru. To the south, Tiahuanaco became a powerful city on Lake Titicaca. The two cities may have been connected through trade or religion because their artistic styles are similar.

The most powerful of the Andean peoples were the Inca. Their civilization began in the 1100s, but greatly expanded its power after 1438. That is when Pachacuti Inca Yupanqui, a skilled warrior and leader, declared himself Sapa Inca, or emperor. Eventually, the Inca empire controlled 2,500 miles along the Andes, from Ecuador to Chile. The Inca built a network of roads of about 14,000 miles, winding through deserts and over mountains. The roads allowed news and armies to travel quickly throughout the empire. All roads led through the capital Cuzco. Various culture groups from all over the empire lived in this city.

The emperor had absolute power and was also the religious leader. Inca rulers ran an efficient government. Nobles ruled provinces, and local officials handled everyday business. Officials kept records on colored, knotted strings called **quipu**. Everyone had to speak the Inca language and follow the Inca religion. Each village, or **ayllu**, had a leader who assigned jobs and organized work for the government. Farmers created terraces to farm the steep hillsides. They spent part of the year farming for their village and part working land for the emperor.

The Inca worshiped many gods, but the chief god was **Inti**, the sun god. Religious festivals occurred each month to celebrate the forces of nature that were important to the Inca.

Lesson Vocabulary

adobe   a mixture of clay and plant fibers that becomes hard as it dries in the sun and that can be used for building

quipu   knotted strings used by Inca officials for record keeping

ayllu   in the Inca empire, a close-knit village

Inti   the Inca sun god

Name_____ Class_____ Date_____

Lesson Summary
THE PEOPLES OF NORTH AMERICA

Before A.D. 1500, there were many Native American culture groups in North America. Scholars have organized early people of North America into culture areas based on where they lived. This section covers the following culture areas: Southwest, Southeast, Arctic, Northwest Coast, and Northeast.

In the deserts of the Southwest, around 300 B.C., the Hohokam built canals to carry river water to crops. Between A.D. 1150 and A.D. 1300, the Ancestral Puebloans built homes on cliffs. The largest of these housing complexes, at Mesa Verde in present-day Colorado, had more than 200 rooms. The cliffs offered protection from enemies. The Ancestral Puebloans also built villages on the ground, which they modeled after the cliff dwellings. The Spanish called these villages **pueblos**. Pueblo Bonito was the largest. It still stands in New Mexico. This huge complex was five stories high and had over 800 rooms. In the center was the **kiva**, a round, underground room used for religious ceremonies and meetings.

The Adena and Hopewell of the Northeast farmed in the Ohio and Mississippi river valleys. They built **earthworks**, which were large piles of earth shaped into burial mounds, bases for structures, and defensive walls. By A.D. 800, these cultures had disappeared. A new people of the Southeast, the Mississippians, began to build large towns and ceremonial centers. They also built mounds. The homes of rulers and nobles sat on top of the mounds. By about 1100 A.D., their great city of Cahokia, in present-day Illinois, had 20,000 people.

The Inuit adapted to the harsh Arctic climate by 2000 B.C. They used seals and other animals for food, clothing, tools, and cooking. They built homes from snow and ice and used dogs to pull sleds that carried goods across the ice.

The Northwest Coast provided Native Americans there with plentiful fish and game, and trees for building permanent homes. Wealth gained from trading surplus goods was shared in **potlatch** ceremonies. In this ceremony, a high-ranking person gave gifts to a large number of guests.

Many Native American groups of the Northeast were known as the Iroquois. To stop constant warfare, they formed the Iroquois League. This was an alliance of five Iroquois groups, known as the Five Nations.

Lesson Vocabulary

pueblos   Native American villages of the North American Southwest

kiva   a large underground chamber that the Anasazi used for religious ceremonies and political meetings

earthworks   an embankment or other construction made of earth

potlatch   among Native American groups of the Northwest Coast, ceremonial gift-giving by people of high rank and wealth

Name_____ Class_____ Date_____

Answer the questions below using the information in the Lesson Summaries on the previous pages.

Lesson 1: Civilizations of Middle America

1. How were Maya city-states connected?

_____

_____

2. Cause and Effect How did the Aztec benefit from war?

_____

_____

Lesson 2: The World of the Incas

3. Which group was the most powerful Andean civilization?

_____

_____

4. What was the responsibility of the village leader?

_____

_____

Lesson 3: The Peoples of North America

5. How were the Hohokam able to grow crops in the desert?

_____

_____

6. Summarize How did the Inuit adapt to their environment?

_____

_____

Name_____ Class_____ Date_____

Focus Question: Why has Greek civilization remained such an important influence on modern society?

As you read the Lesson Summaries on the following pages, complete the graphic organizer below to help you. Note specific examples that support the idea that Greek culture and its many civilizations have had a profound effect on other societies, particularly our own modern civilization.

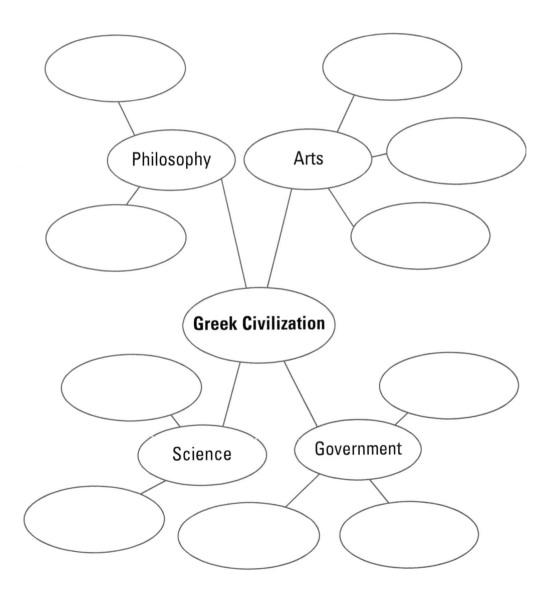

MODIFIED CORNELL NOTES

Lesson Summary
EARLY GREECE

The island of Crete, located on the Aegean Sea, was home to a successful trading civilization known as the Minoan civilization. Minoan rulers lived in a vast palace at Knossos. This palace housed rooms for the royal family, banquet halls, and work areas for artisans. It also included religious **shrines**, areas dedicated to the honor of gods and goddesses. The walls were covered with colorful **frescoes**—watercolor paintings done on wet plaster. The frescoes revealed much about Minoan culture by illustrating scenes from daily life.

By about 1400 B.C., the Minoan civilization vanished. The reasons are unclear, but it is certain that invaders played some role in its destruction. These invaders were the Mycenaeans.

The Mycenaeans ruled the Aegean world from about 1400 B.C. to 1200 B.C. They were also sea traders whose civilization reached as far as Sicily, Italy, Egypt, and Mesopotamia. The Mycenaeans learned skills from the Minoans, such as writing. They also absorbed Egyptian and Mesopotamian customs, which they passed on to later Greeks.

The Myceneans are remembered for their part in the Trojan War, which began about 1250 B.C. The conflict may have started because of economic rivalry between Mycenae and Troy, a rich trading city that controlled the vita **straits**, or narrow water passages, connecting the Mediterranean and Black seas. According to Greek legend, the war erupted when the Mycenaeans, or Greeks, sailed to Troy to rescue the kidnapped wife of the king. The war lasted 10 years, until the Mycenaeans finally burned Troy to the ground.

Much of what we know about the Trojan War and life during this period comes from two epic poems, the Iliad and the Odyssey. These works are credited to the poet Homer, who probably lived about 750 B.C. The Iliad and the Odyssey reveal much about the values of the ancient Greeks. The poems' heroes display honor, courage, and eloquence.

In about 1100 B.C., invaders from the north known as the Dorians conquered the Mycenaeans. After the Dorian invasions, Greece passed several centuries in obscurity. Over time, a new Greek civilization emerged that would extend its influence across the Western world.

Lesson Vocabulary

shrine   altar, chapel, or other sacred place

frescoe   colorful painting completed on wet plaster

strait   narrow water passage

TOPIC 5 LESSON 2

Lesson Summary
THE GREEK CITY-STATES

MODIFIED CORNELL NOTES

As their world expanded, the Ancient Greeks evolved a unique version of the city-state, called the **polis**. The polis consisted of a major city or town and its surrounding countryside. The **acropolis**, or high city with its many temples, stood on a hill. Because the population was small for each city-state, the **citizens** felt a shared sense of responsibility for their polis.

Different forms of government evolved in ancient Greece. At first, there was a monarchy. In a **monarchy**, a hereditary ruler exercises central power. In time, the power shifted to an **aristocracy**—or rule by the landholding elite. As trade expanded and a wealthy middle class emerged, the result was an **oligarchy**—where power is in the hands of a small, wealthy elite.

A new method of fighting also emerged. The **phalanx** was a massive tactical formation of heavily armed foot soldiers. In the city-state of Sparta, Spartans focused on developing strong military skills.

In Athens, government evolved from a monarchy into an aristocracy, but discontent spread among ordinary citizens. Despite government reforms under Solon around 594 B.C., there was still unrest. This led to the rise of **tyrants**, or those who gained power by force. They often won support from the merchant class and the poor by imposing reforms to help these groups. In 507 B.C., the reformer Cleisthenes made the assembly a genuine **legislature**, or lawmaking body. Slowly Athens moved toward **democracy**, or government by the people.

(Continues on the next page.)

Lesson Vocabulary

polis   city-state in ancient Greece

acropolis   highest and most fortified point within a Greek city-state

citizen   a native or resident of a town or city

monarchy   government in which a king or queen exercises central power

aristocracy   government headed by a privileged minority or upper class

oligarchy   government in which ruling power belongs to a few people

phalanx   in ancient Greece, a massive tactical formation of heavily armed foot soldiers

tyrant   ruler who gains power by force

legislature   lawmaking body

democracy   government in which the people hold ruling power

TOPIC 5 LESSON 2 — Lesson Summary
THE GREEK CITY-STATES (continued)

MODIFIED CORNELL NOTES

Despite divisions among city-states, Greeks shared a common culture. They spoke the same language, honored the same ancient heroes, participated in common festivals, and prayed to the same gods.

The Greeks, united by their common culture, were victorious in the Persian Wars, which began in 499 B.C. This victory increased the Greeks' sense of uniqueness. Athens emerged from the wars as the most powerful city-state in Greece. Athens formed an **alliance**, called the Delian League, with other Greek city-states.

After the Persian Wars, a golden age began in Athens under the leadership of Pericles. Because of his wisdom and skill, the economy thrived and the government became more democratic. Periclean Athens was a **direct democracy**. Under this system, citizens take part directly in the daily affairs of government. In addition, Athenians served on juries. A **jury** is a panel of citizens who make the final judgment in a trial. Athenian citizens could also vote to banish a public figure they believed was a threat to their democracy. This was called **ostracism**.

Many Greeks outside Athens resented the growing Athenian domination. In 431 B.C., warfare broke out between Athens and Sparta. This conflict, known as the Peloponnesian War, soon engulfed all of Greece. Sparta defeated Athens with the help of Persia. The defeat ended Athenian domination of the Greek world.

Lesson Vocabulary

alliance formal agreement between two or more nations or powers to cooperate and come to one another's defense

direct democracy system of government in which citizens participate directly in the day-to-day affairs of government rather than through elected representatives

jury group of people with authority to make a decision in a legal case

ostracism practice used in ancient Greece to banish or send away a public figure who threatened democracy

TOPIC 5 LESSON 3

Lesson Summary
GREEK THINKERS, ARTISTS, AND WRITERS

Ancient Greek thinkers used observation and reason to explain events. These thinkers were called **philosophers,** meaning "lovers of wisdom." Philosophers explored many subjects, from mathematics and music to **logic,** or rational thinking. They believed that through reason and observation they could discover laws that governed the universe.

Some philosophers were interested in ethics and morality. In contrast, the Sophists believed that success was more important than moral truth. They developed skills in **rhetoric,** the art of skillful speaking. Ambitious men could use clever and persuasive rhetoric to advance their careers.

The philosopher Socrates was an outspoken critic of the Sophists. He believed in seeking truth and self-knowledge. Most of what we know about Socrates comes from his student Plato. Plato set up a school called the Academy where he taught his own ideas. Like Socrates, Plato emphasized the importance of reason.

Plato's most famous student, Aristotle, also promoted reason as the guiding force for learning. He set up a school, the Lyceum, for the study of all branches of knowledge.

While Plato argued that every object on Earth has an ideal form, ancient Greek artists and architects reflected a similar concern with balance, order, and beauty. The most famous example of Greek architecture is the Parthenon. The basic plan of the Parthenon is a simple rectangle with tall columns supporting a gently sloping roof.

Early Greek sculptors carved figures in rigid poses. Later, they emphasized more natural forms. Sculptors carved their subjects in a way that showed human beings in what was considered their most perfect, graceful form.

(Continues on the next page.)

Lesson Vocabulary

philosophers   someone who seeks to understand and explain life; a person who studies philosophy

logic   rational thinking

rhetoric   art of skillful speaking

TOPIC
5
LESSON 3

Lesson Summary
GREEK THINKERS, ARTISTS, AND WRITERS (continued)

In literature, the Greeks also developed their own style. Some Greek playwrights wrote **tragedies**, or plays that tell stories of human suffering, usually ending in disaster. Others wrote **comedies**, or humorous plays that mock customs or criticize society.

History was also an important subject for ancient Greeks. Herodotus, often called the "Father of History," stressed the importance of research. He visited many lands to collect and chronicle information from witnesses of actual events. Thucydides also recorded events as he experienced them. Both men set standards for future historians.

Lesson Vocabulary

tragedy   in ancient Greece, a play about human suffering often ending in disaster

comedy   in ancient Greece, play that mocked people or social customs

Lesson Summary
ALEXANDER THE GREAT AND THE LEGACY OF GREECE

Soon after Macedonian king Phillip II gained the throne in 359 B.C., he built a powerful army and eventually brought all of Greece under his control. Philip's next goal was to conquer the Persian empire. However, he was assassinated before he could. **Assassination** is the murder of a public figure, usually for political reasons.

After Philip's death, his son, who came to be known as Alexander the Great, acquired the throne and began organizing forces to conquer Persia. Alexander was victorious. Once much of the Persian empire fell under his control, he advanced into India.

Unexpectedly, in 323 B.C., Alexander died at the age of 33 in Persia from a fever. Although his empire collapsed soon after, he is credited with spreading Greek culture from Egypt to the borders of India. Local people **assimilated**, or absorbed, Greek ideas. In turn, Greek settlers adopted local customs. Gradually, a new Hellenistic culture emerged that blended Greek, Persian, Egyptian, and Indian influences.

At the very heart of the Hellenistic world stood the magnificent city of Alexandria, founded in Egypt by Alexander. Its great library was among the greatest scientific and cultural centers of the age. Like Alexandria, cities of the Hellenistic world employed many architects and artists. Temples, palaces, and other public buildings were larger and grander than the buildings of classical Greece. The elaborate new style reflected the desire of Hellenistic rulers to glorify themselves as godlike.

During the Hellenistic age, scholars built on earlier Greek, Babylonian, and Egyptian knowledge. In mathematics, Pythagoras derived a formula to calculate the relationship between the sides of a right triangle. The astronomer Aristarchus developed the theory of a **heliocentric**, or sun-centered, solar system. Another scientist, Archimedes, applied the principles of physics to make practical inventions. In the field of medicine, the Greek physician Hippocrates studied the causes of illnesses and looked for cures.

Greek works in the arts and sciences set a standard for later Europeans. Greek ideas about law, freedom, justice, and government continue to influence political thinking today.

Lesson Vocabulary

assassination   murder of a public figure, usually for political reasons

assimilate   absorb or adopt another culture

heliocentric   based on the belief that the sun is the center of the universe

Name_____ Class_____ Date_____

TOPIC 5	**Review Questions**
	ANCIENT GREECE (1750 B.C.–133 B.C)

Answer the questions below using the information in the Lesson Summaries on the previous pages.

Lesson 1: Early Greece

1. What information about Greek culture can be found in Homer's epic poems?

_____

_____

2. Identify Main Ideas Explain how Mycenaean culture spread.

_____

_____

Lesson 2: The Greek City-States

3. What different forms of governments evolved in ancient Greece?

_____

_____

4. Identify Supporting Details What details in the Summary support the main idea that geography had a role in the development of Greece?

_____

_____

Lesson 3: Greek Thinkers, Artists, and Writers

5. What is direct democracy?

_____

_____

6. Identify Supporting Details How did victory in the Persian Wars strengthen Athens?

_____

_____

Lesson 4: Alexander the Great and the Legacy of Greece

7. What two forms of drama did the Greeks develop?

_____

_____

8. Understand Effects How did Alexander the Great's conquests help create a new Hellenistic culture?

_____

_____

Name_____ Class_____ Date_____

<table>
<tr><td>TOPIC
6</td><td>**Note Taking Study Guide**
ANCIENT ROME AND THE ORIGINS OF CHRISTIANITY (509 B.C.–A.D. 476)</td></tr>
</table>

Focus Question: What enabled Rome to acquire its incomparable wealth and power?

As you read the Lesson Summaries on the next pages, complete the graphic organize below, noting specific actions and achievements that demonstrate how and why Rome acquired wealth and power.

Social/Cultural	Government and Military	Economic and Geographic	Scientific and Technical

Lesson Summary
THE ROMAN REPUBLIC

MODIFIED CORNELL NOTES

Rome's location on the Italian peninsula, centrally located in the Mediterranean Sea, benefited the Romans as they expanded. In addition, Italy had wide, fertile plains, which supported a growing population. Rome began on seven hills near the Tiber River.

Romans shared the Italian peninsula with Greek colonists and the Etruscans—a people who ruled most of central Italy for a time. The Romans learned from the Etruscans, studying their engineering techniques and adapting their alphabet.

In 509 B.C., the Romans drove out the Etruscans and founded the state of Rome. They put in place a new form of government called a **republic**. To keep any individual from obtaining too much power, the republic was run by officials who represented the people. The most powerful governing body was the senate. Its 300 members were all **patricians**, or members of the landholding upper class. Each year, the senators nominated two **consuls** from the patrician class to supervise the administration and command the armies. Also, in the event of war, the senate might choose a temporary **dictator**, or ruler with complete control over the government.

Initially, all government officials were patricians. **Plebeians**, or common people, had little influence. However, the plebeians fought for the right to elect their own officials, called **tribunes**. The tribunes could **veto**, or block, laws that they felt harmed the plebeians. Although the senate still dominated the government, the plebeians had gained access to power and their rights were protected.

The family was the basic unit of Roman society. Although women could own property and, in later Roman times, run businesses, men had absolute power over the family. Romans also believed in education for all children. Religion, too, was a significant part of Roman society.

(Continues on the next page.)

Lesson Vocabulary

republic   form of government in which people choose their officials

patrician   a member of the landholding upper class

consul   public officials responsible for supervising the business of government and commanding the armies

dictator   ruler who has complete control over a government

plebeian   farmers, merchants, and artisans who made up most of the population

tribune   an official elected by the plebeians to protect their interests

veto   block a government action

Lesson Summary
THE ROMAN REPUBLIC (continued)

By 270 B.C., Rome controlled most of the Italian peninsula. This was due mainly to a well-trained army. The basic military unit was the **legion**. Each legion included about 5,000 citizen-soldiers. As Rome occupied new territories, they treated their defeated enemies well. As long as conquered peoples accepted Roman rule and obeyed certain laws, the Romans allowed them to maintain their own customs and governments.

Lesson Vocabulary

legion   basic military unit including about 5,000 citizen-soldiers

TOPIC 6 LESSON 2 — Lesson Summary
THE ROMAN EMPIRE: RISE AND DECLINE

As Rome extended its territory, it encountered Carthage, an empire that stretched across North Africa and the western Mediterranean. These two powers battled in three wars. These Punic Wars lasted from 264 B.C. to 146 B.C., when Rome finally destroyed Carthage.

Rome was committed to a policy of **imperialism**—establishing control over foreign lands. Roman power soon spread from Spain to Egypt. Rome soon controlled busy trade routes that brought tremendous riches. Wealthy families purchased large estates, called **latifundia**, and forced war captives to work as their slaves. The gap between rich and poor grew, leading to corruption and riots.

Rome was in need of social and political reform. Young patrician tribunes Tiberius and Gaius Gracchus were among the first to attempt it. However, the senate felt threatened by their reforms, and in a series of riots, the two brothers and their followers were killed. This power struggle led to a period of civil war.

Out of the chaos emerged Julius Caesar, a brilliant military commander. With Caesar's rising fame, a rivalry erupted between him and another general, Pompey. Caesar eventually defeated Pompey and his soldiers and swept around the Mediterranean, suppressing rebellions. Victorious, Caesar returned to Rome and forced the senate to make him dictator for life.

Caesar pushed through a number of reforms to help solve Rome's many problems. Fearing that Caesar would make himself king, however, his enemies killed him in 44 B.C. His friend, Marc Antony, and his nephew, Octavian, joined forces to avenge Caesar. However, they soon battled one another for power, and Octavian defeated Antony.

With this triumph, the senate gave Octavian the title of Augustus, or "Exalted One." He was the first emperor of Rome and ruled from 27 B.C. to A.D. 14. Augustus built a stable government for the empire. He also undertook economic reforms. To make the tax system fair, he ordered a census, or population count, of the empire. Another influential Roman emperor was Hadrian. He codified Roman law, making it the same for all provinces.

During the Pax Romana, Roman rule brought peace, prosperity, and order to the lands it controlled. Spectacular entertainments were popular across the empire. However, social and economic problems hid beneath the general prosperity.

Lesson Vocabulary

imperialism   establishing control over foreign lands and peoples

latifundium (*pl.* latifundia)   a huge farming estate

Lesson Summary
THE LEGACY OF ROME

MODIFIED CORNELL NOTES

Greek art, literature, philosophy, and scientific developments made a significant impact on Rome. Still, the greatest Roman authors wrote in Latin. In his epic poem the *Aeneid*, the Roman poet Virgil tried to show that Rome was as heroic as Greece. Others used poetry to **satirize**, or make fun of, Roman society. Roman historians pursued their own theme, recalling Rome's triumphant past in an attempt to renew patriotism. In philosophy, Roman thinkers were impressed with the Hellenistic philosophy of Stoicism.

Like their Greek predecessors, Roman sculptors realistically portrayed their subjects, focusing on every detail. However, the Romans distinguished themselves by also focusing on individual character. Art, too, was an important aspect of Roman culture. Artists depicted scenes from Roman literature and daily life in frescoes and **mosaics**—pictures made from chips of colored stone or glass.

Another distinction that set the Romans apart from the Greeks was their architecture. Unlike the Greeks, the Romans emphasized grandeur. They built immense palaces, temples, and stadiums, which stood as impressive monuments to Roman power. The Romans also improved structures such as columns and arches. Utilizing concrete as a building material, they developed the arched dome as a roof for large spaces.

In addition, the Romans excelled in **engineering**, which is the application of science and mathematics to develop useful structures and machines. Roman engineers built roads, bridges, and harbors throughout the empire. They built many **aqueducts**, or bridge-like stone structures that carried water from the hills into Roman cities.

In general, the Romans entrusted the Greeks, who were by that time citizens of the empire, with scientific research. Ptolemy, the astronomer-mathematician, proposed his theory that Earth was at the center of the universe. This mistaken idea was accepted in the Western world for nearly 1,500 years.

Rome was committed to regulating laws and to serving justice. To protect the empire and its citizens, Rome developed the civil law. As Rome expanded, the law of nations was established. This law was applied to both citizens and non-citizens of Rome. When Rome extended citizenship across the empire, the two systems merged.

Lesson Vocabulary

satirize   make fun of

mosaic   picture made from chips of colored stone or glass

engineering   the application of science and mathematics to develop structures and machines

aqueduct   bridge-like stone structure that carried water from the hills into a Roman city

TOPIC **6** LESSON 4	**Lesson Summary** THE ORIGINS OF CHRISTIANITY

Within the Roman empire, there were various religious beliefs. Rome tolerated these different religions, as long as citizens honored Roman gods, too—including the emperor. Because most people were polytheistic, meaning they believed in more than one god, for a long time this was not a problem.

Later, the followers of Judaism became divided about living under Roman rule. Many began to follow a Jewish man named Jesus. They believed Jesus was the **messiah**, or anointed king sent by God. Jesus chose 12 **apostles**, meaning "persons sent forth," to help him preach his message.

While Jesus' teachings were rooted in Jewish tradition, he also preached new, Christian beliefs. Jesus taught the need for justice, morality, forgiveness, and service to others. After Jesus was put to death, the missionary Paul did much to spread Christianity. The message was helped by the *Pax Romana* and the ease of travel on Roman roads. Paul said that those who believed Jesus was the son of God and complied with his teachings would achieve salvation.

Because they did not obey certain Roman practices, many Christians were persecuted. They became known as **martyrs**, or people who suffer or die for their beliefs. Still, Christianity continued to spread. Many found comfort in Jesus' message of love and promise of salvation. Finally, the emperor Constantine issued the Edict of Milan in A.D. 313. This granted freedom of worship to all Roman citizens. By the end of that century, Christianity was the official religion of the empire.

Each Christian community and its **clergy**—those who conduct religious services—were grouped together in a diocese. Every community had its own priest. All the priests in a diocese were supervised by a bishop, a high Church official. Eventually, bishops from five important cities gained more authority and held the honorary title of **patriarch**.

However, as the Church became more structured, differences arose from within. The bishops of Rome came to be called **popes**, and claimed authority over all other bishops. There was also an emergence of **heresies**, or beliefs said to be contrary to official Church teachings. Important teachers helped to define Christian theology. One of these was Augustine, from Hippo in North Africa.

Lesson Vocabulary

messiah   anointed king sent by God

apostle   name that in Greek means "a person sent forth"

martyr   person who suffers or dies for his or her beliefs

clergy   people who conduct worship services

patriarch   church leaders with great authority

pope   father of the Church

heresy   belief said to be contrary to official Church teachings

Answer the questions below using the information in the Lesson Summaries on the previous pages.

Lesson 1: The Roman Republic
1. What governing body in the republic had the greatest power?

_____

_____

2. What were the consuls' responsibilities?

_____

_____

Lesson 2: The Roman Empire: Rise and Decline
3. What was the cause and what was the effect of the establishment of the office of tribune?

_____

_____

4. Who was Octavian?

_____

_____

Lesson 3: The Legacy of Rome
5. What did Virgil wish to accomplish with his poem the *Aeneid*?

_____

_____

6. What theory did Ptolemy propose?

_____

_____

Lesson 4: The Origins of Christianity
7. Why is the missionary Paul an important figure in Christianity?

_____

_____

8. What did the Edict of Milan accomplish?

_____

_____

Name_____ Class_____ Date_____

Note Taking Study Guide
MEDIEVAL CHRISTIAN EUROPE (330–1450)

Focus Question: Which was a more important force of change in medieval Europe—religion or economics?

As you read the Lesson Summaries on the following pages, complete the graphic organizer below to recognize the causes and effects of religious and economic changes in Europe after the fall of the Roman Empire.

Religious developments	Economic developments
•	•
•	•
•	•
•	•
•	•
•	•
•	•
•	•
•	•
•	•

TOPIC 7 — LESSON 1
Lesson Summary
THE EARLY MIDDLE AGES

After the Roman empire fell, Western Europe was cut off from advanced cultures in Asia, overrun by invaders, and divided. The period from 500 to 1000 is sometimes called the Dark Ages. However, it was a time when Greco-Roman, Germanic, and Christian traditions slowly blended to create a new, **medieval** civilization called the Middle Ages.

In the early Middle Ages, Germanic tribes, such as the Franks, divided Western Europe. In 486, Clovis, king of the Franks, conquered Gaul, later to become France. Clovis followed his own customs but also kept Roman customs and converted to Christianity. In the 600s, Islam began in Arabia. Muslims, or believers in Islam, created a huge and expanding empire. When a Muslim army crossed into France, Charles Martel and his Frankish warriors fought them at the battle of Tours in 732. Muslims ruled in Spain, but did not advance farther into Western Europe.

In 768, Charles Martel's grandson, also named Charles, became king of the Franks. He built an empire covering what are now France, Germany, and part of Italy, and he was known as Charlemagne, or Charles the Great. Later, the pope crowned him the new emperor of the Romans. Charlemagne worked, in his 46-year rule, to unite his kingdom by fighting off invaders, conquering peoples, spreading Christianity, and further blending Germanic, Roman, and Christian traditions. He set up an orderly government, naming nobles to rule locally. Charlemagne regarded education as another way to unify his kingdom. He brought back Latin learning across his empire and encouraged the creation of local schools.

After Charlemagne's death in 814, his sons battled for power and his grandsons split up the empire. About 900, nomads called Magyars settled in what is present-day Hungary. They overran Eastern Europe and moved into Germany, France, and Italy, but they were eventually pushed back. Also, in the late 700s the Vikings from Scandinavia began to invade towns along coasts and rivers in Europe. The Vikings were skilled sailors and explorers. They settled and mixed with local peoples in England, Ireland, northern France, and parts of Russia, bringing their culture with them.

Lesson Vocabulary

medieval   referring to the Middle Ages in Europe or the period of history between ancient and modern times

Name_____ Class_____ Date_____

MODIFIED CORNELL NOTES

Medieval society was a network of mutual duties. Even kings and nobles exchanged vows of service and loyalty. These vows were part of a new political and legal system called **feudalism**, which was the basis of European life during the Middle Ages.

Feudalism was a structure of lords and lesser lords, called **vassals**. Lords and their vassals exchanged pledges, and this bond was called the **feudal contract**. In this contract, lords expected military service, payments, and loyalty from vassals. In return, they granted vassals protection and parcels of land, called **fiefs**, or estates. By the 1100s, many nobles lived in castles, which served as fortresses.

All aristocrats had a place in this structured society. For nobles, war was a way of life. Many trained from boyhood to become **knights**. They learned to ride horseback, fight, and care for weapons. They competed in mock battles called **tournaments**. Noblewomen, too, participated in the warrior society. They took over estates while their husbands were at war, and might even have fought to defend their lands. A few learned to read or write. All were expected to learn spinning, weaving, and the supervising of servants.

Knights were expected to follow a code of ideal conduct, called **chivalry**. It required them to be brave, loyal, and honest, to fight fairly, to treat captured knights well, and to protect the weak. **Troubadours**, or wandering musicians, often sang about knights and ladies. Their songs formed the basis for medieval romances, or epic stories and poems.

(Continues on the next page.)

Lesson Vocabulary

feudalism   loosely organized system of government in which local lords governed their own lands but owed military service and other support to a greater lord

vassal   in medieval Europe, a lord who was granted land in exchange for service and loyalty to a greater lord

feudal contract   exchange of pledges between lords and vassals

fief   in medieval Europe, an estate granted by a lord to a vassal in exchange for service and loyalty

knight   a European noble who served as a mounted warrior

tournament   a mock battle in which knights would compete against one another to display their fighting skills

chivalry   code of conduct for knights during the Middle Ages

troubadour   a wandering poet or singer of medieval Europe

TOPIC 7 LESSON 2
Lesson Summary
FEUDALISM AND THE MANOR ECONOMY (continued)

The **manor**, or lord's estate, was central to the feudal economy. Manors were self-sufficient, producing all that their people needed. Most peasants on manors were **serfs**, who were bound to the land. Although they were not slaves, serfs could not leave the manor without permission. They had to work the lord's lands several days a week, pay fees, and get permission to marry. In return, they were allowed to farm several acres for themselves and received protection during war. Their work was harsh, and hunger and disease were common. Yet they found times to celebrate, such as Christmas, Easter, and dozens of Christian festivals each year.

Lesson Vocabulary

manor   during the Middle Ages in Europe, a lord's estate that included one or more villages and the surrounding lands
serf   in medieval Europe, a peasant bound to the lord's land

TOPIC 7 LESSON 3

Lesson Summary
THE MEDIEVAL CHRISTIAN CHURCH

MODIFIED CORNELL NOTES

During the Middle Ages, the Roman Catholic Church controlled the spiritual life of Christians in Western Europe but was also the strongest worldly or **secular** force. Church officials were closely linked to secular rulers. Clergy might even be nobles with lands and armies.

For most people, village churches were the center of community life. Their parish priest celebrated mass and administered **sacraments**, or sacred rites. Church doctrine also taught that men and women were equal before God.

Some chose to live a religious life in monasteries or convents. In about 530, a monk named Benedict created rules governing monastery life. They required vows of obedience, poverty, and chastity, or purity. In time, this Benedictine Rule was used by monasteries and convents across Europe.

As God's representatives on Earth, medieval popes eventually claimed **papal supremacy**, or authority over kings and emperors. The Church had its own courts and body of laws, known as **canon law**, and issued punishments. One was **excommunication**, or the withholding of sacraments and Christian burial. This condemned a sinner to hell. In addition, rulers could be punished by the pope with an **interdict**. This barred entire towns, regions, or kingdoms from receiving sacraments and Christian burial. The Church also used its authority to end warfare among nobles by declaring times of peace known as the Truce of God.

(Continues on the next page.)

Lesson Vocabulary

secular   having to do with worldly, rather than religious, matters; nonreligious

sacrament   sacred ritual of the Roman Catholic Church

papal supremacy   the claim of medieval popes that they had authority over all secular rulers

canon law   body of laws of a church

excommunication   exclusion from the Roman Catholic Church as a penalty for refusing to obey Church law

interdict   in the Roman Catholic Church, excommunication of an entire region, town, or kingdom

Name_____ Class_____ Date_____

MODIFIED CORNELL NOTES

However, as Church wealth and power grew, so did corruption. Monks and nuns ignored their vows. Throughout the Middle Ages, there were calls for reform. In the early 900s, Abbot Berno of Cluny brought back the Benedictine Rule. Over the next 200 years, monasteries and convents copied these reforms. Other reforms came from **friars**, or monks who traveled and preached to the poor, and did not live in monasteries. The first order of friars, the Franciscans, was founded by St. Francis of Assisi. The Franciscans preached poverty, humility, and love of God.

In the Middle Ages, Jewish communities also existed all across Europe. Yet by the late 1000s, prejudice against Jewish people had increased. The Church eventually issued orders forbidding Jews from owning land or having certain jobs.

The Roman emperor Constantine rebuilt the city of Byzantium and renamed it Constantinople. Constantinople grew wealthy from trade. In 330, Constantine made Constantinople the new capital of the Roman empire. In time, the eastern Roman empire became known as the Byzantine empire.

The Byzantine empire reached its peak under Justinian. Byzantine armies reconquered North Africa and parts of southern Europe. However, these victories were only temporary, as Justinian's successors later lost these lands. After a fire in 532, Justinian made Constantinople even grander. One of his most important achievements was rebuilding the church of Hagia Sophia. Justinian also had a commission collect and organize the laws of Rome. This collection became known as Justinian's Code. It helped unify the empire, which Justinian ruled as an autocrat, or with complete authority.

His wife, Theodora, served as his advisor and co-ruler. Christianity was practiced differently in the Byzantine empire than in the West. The Byzantine emperor controlled Church affairs and appointed the patriarch, or highest Church official in Constantinople. Byzantine Christians rejected the pope's claim to authority over all Christians. During the Middle Ages, the eastern and western branches of Christianity grew further apart, partly due to a dispute over the use of **icons**, or holy images. In 1054, other controversies caused a complete split known as the Great Schism. The Byzantine church became known as the Eastern Orthodox Church. The western branch became known as the Roman Catholic Church.

(Continues on the next page.)

Lesson Vocabulary

friar a medieval European monk who traveled from place to place preaching to the poor

icon holy image of Christ, the Virgin Mary, or a saint venerated in the Eastern Orthodox Church

TOPIC 7 LESSON 3

Lesson Summary

THE MEDIEVAL CHRISTIAN CHURCH (continued)

MODIFIED CORNELL NOTES

By this time, the Byzantine empire was in decline. In the 1090s, the Byzantine emperor asked the pope for help in fighting the Muslim Seljuks. This started the First Crusade. In 1204, knights on the Fourth Crusade attacked Constantinople. The Byzantines lost control of trade and much of their wealth. In 1453, Ottoman Turks conquered Constantinople, renamed it Istanbul, and made it the capital of their empire.

The Byzantines left an influential heritage. Their civilization combined Christian beliefs with Greek science, philosophy, and arts. Byzantine artists created unique religious icons and mosaics. Byzantine scholars preserved Greek literature and produced their own great books, especially in the field of history.

| TOPIC **7** LESSON 4 | **Lesson Summary** **ECONOMIC EXPANSION AND CHANGE: THE CRUSADES AND AFTER** |

New farming methods started a series of changes in medieval Europe. By the 800s, farmers were using iron plows instead of wooden ones, and horses rather than slower oxen. Also, a new crop rotation system improved soil fertility. These changes helped farmers produce more food, and Europe's population nearly tripled between 1000 and 1300.

In the 1100s, trade improved, too, as warfare declined. Demand for goods increased and trade routes expanded. Trade centers arose along the routes and slowly grew into the first medieval cities. Merchants in such towns would ask the local lord or king for a **charter**. This was a document establishing rights and privileges for the town in exchange for a large sum of money, a yearly fee, or both.

As trade expanded, new business practices arose. The need for **capital**, or money for investment, stimulated the growth of banks. In addition, merchants sometimes joined together in **partnerships**, pooling their money to finance large-scale ventures. Other business changes included development of insurance and use of credit rather than cash, allowing merchants to travel without having to carry gold. Overall, however, the use of money increased. Peasants began selling their goods to townspeople for cash. Also, by 1300, most peasants were hired laborers or **tenant farmers**, paying rent for their land.

(Continues on the next page.)

Lesson Vocabulary

charter   in the Middle Ages, a written document that set out the rights and privileges of a town

capital   money or wealth used to invest in business or enterprise

partnership   a group of merchants who joined together to finance a large-scale venture that would have been too costly for any individual trader

tenant farmer   someone who would pay rent to a lord to farm part of the lord's land

Name_____ Class_____ Date_____

MODIFIED CORNELL NOTES

By 1000, merchants, traders, and artisans had become a powerful social class between nobles and peasants, called the **middle class**. Members of this class formed **guilds**, associations that controlled and protected specific trades or businesses. To become a guild member, people often began in early childhood as **apprentices**. After seven years, an apprentice became a **journeyman**, or salaried worker. Few became guild masters. Unlike in other areas of medieval life, women dominated some trades and even had their own guilds.

Towns and cities expanded rapidly during medieval times. Typical cities were overcrowded, with narrow streets, multistory houses, and no garbage or sewage systems. They were a fire hazard and breeding ground for disease.

The Crusades were a series of wars in which Christians fought Muslims for control of Middle Eastern lands. The Crusades were destructive, but ultimately opened a wider world to Europeans and increased the pace of change.

In 1071, Seljuk Turks conquered Byzantine lands in Asia Minor and then moved into the Holy Land. The Byzantine emperor asked Pope Urban II for help, and Urban launched the Crusades to free the Holy Land. Only the First Crusade was a success for Christians, who captured Jerusalem in 1099. In the Second Crusade, Jerusalem fell to the great Muslim leader Saladin. He agreed to reopen the city to Christian pilgrims after crusaders failed to take Jerusalem in the Third Crusade. By the Fourth Crusade in 1202, knights were fighting other Christians to help Venice against its Byzantine trade rivals. Crusaders captured and looted the Byzantine capital, Constantinople.

Lesson Vocabulary

middle class   a group of people, including merchants, traders, and artisans, whose rank was between nobles and peasants

guild   in the Middle Ages, an association of merchants or artisans who cooperated to uphold standards of their trade and to protect their economic interests

apprentice   a young person learning a trade from a master

journeyman   a salaried worker employed by a guild master

TOPIC 7 LESSON 5

Lesson Summary
THE FEUDAL MONARCHS AND THE CHURCH

During the early Middle Ages, European monarchs had limited power. However, from 1000 to 1300, increases in royal power and control gradually established the foundations of modern government.

In 1066, William the Conqueror took over England. By 1086, he had completed a census and property survey called the *Domesday Book*. It helped establish an effective taxation system and treasury. In 1154, Henry II ascended the English throne. He expanded the justice system. Royal court decisions became the foundation of English **common law**, a system based on custom and prior rulings. Henry II also set up a jury system that was the forerunner of today's grand jury.

Henry's son, King John, abused his power and was forced to sign the Magna Carta, or Great Charter. It required the king to obey the laws. It also established two important principles: **due process of law**, or protection from arrest without proper legal procedures, and **habeas corpus**, or protection from imprisonment without being charged with a crime. John also agreed not to raise taxes before consulting his Great Council of lords and clergy. Under later rulers, this council evolved into Parliament, England's legislature. Parliament eventually controlled the "power of the purse," meaning it would not approve new taxes unless the monarch met certain demands.

Unlike the English, early French monarchs did not rule a united kingdom. Then in 987, Hugh Capet became king and began expanding royal power. The Capetians stabilized the kingdom over the next 300 years. In 1179, Philip II took the throne. He gained control of English lands in Normandy and expanded territories in southern France, adding vast areas to his domain, and becoming Europe's most powerful ruler.

Louis IX came to power in 1226. Although he persecuted heretics and Jews and led crusades against Muslims, he also outlawed private wars, ended serfdom, and expanded royal courts. By the time of his death in 1270, France was a centralized monarchy ruling over a unified state. In 1302, the Estates General was set up, but this council of clergy, nobility, and townspeople never gained the "power of the purse" over French royalty.

(Continues on the next page.)

Lesson Vocabulary

common law a legal system based on custom and court rulings

due process of law the requirement that the government act fairly and in accordance with established rules in all that it does

habeus corpus principle that a person cannot be held in prison without first being charged with a specific crime

Lesson Summary
THE FEUDAL MONARCHS AND THE CHURCH (continued)

MODIFIED CORNELL NOTES

During the Middle Ages, popes and the Church spread their influence across Europe. European rulers, too, grew more powerful. However, this increase in power often resulted in conflict.

Rulers of the Holy Roman Empire, which extended from Germany to Italy, often confronted the pope over the appointment of Church officials. Pope Gregory VII wanted the Church free from lay (non-church) control. To do this he banned **lay investiture**, in which the emperor rather than the pope named and installed bishops. However, Holy Roman Emperor Henry IV said that bishops held royal lands under his control, so he had the right to appoint them. In 1076 the pope excommunicated him and threatened to crown a new emperor. Henry was forced to humble himself to the pope as a sinner, and Gregory forgave him. Later, Henry led an army to Rome, sending Gregory into exile. Fifty years later, the Concordat of Worms was accepted, giving popes sole power to invest bishops with religious authority and emperors the right to invest them with lands.

Power struggles over land also occurred during the 1100s and 1200s. Holy Roman Emperor Frederick I, called Frederick Barbarossa or "Red Beard," fought but failed to capture wealthy northern Italian cities. Instead, he arranged for his son to marry the heiress to Sicily and southern Italy, expanding his control there. His grandson, Frederick II, also sought but failed to control northern Italy. Ultimately, the Holy Roman Empire broke up into separate feudal states, while southern Italy went through centuries of chaos.

By the 1200s, the Church reached its peak of power. In 1198, Pope Innocent III took office and claimed supremacy over all other rulers. He excommunicated the English and French kings, and placed their kingdoms under interdict, barring people from religious sacraments. He also launched a holy war against heretics in southern France, killing tens of thousands. After Innocent's death, popes continued to claim supremacy, but they were challenged by the monarchs' growing power. In the late 1200s, France's Philip IV successfully challenged the pope on the issue of taxing the clergy. Philip then went on to engineer the election of a French pope.

Lesson Vocabulary

lay investiture   appointment of bishops by anyone who is not a member of the clergy

TOPIC 7 LESSON 6	**Lesson Summary**
	LEARNING, LITERATURE, AND ARTS OF THE MIDDLE AGES

Europe in the High Middle Ages experienced a blossoming of education, literature, and the arts. This was influenced by increased prosperity, contact with other cultures, and the rediscovery of ancient learning.

Education gained importance. By the 1100s, schools had sprung up near cathedrals, some evolving into the first universities. Muslim scholars had translated the works of Aristotle and other Greeks into Arabic. In Muslim Spain, they were translated into Latin, the language of European scholars. In the 1100s, the new translations initiated a revolution in learning. The Greek philosophers had used reason to discover truth; Christians believed that the Church was the final authority. Christian scholars struggled with this reason-based, rather than faith-based, approach. To resolve the conflict, they began to use reason to support Christian beliefs. This method is known as **scholasticism**. The most famous scholastic was Thomas Aquinas. He wrote *Summa theologica* to prove that faith and reason exist in harmony.

Scientific learning also reached Europe, including translations of Hippocrates on medicine and Euclid on geometry. Europeans adopted the more streamlined Hindu-Arabic numerals over cumbersome Roman numerals, allowing later scientists and mathematicians to make great strides.

Latin remained the language of Europe's scholars and churchmen. However, new literature emerged in the **vernacular**, or everyday languages of ordinary people. This change brought a flowering of literary works, including the *Song of Roland*, a French epic poem of chivalry; *Divine Comedy*, the Italian classic poem of heaven, hell, and purgatory by Dante Alighieri; and a portrait of English medieval life, the *Canterbury Tales*, by Geoffrey Chaucer.

(Continues on the next page.)

Lesson Vocabulary

scholasticism   in medieval Europe, the school of thought that used logic and reason to support Christian belief

vernacular   everyday language of ordinary people

Name_____ Class_____ Date_____

MODIFIED CORNELL NOTES

Architecture and the arts also flourished. Fortress-like Romanesque churches gave way to the **Gothic style**. Its key feature was **flying buttresses**—exterior stone supports that permitted thinner, higher walls and massive windows, bringing light and height to cathedrals. Other arts during the period include stained glass, religious paintings, and woven wall hangings. A famous example is the Bayeux Tapestry, an embroidered illustration of the Norman Conquest of England. The Gothic style was also applied to the decoration of books, in an artknown as **illumination**.

Lesson Vocabulary

Gothic style   type of European architecture that developed in the Middle Ages, characterized by flying buttresses, ribbed vaulting, thin walls, and high roofs

flying buttress   stone supports on the outside of a building that allowed builders to construct higher, thinner walls that contained large stained-glass windows.

illumination   the artistic decoration of books and manuscripts

TOPIC 7 / LESSON 7

Lesson Summary

THE LATE MIDDLE AGES: A TIME OF UPHEAVAL

In the mid-1300s a deadly disease called bubonic plague, or the Black Death, reached Europe. It was spread by fleas carried by rats. Eventually, the **epidemic**, or outbreak, killed one third of all Europeans. People were terrified, and normal life broke down. People fled cities or hid in their homes. Without workers, production declined. Survivors demanded higher wages, leading to inflation, or rising prices. Landlords tried to limit wages and forced villagers off the land. The plague not only spread death but also social unrest, as bitter, angry peasants revolted.

By the late Middle Ages, the Church, too, was in crisis. Many monks and priests had died during the plague. Survivors asked tough spiritual questions. The Church could not provide the strong leadership that was needed. For 70 years, a luxury-loving papal court had ruled in Avignon. Reformers arose within the Church, calling for change. In 1378, the reformers elected their own pope in Rome. French cardinals elected a rival pope. This Church schism, or split, finally ended in 1417 when a Church council removed authority from all three popes and elected a compromise candidate.

For most of this time, a destructive war raged. Between 1337 and 1453 England and France fought a series of conflicts known as the Hundred Years' War. Both sides wanted control of lands in France that had once been England's, of the English Channel, and of regional trade. England won early victories with new technology, the **longbow**. However, led by 17-year-old Joan of Arc, France began to win battles. Joan had told the uncrowned king, Charles VII, that God sent her to save France, so he authorized her to lead an army against the English. In one year, her troops won several victories, but she was captured, tried, and burned at the stake. Her martyrdom rallied French forces, and with their powerful new weapon, the cannon, they drove the English out of most of France. Ultimately, the war helped French kings expand their power. In England, it strengthened Parliament.

As Europe recovered from the plague, its population grew, manufacturing expanded, and trade increased. This set the stage for the Renaissance, the Reformation, and the Age of Exploration.

Lesson Vocabulary

epidemic outbreak of a rapidly spreading disease

longbow six-foot-long bow that could rapidly fire arrows with enough force to pierce most armor

Name_____ Class_____ Date_____

MODIFIED CORNELL NOTES

TOPIC **7** LESSON 8	**Lesson Summary**
	RUSSIA AND EASTERN EUROPE

Russia has three main geographic regions that shaped early life there. The northern forests have poor soil and a cold climate. A band of fertile land farther south attracted farmers. The southern **steppe**—an open, treeless grassland—provided pasture for herds. It allowed nomads to migrate easily from Asia into Europe.

Since ancient times, Slavic peoples had lived in areas that later became part of Russia. Vikings came from Scandinavia. The Vikings traveled south along Russia's rivers, trading with the Slavs and with Constantinople. The city of Kiev was at the center of this trade.

Russians date the origins of their country to 862, when a Viking tribe called the Rus began ruling from Novgorod in the north. Rus lands expanded to include Kiev, which became their capital.

In the 800s, Constantinople sent missionaries to Russia. Two Orthodox monks, Cyril and Methodius, developed the **Cyrillic** alphabet, which is still used in Russia. During the reign of the Rus king Vladimir, Orthodox Christianity became the religion of the Rus and they aligned themselves with the Byzantines.

Between 1236 and 1241, Mongols advanced into Russia. They were known as the Golden Horde. They burned Kiev and ruled Russia for the next 240 years. However, as long as they received tribute, the Mongols let Russian princes rule and they tolerated the Russian Orthodox Church. Although trade increased under the Mongols, Mongol rule cut Russia off from Western Europe at a time when Europeans were making great advances.

The princes of Moscow gained power under the Mongols, and Moscow became Russia's political and spiritual center. In 1380, these princes led other Russians in defeating the Golden Horde at the battle of Kulikovo. A driving force behind Moscow's successes was Ivan III, or Ivan the Great. Between 1462 and 1505, he brought much of northern Russia under his rule. He tried to limit the power of the nobles, and sometimes called himself tsar, the Russian word for Caesar. His grandson, Ivan IV, became the first Russian ruler officially crowned tsar. However, Ivan IV became unstable and violent. The ways in which he used his power earned him the title Ivan the Terrible.

Eastern Europe lies between Central Europe to the west and Russia to the east. Included in this region is the Balkan Peninsula. Both goods and cultural influences traveled along its rivers.

(Continues on the next page.)

Lesson Vocabulary

steppe   sparse, dry, treeless grassland

Cyrillic   relating to the Slavic alphabet derived from the Greek and traditionally attributed to St. Cyril; in modified form still used in modern Slavic languages

Name_____ Class_____ Date_____

MODIFIED CORNELL NOTES

Many ethnic groups settled in Eastern Europe. An **ethnic group** is a large group of people who share the same language and culture. The West Slavs settled in Poland and other parts of Eastern Europe, while the South Slavs occupied the Balkans. Asian peoples, like the Magyars, as well as Vikings and other Germanic peoples, also migrated to Eastern Europe. At times, some groups tried to dominate the region.

Many cultural and religious influences spread to Eastern Europe. Byzantine missionaries brought Eastern Orthodox Christianity and Byzantine culture to the Balkans. German knights and missionaries brought Roman Catholic Christianity to Poland and other areas. In the 1300s, the Ottomans invaded the Balkans and introduced Islam. Jews who were persecuted in Western Europe fled to Eastern Europe, especially to Poland, where their liberties were protected.

During the Middle Ages, Eastern Europe included many kingdoms and small states. The marriage in 1386 of Queen Jadwiga of Poland to Duke Wladyslaw Jagiello of Lithuania made Poland-Lithuania the largest state in Europe. However, power gradually shifted from the monarch to the nobles. The nobles met in a **diet**, or assembly, where a single noble could block passage of a law. Without a strong central government, Poland-Lithuania declined and eventually disappeared from the map.

The Magyars settled in Hungary and became Roman Catholics. The Hungarian king was forced to sign the Golden Bull of 1222, which strictly limited royal power. The Mongols overran Hungary in 1241, killing half of its people. Although they soon withdrew, the Ottoman Turks ended Hungarian independence in 1526.

Some of the South Slavs who settled in the Balkans became the ancestors of the Serbs. Most Serbs became Orthodox Christians and set up a state based on a Byzantine model. Serbia reached its height in the 1300s but could not withstand the advance of the Ottoman Turks. It was conquered by the Ottomans in 1389.

Lesson Vocabulary

ethnic group   large group of people who share the same language and cultural heritage

diet   assembly or legislature

Name_____ Class_____ Date_____

TOPIC 7
Review Questions
MEDIEVAL CHRISTIAN EUROPE (330–1450)

Answer the questions below using the information in the Lesson Summaries on the previous pages.

Lesson 1: The Early Middle Ages

1. Name three things that Charlemagne did to unify his kingdom.

_____

_____

2. What happened to Charlemagne's empire after his death?

_____

_____

Lesson 2: Feudalism and the Manor Economy

3. Describe the feudal contract.

_____

_____

4. What were serfs required to do?

_____

_____

Lesson 3: The Medieval Christian Church

5. What two actions could the Church take to punish Christians?

_____

_____

6. How did the Crusades help to weaken the Byzantine empire?

_____

_____

Lesson 4: Economic Expansion and Change: The Crusades and After

7. What advances in agriculture led to greater food production and increased population?

_____

_____

8. What new business practices arose as trade expanded?

_____

_____

Name_____

Lesson 5: The Feudal Monarchs and the ⬛

9. What important English document limited the absolu⬛

_____

_____

10. What did Popes Gregory VII and Innocent III claim?

_____

_____

Lesson 6: Learning, Literature, and Arts of the Middle Ages

11. How did Europeans become aware of Greek thinking?

_____

_____

12. How were Gothic cathedrals different from Romanesque churches?

_____

_____

Lesson 7: The Late Middle Ages: A Time of Upheaval

13. What caused a schism in the Church in the late 1300s?

_____

_____

14. Why did France and England fight the Hundred Years' War?

_____

_____

Lesson 8: Russia and Eastern Europe

15. Why do Russians consider 862 the year when their country began?

_____

_____

16. Why did Poland-Lithuania decline?

_____

_____

Date_____

____de

(____1500)

tions

(330–1450)

Chur

Class____

_, and compare how
and African cultures into

gion influence European and

Name_____

TOPIC
8

owing pages, complete the graphic organizer
uences on other civilizations. Outline the main
amic civilizations influenced European and African

Europe	Muslim Influence in Africa

TOPIC 7

Review Questions
MEDIEVAL CHRISTIAN EUROPE (330–1450) (continued)

Lesson 5: The Feudal Monarchs and the Church

9. What important English document limited the absolute power of the king?

_____

_____

10. What did Popes Gregory VII and Innocent III claim?

_____

_____

Lesson 6: Learning, Literature, and Arts of the Middle Ages

11. How did Europeans become aware of Greek thinking?

_____

_____

12. How were Gothic cathedrals different from Romanesque churches?

_____

_____

Lesson 7: The Late Middle Ages: A Time of Upheaval

13. What caused a schism in the Church in the late 1300s?

_____

_____

14. Why did France and England fight the Hundred Years' War?

_____

_____

Lesson 8: Russia and Eastern Europe

15. Why do Russians consider 862 the year when their country began?

_____

_____

16. Why did Poland-Lithuania decline?

_____

_____

TOPIC 8 — Note Taking Study Guide
THE MUSLIM WORLD AND AFRICA (730 B.C.–A.D. 1500)

Focus Question: Outline the main tenets of Islam, and compare how Arab Islamic civilizations influenced European and African cultures into the 1700s.

How did Arab Islamic civilization and religion influence European and African cultures?

As you read the Lesson Summaries on the following pages, complete the graphic organizer below to recognize examples of Muslim influences on other civilizations. Outline the main tenets of Islam, and compare how Arab Islamic civilizations influenced European and African cultures into the 1700s.

Muslim Influence in Europe	Muslim Influence in Africa

Lesson Summary

THE ORIGINS OF ISLAM

MODIFIED CORNELL NOTES

The religion of Islam, whose followers are called Muslims, emerged in the Arabian Peninsula. There, in A.D. 570, Muhammad was born in Mecca—a trading and religious center. Muhammad worked among nomadic herders called Bedouins. Later, he became a successful merchant and decided to marry at 25. He was known for his honesty in business and devotion to his family.

Muhammad often meditated on the moral ills of Meccan society, including greed. According to Muslim tradition, Muhammad became a prophet at 40 when he was asked by an angel to become God's messenger. When he began teaching, a few listened, but others opposed him with threats. In 622, he and his followers fled Mecca for Yathrib, on a journey called the **hijra**. Later Yathrib was called Medina. In Medina, thousands adopted Islam and formed strong, peaceful communities. When Meccan leaders grew hostile, Muslims defeated them in battle. Muhammad returned to Mecca in 630, where the Kaaba, which Muhammad dedicated to Allah, became the holiest Islamic site. Muhammad died in 632.

The sacred text of Islam is the **Quran**, believed to be the direct word of God as told to Muhammad. All Muslims study it to learn about God's will and living a good life.

Muslims believe that priests are not necessary to mediate between people and God. Muslims gather in **mosques** to pray. They follow the Five Pillars of Islam, which are the following duties: declaring faith, praying five times daily, giving charity to the poor, fasting during their holy month, and making the **hajj**, or pilgrimage to Mecca, if a person is able. Another duty is jihad, which means to struggle in God's service.

Because Jews and Christians worship the same God and study what are considered God's earlier revelations, Muslims call them "People of the Book." In most cases, they have been allowed religious freedom in Muslim societies.

The **Sharia** is a body of laws that interprets the Quran and applies religious principles to legal situations. According to the Quran, women are spiritually equal to men but have different roles. In different places, Muslims interpret women's roles and rights differently. In some cases, Muslims adopted practices of conquered peoples, such as requiring upper-class women to wear veils.

Lesson Vocabulary

hijra   Muhammad's journey from Mecca to Medina in 622

Quran   sacred text of Islam

mosque   Muslim house of worship

hajj   one of the Five Pillars of Islam, the pilgrimage that all Muslims are expected to make at least once in their lifetime

Sharia   body of Islamic law that includes interpretation of the Quran and applies Islamic principles to everyday life

MODIFIED CORNELL NOTES

TOPIC 8 LESSON 2

Lesson Summary
A MUSLIM EMPIRE

In 632, Abu Bakr became the first **caliph**, or successor to Muhammad. He united all Arab tribes as Muslims. Once united, the Arabs defeated the Persian empire and parts of the Byzantine empire. However, a schism between Sunni and Shiite Muslims occurred after Muhammad's death, and still exists today.

Shiites believe that Muhammad's successors must be descendants of his son-in-law, Ali. They also should be religious leaders and interpret the Quran. Sunnis believe that any pious male Muslim from Muhammad's tribe can lead without performing religious functions. Today, about 90 percent of Muslims are Sunni. Both groups believe in the same God, the Quran, and the Five Pillars of Islam, but they differ in religious practices and laws. **Sufis**, who may be Sunni or Shiite, meditate and fast to gain communion with God.

In the 700s, a powerful Meccan clan set up the Sunni Umayyad caliphate. They directed conquests that extended Muslim rule from Spain to the Indus River Valley. Their empire lasted until 750. The Muslims brought many people under their rule. Muslim leaders imposed a special tax on non-Muslims, but Jews, Christians, and Zoroastrians could worship and some held important positions. Many people converted to Islam.

(Continues on the next page.)

Lesson Vocabulary

caliph   successor to Muhammad as political and religious leader of the Muslims

Sufi   Muslim mystic who seeks communion with God through meditation, fasting, and other rituals

TOPIC 8 LESSON 2

Lesson Summary
A MUSLIM EMPIRE (continued)

The Umayyads later faced economic tensions and opposition from those who did not have the same privileges as Muslims. After capturing Damascus in 750, with strong support from Shiites and non-Arabs, Abu al-Abbas founded the Abbasid dynasty. The Abbasids ended conquests and supported education and learning. They enjoyed a golden age, with a more efficient government and a beautiful new capital, Baghdad, in the former Persian empire. Mosques with **minarets**, or slender towers, graced the cities, and markets sold goods from far-off lands.

In Spain, one of the Umayyads established a separate state. Muslims ruled parts of Spain until 1492. They were tolerant of other religions, supported scholars, and constructed grand buildings.

As the empire declined, independent dynasties took power. Seljuk Turks gained power, and their **sultan**, or ruler, controlled Baghdad by 1055, keeping the Abbasid caliph as a figurehead. Beginning in 1216, the Mongols attacked across southwest Asia. In 1258, they burned and looted Baghdad, ending the Abbasid dynasty.

Lesson Vocabulary

minaret   slender tower of a mosque, from which Muslims are called to prayer

sultan   Muslim ruler

TOPIC 8 LESSON 3

Lesson Summary
ACHIEVEMENTS OF MUSLIM CIVILIZATION

MODIFIED CORNELL NOTES

Muslim civilization enjoyed a golden age under the Abbasids. Their empire stretched into Asia, the Middle East, Africa, and Europe. Merchants crossed the Sahara, traveled the Silk Road to China, and sailed to India and Asia. New products and ideas were exchanged, and the religion of Islam was introduced to many regions. All this fueled the Muslim economy, leading to the development of partnerships, the use of credit, and a banking system. Artisans created manufactured goods for trade, and the government helped improve farming through large irrigation systems.

Muslim society allowed some **social mobility**, the ability to move up in social class through religious, scholarly, or military achievements. Most slaves were household servants and some were able to purchase their freedom. The children of some slaves could become free under another system.

The diverse cultures in the empire, as well as Islam, influenced art and literature. Early oral poetry told tales of nomadic life, while later poets developed elaborate rules for poems. Great Muslim poets include Firdawsi, who told the history of Persia, and Omar Khayyám, who wrote about fate and life in *The Rubáiyát*. Storytellers often used short anecdotes to entertain people. In architecture, buildings reflected Byzantine influences, and mosques included domes and minarets. Muslim artists also used **calligraphy**, the art of beautiful handwriting, for decoration on buildings and in books.

Muslims made great strides in education. Both boys and girls were educated so they could study the Quran. Several cities supported learning centers with vast libraries. There, scholars translated Greek, Hindu, and Buddhist texts. Known in Europe as Averröes, the philosopher Ibn Rushd believed that knowledge should meet the standards of reason. Another Muslim thinker, Ibn Khaldun, studied history scientifically and advised others in ways to avoid errors.

In mathematics, al-Khwarizmi pioneered the study of algebra. Muhammad al-Razi, chief physician in the hospital at Baghdad, wrote books on diseases and medical practices. Ibn Sina, a famous Persian physician, compiled an encyclopedia of medical knowledge. Both doctors' works guided medical study in Europe for 500 years. Other physicians improved ways to save eyesight and mix medicines.

Lesson Vocabulary

social mobility   the ability to move between social classes

calligraphy   the art of producing beautiful handwriting

Name_____ Class_____ Date_____

The Ottomans were Turkish-speaking nomads who had expanded into Asia Minor and the Balkan Peninsula by the 1300s. They were successful in capturing Constantinople in 1453. The city was renamed Istanbul and became the capital of the Ottoman empire.

The Ottoman empire enjoyed a golden age under Suleiman, who ruled from 1520 to 1566. He expanded the empire into Asia, Africa, and Europe. Although he was defeated at Vienna in 1529, the empire remained the largest and most powerful in Europe and the Middle East for centuries. Suleiman had absolute power, but a council helped him govern. He based the justice system on the Sharia, as well as royal edicts.

The top two social classes in Ottoman society—military men and intellectuals, such as scientists and lawyers—were nearly all Muslims. Below them were men involved in trade and production, and then farmers. All people belonged to religious communities, which provided for education and legal matters. The Jewish community, which had been expelled from Spain, possessed international banking connections that benefited the Ottomans.

Ottomans converted some young Christian boys to Islam and trained them for government service. Some were chosen for the **janizaries**, an elite force of the Ottoman army. The brightest became government officials.

Ottoman culture included great poets, painters, and architects. However, after Suleiman's death, the empire declined. By the 1700s, it had lost control of areas in Europe and Africa.

By the early 1500s, the Safavids united an empire in Persia (modern Iran). They were Shiite Muslims who fought with Sunni Ottomans to the west and the Mughals in India to the east. Their greatest king, or **shah**, was Shah Abbas who ruled from 1588 to 1629. He created a strong military and developed military alliances with Europeans. Abbas lowered taxes and encouraged industry. He tolerated other religions and built a capital at Isfahan, which became a center for silk trading.

After Abbas's death, the empire suffered from religious disputes until its end in 1722. In the late 1700s, a new dynasty, the Qajars, won control of Iran, made Tehran the capital, and ruled until 1925.

Lesson Vocabulary

janizary   a member of the elite forces of the Ottoman army

shah   king

TOPIC 8 LESSON 5

Lesson Summary

EARLY CIVILIZATIONS OF AFRICA

Africa includes tropical rain forests, grassy plains called **savannas**, and deserts such as the vast Sahara. Deserts, rain forests, the interior plateau, and rivers with **cataracts**, or waterfalls, limited travel and trade. On the other hand, an interior valley and the Mediterranean and Red seas provided overseas trade routes to Asia and Europe. By A.D. 200, camel caravans helped transport goods across the Sahara. Valuable minerals also encouraged trade.

Before 2500 B.C., there were grasslands and savanna in the Sahara. Due to climate change, however, the area slowly dried up and became desert—a process called **desertification**. As a result, people migrated to find new farmland. Between 1000 B.C. and A.D. 1000, people from West Africa moved south and east. They spoke Bantu languages. These Bantu peoples merged with existing peoples and brought skills in farming and ironworking.

About 2700 B.C., the civilization of Nubia, or Kush, developed on the upper Nile. Egypt controlled Nubia for about 500 years beginning in 1500 B.C. Early Nubian culture was influenced by Egyptian architecture and religion.

Forced to move by Assyrian invaders, the Nubians established a new capital in Meroë about 500 B.C. Meroë developed into a successful trade center. Nearby areas were rich in iron ore and timber. Using wood to fuel smelting furnaces, the Nubians made iron tools and weapons, improving their defense. The Nubians also established a new religion and a system of writing. In A.D. 350, Nubia was conquered by an invader from the south, King Ezana of Axum.

While Nubia was thriving along the Nile, Carthage emerged along the Mediterranean in North Africa. Founded by Phoenician traders, Carthage forged a huge empire from 800 B.C. to 146 B.C. At the end of the Third Punic War, however, Rome destroyed Carthage. The Romans then utilized North Africa's farmlands to provide grain for their armies. They also built roads and cities, and later brought Christianity to the area.

Muslim Arabs took control of North Africa in the 690s. Islam replaced Christianity, and traders later carried the religion to West Africa. Arabic replaced Latin as North Africa's main language.

Lesson Vocabulary

savanna   grassy plain with irregular patterns of rainfall

cataract   waterfall

desertification   process by which fertile or semi-desert land becomes desert

Lesson Summary
KINGDOMS OF WEST AFRICA

MODIFIED CORNELL NOTES

After early farmers moved from the Sahara to more fertile lands to the south, they began to produce more food than they needed, or a **surplus**. They were then able to trade surplus food for goods from other villages. A trade network developed that eventually connected Africa with Asia and Europe. Cities developed along the trade routes.

Much of the trade exchanged gold for salt, each a valuable product or **commodity**. Gold was common in West Africa, while salt was plentiful in the Sahara. People needed salt to stay healthy and preserve food. In fact, traders might exchange one pound of salt for one pound of gold.

In about A.D. 800, the ancient West African kingdom of Ghana became a center of trade. From there, the king controlled the salt and gold trade. In addition, the king administered justice and other government activities, and kept the peace. Ghana was very prosperous and attracted Muslims from the north. They brought new ideas about military technology and business. Later, Ghana was swallowed up by a new power, the rising kingdom of Mali.

About 1235, Sundiata established the empire of Mali. He gained control of trade routes, the gold mining regions, and the salt supplies. Mansa Musa, Mali's greatest ruler, came to power in about 1312. He fostered justice and religious freedom. His pilgrimage to Mecca created ties to Muslim states and brought Islamic scholars to Mali to provide religious instruction.

After Mali weakened, another kingdom, Songhai, developed in West Africa. After 1492, Songhai's emperor Askia Muhammad established a Muslim dynasty, expanded the territory, and improved the government. He strengthened ties to other Muslim states and built mosques and schools. However, internal conflicts weakened the empire, which was conquered by the sultan of Morocco around 1591.

Smaller societies, such as Benin, also flourished in the region from A.D. 500 to 1500. In the rain forests of the Guinea coast in the 1300s, the people of Benin built farming villages. They also traded pepper, ivory, and slaves to neighbors. At the same time, the Hausa built clay-walled cities. These cities grew into commercial centers, where artisans produced goods, and merchants traded with Arabs. Many Hausa rulers were women.

Lesson Vocabulary

surplus an amount that is more than needed; excess

commodity valuable product

TOPIC
8
LESSON 7

Lesson Summary
TRADING STATES OF EAST AFRICA

After 100 B.C., the kingdom of Axum spread from the Ethiopian highlands to the Red Sea coast. Axum included the upland capital city of Axum and the port of Adulis on the Red Sea. The peoples of Axum were descended from African farmers and people from the Middle East. By about A.D. 400, Axum controlled a rich trade network connecting Africa, India, and the Mediterranean. Traders exchanged many cultural influences in their travels.

Axum became a Christian kingdom in the 300s. At first, this helped strengthen trade ties with other Christian countries. When Islam began spreading across North Africa in the 600s, however, Axum became isolated and lost power. Civil war and economic decline combined to weaken Axum.

Axum's legacy, however, survived for centuries in a portion of present-day Ethiopia. There, Christianity was a unifying influence that helped give Ethiopia a unique identity among Muslim neighbors. A distinct culture developed in Ethiopia. In the 1200s, under King Lalibela, Christian churches were carved below ground into mountain rocks. Ethiopian Christianity absorbed local customs.

After Axum declined, Arab and Persian traders established Muslim communities along the East African coast. By the 600s, ships regularly took advantage of monsoon winds to sail to India and back, and the cities in East Africa grew wealthy by trading goods with Africa, Southeast Asia, and China. The cities were independent, and although they competed for power, relations among them were generally peaceful. By the 1000s, the mixture of cultures created unique architecture, as well as a new language and culture, both called **Swahili**. The language was Bantu-based, using some Arabic words and written in Arabic.

Great Zimbabwe, the capital of a great inland Zimbabwe empire, was built by a succession of Bantu-speaking peoples between 900 and 1500. It reached its height around 1300. The city included great stone buildings, and its people mined gold and traded goods across the Indian Ocean. By the 1500s, the empire of Zimbabwe was in decline. Later, Portuguese traders tried, but failed, to find the region's source of gold.

Lesson Vocabulary

Swahili   an East African culture that emerged in about A.D. 1000; also a Bantu-based language, blending Arabic words and written in Arabic script

TOPIC 8 — LESSON 8

Lesson Summary
DIVERSE PEOPLES AND TRADITIONS IN AFRICA

In small societies in medieval Africa, the **nuclear family**, or one set of parents and their children, lived and worked together. In other societies, the family included several generations. **Patrilineal** families passed inheritances through the father's side of the family, while **matrilineal** families passed property down through the mother's side. Each family belonged to a **lineage**, a group of households with a common ancestor, and a clan included several lineages descended from a common ancestor.

Political patterns depended on the size and culture of a community. In small societies, political power was often shared among a number of people. Village decisions were often made by **consensus**, or general agreement, after open discussions. Because elders had experience, their opinions usually carried the greatest weight. Women sometimes took strong roles in the marketplace or as peacemakers.

Large empires usually required villages to obey decisions made by distant rulers and their courts. Another form of government that developed grouped many villages into districts and provinces governed by the king's officials. Around A.D. 1500, Kongo, a kingdom in central Africa, governed in this way. The king had limited powers. Villagers were governed by appointed royal officials, but each village had its own chief.

Early African religions were varied and complex. They involved many gods, goddesses, rituals, and ceremonies. Many people believed in one supreme being, and some honored the spirits of ancestors. By A.D. 1000, Christianity and Islam had spread and absorbed many local practices and beliefs.

The tradition of African arts includes the Egyptian pyramids, built 4,000 years ago. Much art served decorative, religious, or ceremonial purposes, such as cloths, pottery, and jewelry. Objects often had symbolic meanings, such as the bright blue-and-gold kente cloth of West Africa, which was reserved for the wealthy and powerful.

Medieval written histories from Africa provide records of laws, religion, and society. Arabic provided a common written language in Muslim areas, and Muslim scholars gathered in important cities. In West Africa, **griots**, or professional storytellers, kept traditions alive by reciting ancient stories and histories. Folktales and other stories encouraged a sense of community and common values.

Lesson Vocabulary

nuclear family   family unit consisting of parents and children

patrilineal   kinship ties that are passed on through the father's side of the family

matrilineal   kinship ties that are passed on through the mother's side of the family

lineage   a group claiming a common ancestor

consensus   widespread agreement among all members of a group

griot   professional storyteller in early West Africa

Name_____ Class_____ Date_____

TOPIC 8 — Review Questions
THE MUSLIM WORLD AND AFRICA (730 B.C.–A.D. 1500)

Answer the questions below using the information in the Lesson Summaries on the previous pages.

Lesson 1: The Origins of Islam
1. What is the Quran?

_____

_____

2. Why do Muslims call Jews and Christians "People of the Book"?

_____

_____

Lesson 2: A Muslim Empire
3. What are the differences between Shiite and Sunni beliefs?

_____

_____

4. What two groups took power from the Abbasid dynasty?

_____

_____

Lesson 3: Achievements of Muslim Civilization
5. How did trade affect the Abbasid empire?

_____

_____

6. How did Muslim poetry change during this time?

_____

_____

Lesson 4: The Ottoman and Safavid Empires
7. What social classes existed in the Ottoman empire?

_____

_____

8. What religious difference existed between the Ottoman and Safavid empires?

_____

_____

Name_____ Class_____ Date_____

TOPIC 8	**Review Questions**
	THE MUSLIM WORLD AND AFRICA (730 B.C.–A.D. 1500) (continued)

Lesson 5: Early Civilizations of Africa

9. How did the Bantu migrations affect existing cultures?

_____

_____

10. How did Meroë's resources strengthen Nubia?

_____

_____

Lesson 6: Kingdoms of West Africa

11. The king of Ghana controlled the trade of which two commodities?

_____

_____

12. What were Mansa Musa's contributions to Mali?

_____

_____

Lesson 7: Trading States of East Africa

13. How did the spread of Islam in North Africa affect the Axum empire?

_____

_____

14. How did Axum's decline affect trade in East Africa?

_____

_____

Lesson 8: Diverse Peoples and Traditions in Africa

15. What are a lineage and a clan?

_____

_____

16. How did the rulers of the Kongo control their lands?

_____

_____

Name _____ Class _____ Date _____

Focus Question: How did the civilizations of China and India influence their neighbors in Asia and Southeast Asia?

As you read the Lesson Summaries on the following pages, complete the graphic organizer by listing some features of each area's culture to help you understand the influences these countries or regions had on each other.

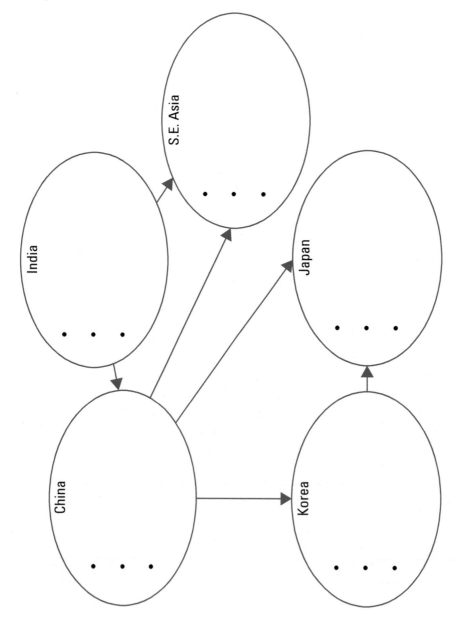

TOPIC 9 LESSON 1 — Lesson Summary
THE DELI SULTANATE AND MUGHAL INDIA

After 550, rival princes fought for control of India. Around 1000, Muslim armies moved in. Muslim attacks included onslaughts that killed many Hindus and destroyed Buddhist temples. Muslims triumphed due to military superiority, rivalries among Hindu princes, and the many Hindus who converted to Islam. By the 1100s, a **sultan** controlled northern India. From the capital in Delhi, the Delhi sultanate ruled from 1206 to 1526.

Muslim rulers reorganized Indian government and increased trade. During the Mongol raids of the 1200s, scholars fled from Baghdad to India, bringing Persian and Greek learning with them. These newcomers helped turn Delhi into a place where art and architecture flourished. However, in 1389, Mongols attacked Delhi, destroying much of its culture.

The Muslim advance brought two very different religious groups—Hindus and Muslims—face to face. Muslims worshiped a single god, while Hindus prayed to many. Hindus accepted the caste system, while Islam promoted equality.

Gradually, the cultures blended. Hindus were allowed to practice their religion, and some **rajahs**, or local Hindu rulers, continued governing. Many Hindus converted to Islam because it rejected the caste system. Muslims followed some Hindu customs and ideas. A new language, called Urdu, blended Arabic, Persian, and the Indian language spoken in Delhi. A new religion, Sikhism, emerged. It taught that there was one God for all people and that all people were equal regardless of race, gender, social status, or religious beliefs.

In 1526, Babur led Turkish and Mongol armies into northern India to establish the Mughal dynasty, which would last until 1857. Babur's grandson, Akbar, known as Akbar the Great, ruled from 1556 to 1605. He established a strong central government that had paid officials; he also modernized the army and encouraged international trade. He allowed Hindus to work in government and promoted peace through religious tolerance.

After Akbar's death, his son's wife, Nur Jahan, managed the government skillfully. She was the most powerful woman in Indian history until the twentieth century. Akbar's grandson, Shah Jahan, ruled when Mughal literature, art, and architecture were at their height. He built the Taj Mahal, a tomb for his wife. It is a spectacular building and a great monument of the Mughal empire.

Lesson Vocabulary

sultan   Muslim ruler

rajah   in ancient India, an elected warrior chief of an Aryan tribe

MODIFIED CORNELL NOTES

Lesson Summary
GOLDEN AGES IN CHINA: TANG AND SONG DYNASTIES

After the Han dynasty collapsed, China broke apart. During the Sui dynasty (589–618), the emperor Sui Wendi reunited north and south. In 618, the general Li Yuan and his son Li Shimin led a revolt and established the Tang dynasty. Eight years later, Li Shimin compelled his aging father to step down. Li Shimin then took the throne under the name Tang Taizong. Later Tang rulers conquered many territories and forced Vietnam, Tibet, and Korea to become **tributary states**, or self-governing states that sent tribute. Other Tang rulers, such as Empress Wu Zhao, restored the Han system of uniform government. Tang emperors also undertook **land reform** in which they redistributed land to peasants. However, the Tang dynasty eventually weakened. In 907, the last Tang emperor was overthrown.

In 960, Zhao Kuangyin founded the Song dynasty. The Song ruled for 319 years. They faced the constant threat of invaders from the north. Nonetheless, the Song period was a time of great achievement. A new type of faster-growing rice was imported from Southeast Asia. The rise in productivity created food surpluses, freeing more people to pursue commerce, learning, or the arts.

Under the Tang and Song, China was a well-ordered society. At its head was the emperor. Scholar-officials had the highest social status. Most of them came from the **gentry**, or wealthy, landowning class. The vast majority of Chinese were poor peasant farmers. Merchants had the lowest status because their riches came from the labor of others. Women had higher status during this period than they did later. However, when a woman married, she could not keep her **dowry**, the payment that a woman brings to a marriage. She could also never remarry.

The Tang and Song developed a rich culture. Song landscape painting was influenced by Daoist beliefs. Buddhist themes influenced Chinese sculpture and architecture. The Indian stupa evolved into the Chinese **pagoda**. The Chinese also perfected the making of porcelain. Among the gentry, poetry was the most respected form of literature. Probably the greatest Tang poet was Li Bo, who wrote some 2,000 poems.

Lesson Vocabulary

tributary state   independent state that has to acknowledge the supremacy of another state and pay tribute to its ruler

land reform   a break-up of large agricultural holdings for redistribution among peasants

gentry   wealthy, landowning class

dowry   in some societies, payment a bride's family makes to the bridegroom and his family; payment a woman brings to a marriage

pagoda   multi-storied Buddhist temple with eaves that curve up at the corners

TOPIC 9 LESSON 3	Lesson Summary
	THE MONGOL EMPIRE AND MING CHINA

The Mongols were nomads who grazed their animals on the **steppes**, or treeless plains, of Central Asia. Mongol clans spent much of their time warring with one another. In the early 1200s, however, a Mongol chieftain united these clans. He took the name Genghis Khan, meaning "Universal Ruler." Under his leadership, Mongol forces conquered a vast empire. After his death, his heirs continued to expand the Mongol empire. For the next 150 years, they dominated much of Asia. The Mongols established peace and order within their domains. They controlled and protected the Silk Road, and trade flourished.

Genghis Khan's grandson, Kublai Khan, toppled the last Song emperor in China in 1279. He named his dynasty the Yuan. Only Mongols could serve in his military and in the highest government jobs, but he allowed Chinese officials to continue to rule in the provinces. He welcomed many foreigners to his court, including Ibn Battuta and Marco Polo. Polo's writings about the wealth and splendor of China sparked European interest in Asia. Chinese products, including gunpowder and porcelain, made their way to Europe.

The Yuan dynasty declined after Kublai Khan's death in 1294. Finally, Zhu Yuanzhang formed a rebel army that toppled the Mongols. In 1368, he founded the Ming, or "brilliant," dynasty.

Ming China was immensely productive. Better methods of fertilizing improved farming. The Ming repaired the canal system, which made trade easier and allowed cities to grow.

The Ming carefully limited trade with Europeans. By accepting only silver or gold in exchange for goods in high demand in Europe, such as silk, tea, and porcelain, the Ming caused a massive flow of precious metals into China.

The arts and literature also flourished in Ming China. Ming artists developed their own styles of painting and created beautiful blue-and-white porcelain. Ming writers composed novels and the world's first detective stories.

Mathematicians during the Ming period turned to popular and practical application. The use of the **abacus**, a much earlier invention for making calculations, now spread swiftly within and beyond China.

(Continues on the next page.)

Lesson Vocabulary

steppe   sparse, dry, treeless plain

abacus   a device used for counting and calculating by sliding small balls or beads along rods or in grooves

TOPIC 9 LESSON 3

Lesson Summary
THE MONGOL EMPIRE AND MING CHINA (continued)

Many Ming scholars sought to integrate their own traditions with the Western science and technology they were learning from Jesuit missionaries. In 1629, Xu Guangqi led an imperial research program to reform the inaccurate Chinese calendar. Assisted by Jesuits, Chinese scholars used Western ideas and technology, including telescopes, to make observations of the heavenly bodies.

Early Ming rulers sent Chinese fleets into distant waters to show the glory of their empire. The most famous voyages were those of Zheng He. Between 1405 and 1433, he commanded seven **expeditions** that explored the coasts of Southeast Asia, India, the Persian Gulf, and East Africa. However, after Zheng He died in 1435, the Ming emperor banned the building of seagoing ships, and overseas expeditions came to a halt. Historians are not sure why.

Lesson Vocabulary

expedition   voyage to explore unknown lands

Lesson Summary
KOREA AND ITS TRADITIONS

MODIFIED CORNELL NOTES

Korea is located on a peninsula that juts south from the Chinese mainland. Because of its location, Korea has been strongly influenced by China. The earliest Koreans probably migrated from Siberia and northern Manchuria. They evolved their own ways of life before they were influenced by China. In 108 B.C., the Han emperor, Wudi, invaded Korea. The invasion brought with it Confucian traditions and Chinese ideas.

Between A.D. 100 and 668, local rulers forged three kingdoms in Korea: Koguryo, Paekche, and Silla. The three kingdoms often warred with one another or with China. Still, Chinese ideas continued to spread there. Missionaries brought Buddhism to Korea. Korean monks then traveled to China and brought home Chinese arts and learning. In 668, the Silla kingdom united the Korean peninsula. Under the Silla dynasty, Korea became a tributary state of China. As Chinese influence increased, Confucian views took root. However, Koreans adapted Confucian ideas to fit their own traditions.

The Koryo dynasty replaced the Silla in 935. Confucianism and Buddhism were both influential during this time. Koreans used woodblock printing from China to produce Buddhist texts. They learned to make Chinese porcelain. They then perfected the technique for making **celadon**, a porcelain with an unusual blue-green glaze.

The Mongols first invaded Korea in 1231 and occupied the country until the 1350s. When their rule collapsed, the Koryo returned to power. However, in the late 1300s the Korean general Yi Song-gye overthrew them and set up the Choson dynasty. This was the longest-lasting, but final, Korean dynasty.

In 1443, King Sejong decided to replace complex Chinese writing. Sejong had experts develop **hangul**, the Korean phonetic alphabet. Hangul spread quickly because it was easier to use than written Chinese. Its use led to an extremely high **literacy rate**.

In the 1590s, the Japanese armies invaded Korea. To stop the invaders at sea, Korean Admiral Yi Sun-shin sailed armored ships into the Japanese fleet. Eventually, the Japanese armies withdrew from Korea. As they left, they carried off many Korean artisans in order to introduce their skills to Japan.

Lesson Vocabulary

celadon   porcelain made in Korea with an unusual blue-green glaze

hangul   alphabet that uses symbols to represent the sounds of spoken Korean

literacy rate   percentage of people who can read and write

MODIFIED CORNELL NOTES

Lesson Summary
THE ISLAND KINGDOM OF JAPAN

Japan felt the influence of Chinese civilization early in its history yet continued to maintain its own distinct culture. Japan sits on an archipelago, or chain of islands. In early times, surrounding seas both protected and isolated Japan. This region has many volcanoes, earthquakes, and tidal waves called **tsunamis**.

Early Japanese society was divided into clans. The clans honored kami, or powers that were natural or divine. The worship of these forces of nature became known as Shinto. Missionaries from Korea introduced Buddhism to Japan in the 500s. They also brought knowledge of Chinese culture. In the 600s, Prince Shotoku sent nobles to study in China. The visitors brought back Chinese technology and arts. In 710, the Japanese emperor built a new capital at Nara, modeled after the Chinese capital.

The Japanese kept some Chinese ways but discarded others. This process is known as **selective borrowing**. The Japanese revised the Chinese writing system and added **kana**, symbols representing syllables. From 794 to 1185, Heian was the Japanese capital. Heian women, such as Murasaki Shikibu, produced some of the most important works of Japanese literature.

Japan evolved into a feudal society. Theoretically, the emperor was the head of this society, but really he was powerless. The shogun, or supreme military commander, had the real power. Minamoto Yoritomo was appointed shogun in 1192. He set up the Kamakura shogunate. The shogun distributed land to lords, called daimyo, who agreed to support him with their armies. They, in turn, granted land to lesser warriors called **samurai**. Samurai developed a code of values, known as **bushido** or the "way of the warrior." The code emphasized honor, bravery, and loyalty to one's lord.

(Continues on the next page.)

Lesson Vocabulary

tsunami   a very large wave caused by an earthquake or very strong wind

selective borrowing   adopting or adapting some cultural traits but discarding others

kana   in the Japanese writing system, phonetic symbols representing syllables

samurai   member of the warrior class in Japanese feudal society

bushido   code of conduct for samurai during the feudal period in Japan

TOPIC 9

LESSON 5

Lesson Summary

THE ISLAND KINGDOM OF JAPAN (continued)

The Mongol conquest of China and Korea threatened Japan. Kublai Khan tried to invade Japan in 1274 and 1281, but typhoons wrecked the Mongol ships during both invasions. However, after the attempted invasions, the Kamakura shogunate crumbled. By 1590, Toyotomi Hideyoshi had brought most of Japan under his control. In 1600, Tokugawa Ieyasu defeated his rivals to become master of Japan. The Tokugawa shoguns created an orderly society. With peace restored to the countryside, agriculture improved and trade flourished.

During Japan's feudal age, a Buddhist sect known as Zen won widespread acceptance. Zen monks were great scholars, yet they stressed the importance of reaching a moment of "non-knowing."

MODIFIED CORNELL NOTES

Southeast Asia is made up of two regions: mainland Southeast Asia, which includes present-day Myanmar, Thailand, Cambodia, Laos, Vietnam, and Malaysia; and island Southeast Asia, which consists of more than 20,000 islands. These islands include the present-day nations of Indonesia, Singapore, Brunei, and the Philippines. Historically, sea trade between China and India had to pass through the Malacca or Sunda straits, so the islands that controlled these straits were strategically important. Women took part in the spice trade and had greater equality there than they did elsewhere in Asia. Matrilineal descent, or inheritance through the mother, was an accepted custom in this region.

In the early centuries A.D., Indian merchants and Hindu priests slowly spread their culture through Southeast Asia. Later, monks introduced Theravada Buddhism. Indian traders eventually carried Islam to Indonesia, and as far east as the Philippines. Trade with India brought prosperity. Merchants exchanged cotton cloth, jewels, and perfume for timber, spices, and gold.

A series of kingdoms and empires developed in Southeast Asia. The kingdom of Pagan arose in present-day Myanmar. In 1044, King Anawrahta united the region and brought Buddhism to his people. He filled his capital city with magnificent **stupas**, or dome-shaped shrines.

Indian influences also shaped the Khmer empire, which reached its peak between 800 and 1350. Its greatest rulers controlled much of present-day Cambodia, Thailand, and Malaysia. A crowning achievement was the building of the temple at Angkor Wat by King Suryvarman II. Khmer rulers became Hindus, but most people were Buddhists.

In Indonesia, the trading empire of Srivijaya flourished from the 600s to the 1200s. Both Hinduism and Buddhism reached Srivijaya. The heart of northern Vietnam was the Red River delta. There, the river irrigated fertile rice paddies. In 111 B.C., Han armies conquered the region, and China remained in control for the next 1,000 years. During that time, the Vietnamese absorbed Confucian ideas. Unlike the rest of Southeast Asia, where Theravada Buddhism had the strongest impact, Vietnam adopted Mahayana Buddhism from China. In A.D. 39, two noble sisters, Trung Trac and Trung Nhi, led an uprising that briefly drove out the Chinese. Finally, in 939, Vietnam was able to break free from China.

Lesson Vocabulary

stupa   large, domelike Buddhist shrine

TOPIC 9 — Review Questions
CIVILIZATIONS OF ASIA (500–1650)

Answer the questions below using the information in the Lesson Summaries on the previous pages.

Lesson 1: The Deli Sultanate and Mughal India

1. What were Nur Jahan's contributions to the Mughal empire?

_____

_____

2. Identify Supporting Details Record details that support this statement: In India, the Hindu and Muslim cultures blended.

_____

_____

Lesson 2: Golden Ages in China: Tang and Song Dynasties

3. What are tributary states?

_____

_____

4. Compare and Contrast Compare and contrast the social classes in Tang and Song China.

_____

_____

Lesson 3 The Mongol Empire and Ming China

5. Why did trade flourish under the Mongols?

_____

_____

6. Recognize Sequence List in correct chronological order the three Chinese dynasties mentioned in the Summary.

_____

_____

Lesson 4: Korea and Its Traditions

7. What is hangul?

_____

_____

8. Categorize List events and developments during each of the three Korean dynasties

_____

_____

Lesson 5: The Island Kingdom of Japan

9. **Categorize** List the levels in Japanese feudal society and give details about each level.

_____

_____

10. How did the shogun gain the support of the daimyo?

_____

_____

Lesson 6: The Many Cultures of Southeast Asia

11. **Summarize** Summarize the influence of India on Southeast Asia.

_____

_____

12. What is matrilineal descent?

_____

_____

Name_____ Class_____ Date_____

<table>
<tr><td>TOPIC
10</td><td>**Note Taking Study Guide**
THE RENAISSANCE AND REFORMATION (1300–1650)</td></tr>
</table>

Focus Question: What ideas of the Renaissance both influenced and were carried forth through the Reformation?

As you read the Lesson Summaries on the following pages, complete the graphic organizer below to identify examples of Renaissance thought that both led to the Reformation and were important aspects of the Reformation.

Cause	Effect
Renaissance Idea or Practice	**Reformation Idea or Practice**
Humanism's emphasis on individual achievement	Each individual can interpret Scripture for him- or herself

Name_____ Class_____ Date_____

MODIFIED CORNELL NOTES

A new age called the Renaissance, meaning "rebirth," marked a great change in culture, politics, society, and economics. In Italy, it began in the 1300s and reached its peak around 1500. Instead of focusing on religion, as in the Middle Ages, the Renaissance explored the human experience. At the same time, there was a new emphasis on individual achievement. At the heart of the Renaissance was an intellectual movement called **humanism**. Renaissance **humanists** studied the classical cultures of Greece and Rome to try to better understand their own times. They emphasized the humanities—subjects such as rhetoric, poetry, and history.

Poet Francesco Petrarch was an early Renaissance humanist. He gathered a library of Greek and Roman manuscripts. This opened the works of Cicero, Homer, and Virgil to Western Europeans. Italy was the birthplace of the Renaissance for many reasons. It had been the center of the Roman empire; remains of that ancient culture were all around. Rome was also the seat of the Roman Catholic Church, an important **patron** of the arts. Furthermore, Italy's location encouraged trade with markets on the Mediterranean, in Africa, and in Europe. Trade provided the wealth that fueled the Renaissance. In Italy's city-states, powerful merchant families, such as the Medici family of Florence, lent political and economic leadership and supported the arts.

Renaissance art reflected humanism. Renaissance painters returned to the realism of classical times by developing improved ways to represent humans and landscapes. For example, the discovery of **perspective** allowed artists to create realistic art and to paint scenes that appeared three-dimensional. The greatest of the Renaissance artists were Leonardo da Vinci, Michelangelo, and Raphael.

Some Italian writers wrote guidebooks to help ambitious people who wanted to rise in the Renaissance world. The most widely read of these was The Book of the Courtier, by Baldassare Castiglione. His ideal courtier was a well-educated, well-mannered aristocrat who mastered many fields. Niccolò Machiavelli wrote a guide for rulers, titled The Prince, on how to gain and maintain power.

Lesson Vocabulary

humanism   an intellectual movement at the heart of the Renaissance that focused on education and the classics

humanist   someone who studies subjects such as grammar, rhetoric, poetry, and history that were taught in ancient Greece and Rome

patron   a person who provides financial support for the arts

perspective   artistic technique used to give paintings and drawings a three-dimensional effect

TOPIC 10 LESSON 2 — Lesson Summary
THE RENAISSANCE IN NORTHERN EUROPE

By the 1400s, northern Europe began to enjoy the economic growth needed to develop its own Renaissance. An astounding invention—the printing press—helped to spread Renaissance ideas. In about 1455, Johann Gutenberg printed the first complete edition of the Bible using the new printing press. The printing press caused a printing revolution. Before, books were made by hand. They were rare and expensive. Printed books were cheaper and easier to produce. Now more books were available, so more people learned to read. Printed books exposed Europeans to new ideas and new places.

The northern Renaissance began in the prosperous cities of Flanders, a thriving center of trade. Flemish painters pursued realism in their art. One of the most important Flemish painters was Jan van Eyck. He portrayed townspeople and religious scenes in rich detail. Pieter Bruegel used vibrant color to portray lively scenes of peasant life. Peter Paul Rubens blended the tradition of Flemish realism with themes from mythology, the Bible, and history. German painter Albrecht Dürer traveled to Italy to study the techniques of the Italian masters. He soon became a pioneer in spreading Renaissance ideas to northern Europe. Dürer applied the painting techniques he learned in Italy to engraving. Many of his **engravings** and paintings portray the theme of religious upheaval.

Northern European humanists and writers also helped spread Renaissance ideas. The Dutch priest and humanist Desiderius Erasmus called for a translation of the Bible into the **vernacular** so it could be read by a wider audience. The English humanist Sir Thomas More called for social reform in the form of a **utopian**, or ideal, society in which people live together in peace and harmony.

The towering figure of Renaissance literature, however, was the English poet and playwright William Shakespeare. His 37 plays are still performed around the world. Shakespeare's genius was in expressing universal themes, such as the complexity of the individual, in everyday, realistic settings. He used language that people understand and enjoy. Shakespeare's love of words also enriched the English language with 1,700 new words.

Lesson Vocabulary

engraving   art form in which an artist etches a design on a metal plate with acid and then uses the plate to make multiple prints

vernacular   everyday language of the native people

utopian   idealistic or visionary, usually used to describe a perfect society

Name_____ Class_____ Date_____

MODIFIED CORNELL NOTES

In the 1500s, the Renaissance in northern Europe sparked a religious upheaval that affected Christians at all levels of society. This movement is known as the Protestant Reformation. In the late Middle Ages, the Catholic Church had become caught up in worldly affairs. Popes led lavish lives and hired artists to enhance churches. To finance such projects, the Church increased fees for services. Many Christians protested such acts. They also questioned why the Church in distant Rome should have power over their lives.

In 1517, protests against Church abuses turned into a revolt. A German monk named Martin Luther triggered it over an event in Wittenberg, Germany. There, a priest sold **indulgences** to Christians to raise money to rebuild St. Peter's Cathedral in Rome. To Luther, the priest's actions were the final outrage. He wrote 95 Theses, or arguments, against indulgences. He said that they had no biblical basis, that the pope did not have the authority to release souls from purgatory, and that Christians could be saved only through faith. Throughout Europe, Luther's 95 Theses stirred furious debate. The new Holy Roman emperor, Charles V, summoned Luther to the **diet**, or assembly, at the city of Worms. Luther refused to change his views. Thousands hailed Luther as a hero and renounced the authority of the pope. At the heart of Luther's doctrines were several beliefs, including the idea that all Christians have equal access to God through faith and the Bible. Printing presses spread Luther's writings and ideas throughout Germany and Scandinavia. By 1530, Luther's many followers were using a new name, "Protestants," for those who "protested" papal authority.

In Switzerland, the reformer John Calvin also challenged the Catholic Church. Calvin shared many of Luther's beliefs but also preached **predestination**. Protestants in Geneva asked Calvin to lead them. In keeping with his teachings, Calvin set up a **theocracy**. Reformers from all over Europe visited Geneva and then returned home to spread Calvin's ideas. This new challenge to the Roman Catholic Church set off fierce wars of religion across Europe. In the 1600s, English Calvinists sailed to America to escape persecution.

Lesson Vocabulary

indulgence   in the Roman Catholic Church, pardon for sins committed during a person's lifetime

diet   assembly or legislature

predestination   Calvinist belief that God long ago determined who would gain salvation

theocracy   government run by religious leadersr

Name_____ Class_____ Date_____

As the Reformation continued, hundreds of new Protestant **sects** arose, influencing Protestant thinking in many countries. In England, the break with the Catholic Church came from Henry VIII. He and his wife, Catherine of Aragon, had one child, Mary Tudor. Henry wanted to divorce Catherine and marry another woman whom he hoped would bear him a male heir. However, the pope refused to annul Henry's marriage. Furious, Henry had Parliament pass laws to take the English church from the pope's control. Henry appointed Thomas Cranmer archbishop of the new English church. Cranmer annulled the king's marriage. In 1534, Parliament passed the Act of Supremacy, making Henry the head of the Church of England.

Many Catholics, including Sir Thomas More, refused to accept the Act of Supremacy and were executed. The Catholic Church later **canonized** More for his stand against Henry. When Henry died in 1547, his son Edward VI inherited the throne. Under Edward, Parliament passed laws bringing more Protestant reforms to England. When Edward died, his half-sister Mary Tudor, a Catholic, became queen. She wanted to return England to the Catholic faith. Hundreds of English Protestants were burned at the stake.

On Mary's death in 1558, the throne passed to her half-sister, Elizabeth. She made reforms that became known as the Elizabethan settlement—a **compromise** between Protestant and Catholic practices. Elizabeth restored unity to England; she kept many Catholic traditions but made England a Protestant nation.

As the Protestant Reformation swept northern Europe, the Catholic Church began a Counter-Reformation. The pope's Council of Trent reaffirmed Catholic beliefs that Protestants had challenged. Ignatius of Loyola founded a new religious order, the Jesuits. They followed a rigorous program of strict discipline, thorough religious training, and absolute obedience to the Church. Teresa of Avila established her own order of nuns dedicated to prayer and meditation. Both Catholics and Protestants fostered intolerance and persecuted radical sects. Innocent people were executed for witchcraft. In Venice, Jews were pressured to convert and forced to live in a separate part of the city called the **ghetto**.

Lesson Vocabulary

sect   subgroup of a major religious group

canonize   recognize a person as a saint

compromise   an agreement in which each side makes concessions; an acceptable middle ground

ghetto   separate section of a city where members of a minority group are forced to live

MODIFIED CORNELL NOTES

In the mid-1500s, a big shift in scientific thinking caused the Scientific Revolution. At the heart of this movement was the idea that mathematical laws governed nature and the universe. Before the Renaissance, Europeans thought that Earth was the center of everything in the heavens. In 1543, Polish scholar Nicolaus Copernicus proposed a **heliocentric**, or sun-centered, model of the solar system. In the late 1500s, the Danish astronomer Tycho Brahe provided evidence that supported Copernicus's theory. The German astronomer and mathematician Johannes Kepler used Brahe's data to calculate the orbits of the planets revolving around the sun. His calculations also supported Copernicus's heliocentric view.

Scientists from different lands built on the foundations laid by Copernicus and Kepler. In Italy, Galileo assembled a telescope and observed that the four moons of Jupiter move slowly around that planet. He realized that these moons moved the same way that Copernicus had said that Earth moves around the sun. Galileo's findings caused an uproar. Other scholars attacked him because his observations contradicted ancient views about the world. The Church condemned him because his ideas challenged the Christian teaching that the heavenly bodies were fixed in relation to Earth, and perfect.

Despite the opposition of the Church, a new approach to science had emerged, based upon observation and experimentation. To explain their data, scientists used reasoning to propose a logical **hypothesis**, or possible explanation. This process became known as the **scientific method**. The new scientific method was a revolution in thought. Two giants of this revolution were the Englishman Francis Bacon and the Frenchman René Descartes. Both were devoted to understanding how truth is determined, but they differed in their approaches. Bacon stressed experimentation and observation. Descartes focused on reasoning.

The 1500s and 1600s saw dramatic changes in many branches of science. English chemist Robert Boyle explained that matter is composed of particles that behave in knowable ways. Isaac Newton used mathematics to show that a single force keeps the planets in their orbits around the sun. He called this force **gravity**. To help explain his laws, Newton developed a branch of mathematics called **calculus**.

Lesson Vocabulary

heliocentric   based on the belief that the sun is the center of the universe

hypothesis   an unproved theory accepted for the purpose of explaining certain facts or to provide a basis for further investigations

scientific method   careful, step-by-step process used to confirm findings and to prove or disprove a hypothesis

gravity   force that pulls objects in Earth's sphere to the center of Earth

calculus   a branch of mathematics in which calculations are made using special symbolic notations, developed by Isaac Newton

TOPIC 10 — Review Questions
THE RENAISSANCE AND REFORMATION (1300–1650)

Answer the questions below using the information in the Lesson Summaries on the previous pages.

Lesson 1: The Italian Renaissance

1. What was significant about the discovery of perspective?

_____

_____

2. **Identify Main Ideas** Identify three of the main characteristics of the Renaissance.

_____

_____

Lesson 2: The Renaissance in Northern Europe

3. What changes did the invention of the printing press bring about?

_____

_____

4. **Compare and Contrast** Compare and contrast the northern European humanists Desiderius Erasmus and Sir Thomas More.

_____

_____

Lesson 3: The Protestant Reformation

5. What factors encouraged the Protestant Reformation?

_____

_____

6. **Identify Main Ideas** What was one of the main beliefs at the heart of Luther's doctrines?

_____

_____

Lesson 4: Reformation Ideas Spread

7. What caused Henry VIII to break with the Catholic Church and establish the Church of England?

_____

_____

8. **Identify Main Ideas** How did Elizabeth restore unity to England?

_____

_____

Lesson 5: The Scientific Revolution

9. What assumption was at the heart of the Scientific Revolution?

_____

_____

10. Identify Main Ideas How did Copernicus's proposed model of the solar system differ from earlier beliefs?

_____

_____

Note Taking Study Guide

TOPIC 11

NEW GLOBAL CONNECTIONS (1415–1796)

Focus Question: How did the European desire for trade connections in Asia and Africa often result in the exploration of unexpected places and the later colonization of North and South America?

As you read the Lesson Summaries on the following pages, complete the graphic organizer below to understand how trade became an important force for exploration and colonization.

Exploration	Goal	Actual Accomplishment	Significance
Prince Henry (sponsor, not explorer)	Trace with Africa and reach Asia	Foothold in Africa	Led to further exploration

Name_____ Class_____ Date_____

MODIFIED CORNELL NOTES

By the 1400s, Europe's population and its demand for trade goods from Asia were growing. Especially desirable were spices. The chief source of spices was the Moluccas, an island chain in present-day Indonesia. Arab and Italian merchants controlled most trade between Asia and Europe. Europeans outside Italy wanted direct access to Asia's trade goods. They also desired to spread Christianity, compete with other European countries, and gain glory for their country.

In Portugal, Prince Henry encouraged sea exploration. He believed that Africa was the source of the riches the Muslim traders controlled. He also hoped to find a way to reach Asia by sailing along the coast. **Cartographers** prepared maps for the voyages. Then Henry's ships sailed south to Africa. Soon, the Portuguese sailed around the southern tip of the continent.

The Portuguese established footholds on the coast of Africa, building small forts and trading posts. In addition, they attacked coastal cities of East Africa, such as Mombasa and Malindi, which were hubs of international trade. They also took over the Arabs' thriving East African trade network. In 1497, Vasco da Gama led four Portuguese ships around the tip of Africa, across the Indian Ocean, and reached the great spice port of Calicut in India. Soon, the Portuguese seized ports around the Indian Ocean, creating a vast trading empire.

Portugal's successes spurred others, including Christopher Columbus, to look for a western sea route to Asia. Columbus persuaded Ferdinand and Isabella of Spain to finance his voyage. In 1492, Columbus sailed west with three small ships. When the crew members spotted land, they thought they had reached the Indies. What Columbus had actually found, however, were previously unknown continents. The rulers of Spain appealed to the Spanish-born Pope Alexander VI to support their claims to the lands of this "new world." The pope set the Line of Demarcation, which divided the non-European world into two trading and exploration zones— one for Spain and one for Portugal. The two nations agreed to these terms in the Treaty of Tordesillas.

(Continues on the next page.)

Lesson Vocabulary

cartographer   a person who makes maps

Lesson Summary
EUROPEANS EXPLORE OVERSEAS (continued)

MODIFIED CORNELL NOTES

Although Europeans had claimed vast territories, they had not yet found a western sea route to Asia. In 1519, a Portuguese nobleman named Ferdinand Magellan set out west from Spain to find a way to the Pacific Ocean. In 1520, he found a passageway at the southern tip of South America. Survivors of the long voyage, who did not include Magellan, finally returned to Spain nearly three years later. They were hailed as the first to **circumnavigate** the world.

By the 1600s, several other European powers had established forts along the west coast of Africa. In 1652, Dutch immigrants arrived at the southern tip of the continent. They built Cape Town, the first permanent European settlement in Africa, to supply ships sailing to or from the East Indies. Dutch farmers, called Boers, settled the lands around the port.

Lesson Vocabulary

circumnavigate   to travel completely around the world

TOPIC 11 LESSON 2	**Lesson Summary**
	EUROPEANS GAIN FOOTHOLDS IN ASIA

MODIFIED CORNELL NOTES

After Vasco da Gama's voyage to India, the Portuguese burst into the Indian Ocean. Muslim rulers had established the Mughal empire throughout much of India. The Portuguese gained footholds in southern India, however, by promising local princes aid against other European rulers. In 1510, the Portuguese seized the island of Goa; then they took Malacca. The Portuguese built a trading empire with military and merchant **outposts**. For most of the 1500s, they controlled the spice trade between Europe and Asia.

The Dutch challenged Portuguese domination of Asian trade. Dutch warships and trading vessels made the Netherlands a leader in global commerce. The Dutch set up colonies and trading posts around the world. In 1602, wealthy Dutch merchants formed the Dutch East India Company, which had full **sovereign** powers. With its power to wage war, negotiate treaties, and govern colonies, the Dutch East India Company dominated Southeast Asia. Meanwhile, Spain took over the Philippines, which became a key link in Spain's colonial empire.

When Europeans sought more trading rights in India, the once powerful Mughal emperors saw no threat in granting them. The Portuguese—and later the Dutch, British, and French—were permitted to build forts and warehouses in coastal towns. Over time, the Mughal empire weakened, and French and British traders fought for power. Like the Dutch, both the British and the French established East India companies. Each company organized its own army of **sepoys**, or Indian troops. By the late 1700s, however, the British East India Company controlled most of India.

Portuguese traders reached China in 1514 seeking Chinese silks and porcelains. The Chinese considered European goods inferior and therefore demanded payment in gold or silver. The Ming rulers eventually allowed the Portuguese and other Europeans a trading post at Macao. With the traders came Portuguese missionaries. The brilliant Jesuit priest Matteo Ricci made a strong impression on the Chinese, who welcomed learning about Renaissance Europe.

(Continues on the next page.)

Lesson Vocabulary

outpost   a distant military station or a remote settlement

sovereign   having full, independent power

sepoy   Indian soldier who served in an army set up by the French or English trading companies

MODIFIED CORNELL NOTES

In 1644, the Manchus, who ruled Manchuria, succeeded in seizing Beijing. They set up a new **dynasty** called the Qing. The Chinese economy expanded. The Qing maintained the Ming policy of restricting foreign traders, however. In 1793, Lord Macartney led a British diplomatic mission to China, but his attempt to negotiate for expanded trade failed.

Like China, Korea also restricted contacts with the outside world. In the 1590s, a Japanese invasion devastated Korea. Then, in 1636, the Manchus conquered Korea. In response, the Koreans chose isolation, excluding all foreigners except the Chinese and a few Japanese.

The Japanese at first welcomed Westerners. Japanese warrior lords quickly adopted Western firearms. Jesuit priests converted many Japanese to Christianity. The Tokugawa **shoguns**, however, worried that Japanese Christians owed their allegiance to the foreign pope and that foreigners would try to dominate Japan. In response, the shoguns expelled foreigners and barred all European merchants. To keep informed about world events, however, they permitted just one or two Dutch ships each year to trade at a small island in Nagasaki harbor.

Lesson Vocabulary

dynasty   a family of rulers who rule for a long time

shogun   one of the military leaders who ruled Japan prior to 1868

Name_____ Class_____ Date_____

MODIFIED CORNELL NOTES

TOPIC 11 / LESSON 3

Lesson Summary
EUROPEAN CONQUESTS IN THE AMERICAS

In 1492, Christopher Columbus reached the Caribbean islands now called the West Indies. Columbus's first meeting with Native Americans there began a recurring cycle of encounter, conquest, and death across the Western Hemisphere.

Columbus first encountered the Taíno people and claimed their land for Spain, taking prisoners back with him. A wave of Spanish **conquistadors**, or conquerors, followed. Ultimately, small armies of Spanish, using superior weapons and horses, were able to overpower millions of native people. Unknowingly, the Spanish also brought diseases like smallpox, measles, and influenza. This wiped out village after village of Native Americans who had no **immunity**, or resistance, to these diseases.

One of the earliest explorers, Hernán Cortés, reached Mexico in 1519 and moved toward the Aztec capital, Tenochtitlán. Cortés was aided by an Indian woman, Malinche, who helped him form **alliances** with native peoples previously conquered by the Aztecs. Aztec ruler Moctezuma tried but failed to keep Cortés from coming to Tenochtitlán. Cortés later imprisoned Moctezuma and compelled him to sign over lands and treasure to the Spanish. Cortés was driven out, but he returned in 1521 and destroyed Tenochtitlán.

Another Spanish adventurer, Francisco Pizarro, sought riches from Peru's Incan empire. Pizarro reached Peru in 1532. The Incan ruler, Atahualpa, had just won a **civil war**, or conflict between people of the same nation. Pizarro captured Atahualpa and demanded a huge ransom. This was paid, but Pizarro had the Incan ruler killed anyway. Spanish forces overran Incan lands, adding much of South America to the Spanish empire.

Soon, other European countries sent explorers and conquerors to the Americas. Portugal established a large colony in Brazil. Portugal granted land to nobles, who sent settlers to develop the area. As in Spanish colonies, Native Americans in Brazil were nearly wiped out from disease. Brazil's rulers also used African slaves and forced Native American labor. A new culture emerged, blending European, Native American, and African traditions.

(Continues on the next page.)

Lesson Vocabulary

conquistador "conqueror" in Spanish; a leader in the Spanish conquests of America, Mexico, and Peru in the sixteenth century

immunity resistance, such as the power to keep from being affected by a disease

alliance a relationship in which people agree to work together

civil war a war fought between groups of people in the same nation

TOPIC 11
LESSON 3

Lesson Summary
EUROPEAN CONQUESTS IN THE AMERICAS (continued)

In the 1500s, wealth from the Americas made Spain and Portugal Europe's most wealthy and powerful countries. Pirates often attacked treasure ships from the colonies. Some pirates, called **privateers**, even did so with the support of their nations' monarchs.

Spain long remained the dominant European power in the Americas. Spanish settlers and missionaries followed the explorers and conquerors. They built colonies and created a culture that blended European, Native American, and African traditions. By the mid-1500s, Spain's empire reached from modern California to South America.

The Spanish monarch appointed **viceroys**, or representatives who ruled in his name. They closely monitored Spanish colonies and managed their valuable raw materials. Conquistadors received **encomiendas**, or rights to demand work from Native Americans. Under this system, Native Americans were forced to work under brutal conditions. Disease, starvation, and cruel treatment caused drastic declines in the Native American population. A priest, Bartolomé de Las Casas, begged the Spanish king to end the abuse, and laws were passed in 1542, banning enslavement and mistreatment. But Spain was too far away to enforce the laws. Some landlords forced people to become **peons**, paid workers who labored to repay impossibly high debts created by their landlord. To fill a labor shortage, colonists also brought in millions of Africans as slaves.

(Continues on the next page.)

Lesson Vocabulary

privateer   Dutch, English, and French pirates who preyed on treasure ships from the Americas in the 1500s, operating with the approval of European governments

viceroy   representative of the king of Spain who ruled colonies in his name

encomienda   the right, granted by Spanish monarchs to conquistadors, to demand labor or tribute from Native Americans in a particular area

peon   a worker forced to labor for a landlord to pay off a debt that is impossible to pay off in his or her lifetime, which is incurred by food, tool, or seeds the landlord has advanced to him or her

MODIFIED CORNELL NOTES

A blending of diverse cultures resulted. Native Americans contributed building styles, foods, and arts. The Spanish brought Christianity and the use of animals, especially horses. Africans contributed farming methods, crops, and arts.

However, society in the colonies was strictly structured. **Peninsulares**, or people born in Spain, filled the highest positions. Next were **creoles**, or American-born descendants of Spanish settlers. Lower groups included **mestizos**, people of Native American and European descent, and **mulattoes**, people of African and European descent. At the bottom were Native Americans and African slaves.

Lesson Vocabulary

peninsular   in Spanish colonial America, a person born in Spain

creole   in Spanish colonial America, an American-born descendant of Spanish settlers

mestizo   in Spanish colonial America, a person of Native American and European descent

mulatto   in Spanish colonial America, a person of African and European descent

Lesson Summary
EUROPEAN COLONIES IN NORTH AMERICA

MODIFIED CORNELL NOTES

In the 1600s, the French, Dutch, English, and Spanish competed for lands in North America. By 1700, France and England dominated large parts of the continent. Their colonies differed from one another in terms of language, government, resources, and society.

In 1534, Jacques Cartier explored and claimed for the French much of eastern Canada, called New France. However, a permanent French settlement was not established until 1608 in Quebec. Eventually, France's empire stretched from Quebec to the Great Lakes and down the Mississippi River to Louisiana. Harsh Canadian winters discouraged settlers, and many abandoned farming for more profitable fur trapping and fishing. In the late 1600s, the French king Louis XIV wanted greater **revenue**, or income from taxes. He appointed officials to manage economic activities in North America and sent soldiers and more settlers.

In the early 1700s, while New France's population remained small, English colonies expanded along the Atlantic coast. Jamestown in Virginia, the first permanent English colony, was established in 1607. In 1620, Pilgrims, or English Protestants who rejected the Church of England, landed at what became Plymouth, Massachusetts. They wrote a **compact**, or agreement, called the Mayflower Compact. It set guidelines for governing their colony. In the 1600s and 1700s, the English created additional colonies. Many were commercial ventures or havens for religious groups. English monarchs exercised control through royal governors. Yet English colonists enjoyed a greater degree of self-government than French and Spanish colonists. They had their own representative assemblies that could advise the governor and decide local issues.

During the 1700s, England and France emerged as powerful rivals. In 1754, the French and Indian War erupted in North America and then spread to other parts of the world by 1756, where it became known as the Seven Years' War. British and colonial troops eventually captured New France's capital city, Quebec. Although the war dragged on, the British ultimately prevailed. The 1763 Treaty of Paris ended this worldwide conflict. France surrendered Canada and other North American possessions to Britain. Its Louisiana Territory passed to Spain.

Lesson Vocabulary

revenue   money taken in through taxes

compact   an agreement among people

Lesson Summary
THE SLAVE TRADE AND ITS IMPACT ON AFRICA

MODIFIED CORNELL NOTES

Slavery had existed in Africa since ancient times. By the 1500s, European participation had encouraged a much broader Atlantic slave trade, and it grew into a huge and profitable business to fill the need for cheap labor. Europeans especially needed workers on their **plantations** in the Americas. Some African leaders tried to slow down or stop the transatlantic slave trade. The ruler of Kongo, Affonso I, who had been tutored by Portuguese **missionaries**, wanted to maintain contact with Europe but end the slave trade. The slave trade, however, continued.

The slave trade had major effects on African states. Because of the loss of countless numbers of young Africans, some small states disappeared forever. At the same time, new states arose, with ways of life that depended on the slave trade. The Asante kingdom emerged in the area occupied by present-day Ghana. In the late 1600s, an able military leader, Osei Tutu, conquered neighboring peoples and unified the Asante kingdom. Under Osei Tutu, the Asante kingdom held a **monopoly** over both gold mining and the slave trade.

The Oyo empire arose from successive waves of settlement by the Yoruba people in the region of present-day Nigeria. Its leaders used wealth gained from the slave trade to build a strong army.

The trade of slaves became part of the trade network known as the **triangular trade**, a series of Atlantic sea routes joining Europe, Africa, and the Americas. On the first leg of the triangle, merchant ships brought European goods, such as guns and cloth, to Africa, where they were traded for slaves. On the second leg, known as the Middle Passage, slaves were brought to the Americas, where they were traded for sugar, molasses, and cotton from European-owned plantations. On the final leg, these products were traded for other colonial goods, such as furs and salt fish, which were then shipped to Europe, where they were traded for European goods.

(Continues on the next page.)

Lesson Vocabulary

plantation   large estate run by an overseer with laborers working and living there

missionary   someone sent to do religious work in a territory or foreign country

monopoly   complete control of a product or business by one person or group

triangular trade   colonial trade routes among Europe and its colonies, the West Indies, and Africa in which goods were exchanged for slaves

Lesson Summary

THE SLAVE TRADE AND ITS IMPACT ON AFRICA (continued)

MODIFIED CORNELL NOTES

During the Middle Passage, slaves were captured, bound, and forced to walk as many as a thousand miles. Many died on the way. Those who lived were restrained in holding pens in African port cities until European ships arrived. Hundreds were crammed below deck for the three-week to three-month voyages. Some committed suicide. Many died from disease, brutality, or other dangers, like storms; pirate raids; and **mutinies**, or revolts, by captives trying to return home.

The triangular trade continued, in part, because it was so profitable. It brought riches to merchants and traders, helped the colonial economies succeed, and helped European and American port cities grow. However, for Africans the outcome was devastating. African societies were torn apart, and lives were cut short or brutalized. By the mid-1800s, when the slave trade finally ended, an estimated 11 million Africans had been brought to the Americas, and another 2 million had died during the Middle Passage.

Lesson Vocabulary

mutiny   revolt, especially of soldiers or sailors against their officers

Name_____ Class_____ Date_____

Lesson Summary
EFFECTS OF GLOBAL CONTACT

European exploration and expansion in the 1500s and 1600s led to European domination of the globe. By the 1700s, worldwide contact brought major changes to people in Europe, the Americas, Asia, and Africa.

When Columbus returned to Europe in 1493, he brought back American plants and animals. Later, he carried European plants, animals, and settlers back to the Americas. This began a vast global interchange named for Columbus, called the Columbian Exchange. Sharing different food and livestock helped people around the world. The dispersal of new crops from the Americas also contributed to worldwide population growth by the 1700s. Additionally, the Columbian Exchange started a migration to the Americas, including the forcible transfer of millions of slaves. The unintentional transfer of viruses and bacteria brought disease and death to millions of Native Americans.

Another effect of global contact was great economic change. In the 1500s, the pace of **inflation** increased in Europe, fueled by silver and gold flowing in from the Americas. Inflation is a rise in prices linked to sharp increases in the money supply. This period of rapid inflation in Europe is known as the **price revolution**. Expanded trade and an increased money supply spurred the growth of **capitalism**, an economic system of private business ownership and free competition with limited regulation by government. The key to capitalism was **entrepreneurs**, or people who take financial risks for profits. European entrepreneurs hired workers, paid production costs, joined investors in overseas ventures, and ultimately helped convert local economies into international trading economies.

(Continues on the next page.)

Lesson Vocabulary

inflation   economic cycle that involves a rapid rise in prices linked to a sharp increase in the amount of money available

price revolution   period in European history when inflation rose rapidly

capitalism   economic system in which the means of production are privately owned and operated for profit

entrepreneur   person who assumes financial risk in the hope of making a profit

Name_____ Class_____ Date_____

Section Summary
EFFECTS OF GLOBAL CONTACT (continued)

Fierce competition for trade and empires led to a new economic system called **mercantilism**, which measured wealth by a nation's gold and silver. Mercantilists believed the nation must export more than it imports. They also pushed governments to impose **tariffs**, or taxes on foreign goods, giving an advantage to local goods over imports that became costly because of the tariffs.

But by the 1700s, many social changes had taken place in Europe, too. Nobles, whose wealth was in land, were hurt by the price revolution. Merchants who invested in overseas ventures grew wealthy, and skilled workers in Europe's growing cities thrived. A thriving middle class of entrepreneurs and business people also developed.

Lesson Vocabulary

mercantilism   policy by which a nation sought to export more than it imported in order to build its supply of gold and silver

tariff   tax on imported goods

TOPIC 11 Review Questions
NEW GLOBAL CONNECTIONS (1415–1796)

Answer the questions below using the information in the Lesson Summaries on the previous pages.

Lesson 1: Europeans Explore Overseas
1. What motivated Europeans to explore the seas?

_____

_____

2. **Cause and Effect** Identify two effects of Prince Henry's encouragement of sea exploration.

_____

_____

Lesson 2: Europeans Gain Footholds in Asia
3. How did the Dutch come to dominate trade in Southeast Asia?

_____

_____

4. **Identify Causes and Effects** Identify one cause and one effect of the Mughal emperors' decision to grant trading rights to Europeans.

_____

_____

Lesson 3: European Conquests in the Americas
5. Name two factors that helped hundreds of Spanish soldiers conquer millions of Native Americans.

_____

_____

6. **Recognize Sequence** Sequence the following events: Spanish forces take over Inca lands. Pizarro arrives in Peru. Columbus takes the Taínos as prisoners. Cortés captures Tenochtitlán.

_____

_____

Lesson 4: European Colonies in North America
7. In what way did English colonists have a greater degree of self-government than French or Spanish colonists?

_____

_____

**TOPIC
11** | **Review Questions**
NEW GLOBAL CONNECTIONS (1415–1796) (continued)

8. **Recognize Sequence** What happened after the signing of the Treaty of Paris in 1763?

_____

_____

Lesson 5: The Slave Trade and Its Impact on Africa

9. Why did the triangular trade continue, even though it devastated the lives of millions of people?

_____

_____

10. **Recognize Sequence** List the three "legs" of the triangular trade.

_____

_____

Lesson 6: Effects of Global Contact

11. Why did mercantilists push governments to impose tariffs?

_____

_____

12. **Cause and Effect** What happened in the 1500s that caused inflation in Europe?

_____

_____

Name _____ Class _____ Date _____

Focus Question: What forces did the Enlightenment release that brought about major changes in Europe and the English colonies of North America?

As you read the Lesson Summaries on the following pages, complete the graphic organizer below to help you explain how Enlightenment ideas sparked changes in Europe and the Americas.

Cause		Effect

Name _____ Class _____ Date _____

MODIFIED CORNELL NOTES

Between 1500 and 1800, states in Europe were becoming more unified. Their kings and queens ruled as **absolute monarchs**, with complete authority over their government and the lives of their people. These monarchs declared that they ruled by **divine right**. This meant they believed that their authority to rule came directly from God.

In 1519, Charles V, the king of Spain and ruler of the Spanish colonies in the Americas, inherited the Hapsburg empire. This included the Holy Roman Empire and the Netherlands. Ruling two empires involved Charles in constant religious warfare. Additionally, the empire's vast territory became too cumbersome for Charles to rule effectively. Charles V abdicated the throne and divided his kingdom between his brother Ferdinand and his son Philip.

Under Philip II, Spanish power increased. Philip fought many battles in the Mediterranean and the Netherlands to advance or preserve Spanish Catholic power and defend the Catholic faith against the Protestant Reformation.

To expand his empire, Philip II needed to eliminate his rivals. He saw Elizabeth I of England as his chief Protestant enemy. Philip prepared a huge **armada**, or fleet, to carry an invasion force to England. However, several disasters led to the defeat of this powerful Spanish fleet. This defeat marked the beginning of a decline in Spanish power.

Wars were costly and contributed to Spain's economic problems. However, while Spain's strength and wealth decreased, art and learning took on new importance. The arts flourished between 1550 and 1650, during the *Siglo de Oro*, or "golden century." Among the outstanding artists of this period was a painter called El Greco. This period also produced several remarkable writers, including Miguel de Cervantes, author of *Don Quixote*.

(Continues on the next page.)

Lesson Vocabulary

absolute monarch   a ruler who has complete authority over the government and lives of the people he or she governs

divine right   idea that a ruler's authority came directly from God

armada   fleet of ships

Name _____ Class _____ Date _____

MODIFIED CORNELL NOTES

In the late 1500s, France was also torn apart by religious conflict. Fighting between French Protestants, called Huguenots, and Catholics led to the St. Bartholomew's Day Massacre, in which thousands of Huguenots were slaughtered. In 1598, King Henry IV issued the Edict of Nantes to protect Protestants and protect religious toleration.

After Henry's assassination in 1610, his nine-year-old son, Louis XIII, inherited the throne. Louis appointed Cardinal Richelieu as his chief minister. Richelieu sought to strengthen royal power by crushing any groups that did not bow to royal authority. In 1643, five-year-old Louis XIV inherited the French throne. Louis XIV later took complete control of the government. He believed in his divine right to rule and even called himself the Sun King to symbolize his vital role within the nation.

Louis XIV expanded the royal government and appointed **intendants**—royal officials who collected taxes, recruited soldiers, and carried out his policies in the provinces. Louis's finance minister, Jean Baptiste Colbert, expanded commerce and trade. Taxes helped finance the king's extravagant lifestyle.

Outside Paris, Louis XIV transformed a royal hunting lodge into the grand palace of Versailles. The palace represented the king's great power and wealth. Elaborate court ceremonies were held to emphasize the king's importance. Under Louis XIV, France became the strongest state in Europe.

However, the country's prosperity began to erode. This loss of wealth was caused by some of Louis's decisions. He fought costly wars to extend French borders, but rival rulers resisted in order to maintain the **balance of power**. Louis also revoked the Edict of Nantes, driving over 100,000 hard-working and prosperous Huguenots out of France.

Lesson Vocabulary

intendant   official appointed by French king Louis XIV to govern the provinces, collect taxes, and recruit soldiers

balance of power   distribution of military and economic power that prevents any one nation from becoming too strong

TOPIC 12 LESSON 2

Lesson Summary
RISE OF AUSTRIA, PRUSSIA, AND RUSSIA

By the seventeenth century, the Holy Roman Empire had become a mix of several hundred small, separate states. The emperor had little power over the many princes of the states. This power vacuum led to a series of brutal wars that are together called the Thirty Years' War, a widespread European war.

The war devastated the German states. **Mercenaries**, or soldiers for hire, burned villages, destroyed crops, and murdered and tortured villagers. This led to famine and disease, which caused severe **depopulation**, or reduction in population.

In 1648, a series of treaties known as the Peace of Westphalia were established. These treaties aspired to bring peace to Europe and also settle other international problems.

Out of the chaos of war, two powerful new states emerged. Austria, still ruled by the Hapsburg family, was becoming a strong Catholic state. But a region within the German states called Prussia emerged as a new Protestant power. The Prussian ruler Frederick William I came to power in 1713. He created a new bureaucracy and placed great emphasis on military values.

Maria Theresa became empress of Austria after her father's death in 1740. That same year, Frederick II of Prussia seized the Hapsburg province of Silesia. This action sparked the eight-year War of the Austrian Succession. Despite her efforts, Maria Theresa did not succeed in forcing Frederick out of Silesia. However, she did preserve her empire and won the support of most of her people. She also strengthened Hapsburg power by reorganizing the bureaucracy and improving tax collection. Frederick II continued to expand Prussia's military and make it a leading power.

(Continues on the next page.)

Lesson Vocabulary

mercenary   soldier serving in a foreign country for pay

depopulation   reduction in the number of people in an area

Name _____ Class _____ Date _____

MODIFIED CORNELL NOTES

In the early 1600s, Russia was isolated from the nations of Western Europe and had remained a medieval state. It was not until the end of that century that a new tsar, Peter the Great, transformed Russia into a leading power through a new policy of **westernization**—the adoption of Western ideas, technologies, and culture. He forced **boyars** to shave their traditional beards and wear Western-style clothing. Many resisted change. To enforce his new policy, Peter became an **autocratic** monarch—one who ruled with unlimited authority.

Peter pushed through social and economic reforms. He also increased Russia's military power and extended its borders. Peter waged a long war against Sweden to win territory along the Baltic Sea. On this territory, he built a new capital city, St. Petersburg. When Peter died in 1725, he left a mixed legacy. Although he had modernized Russia, he had used terror to enforce his absolute power.

In 1762, Catherine the Great ruled as an absolute monarch. She followed Peter's lead in embracing Western ideas and expanding Russia's borders. She was an efficient and energetic empress. Under her rule, laws were codified, and state-supported education began for both boys and girls. After waging war, she defeated the Ottoman Empire and won a **warm-water port** on the Black Sea, a goal that had been set under Peter the Great.

In the 1770s, Russia, Prussia, and Austria each wanted Poland as part of their territory. In order to avoid war, the three kingdoms agreed to **partition**, or divide up, Poland. In 1772, Russia gained part of eastern Poland, while Prussia and Austria took over the West. Poland vanished from the map.

By 1750, the great European powers included Austria, Prussia, France, Britain, and Russia. These nations formed various alliances to maintain the balance of power. Austria and Prussia were great rivals, as were Britain and France.

Lesson Vocabulary

westernization   adoption of western ideas, technology, and culture

boyar   landowning noble in Russia under the tsars

autocrat   leader with unlimited power

warm-water port   port that is free of ice year round

partition   a division into pieces

Name _____ Class _____ Date _____

From 1485 to 1603, England was ruled by the Tudors. While believing in divine right, Tudor monarchs Henry VIII and Elizabeth I also recognized the value of good relations with Parliament.

This was not the view of the first Stuart king, James I. He inherited the throne after Elizabeth I died childless in 1603. He claimed absolute power. Parliament, however, resisted the king's claim. James clashed often with Parliament over money. James was also at odds with **dissenters**—Protestants who disagreed with the Church of England. One such group, the Puritans, wanted simpler services and a more democratic church with no bishops.

In 1625, Charles I inherited the throne. He too behaved like an absolute monarch. Tensions between Charles and Parliament escalated into civil war. The English Civil War lasted from 1642 to 1651. Supporters of Charles were called Cavaliers. The supporters of Parliament were known as Roundheads. Oliver Cromwell, the leader of the Parliament forces, guided them to victory. In January 1649, Charles I was beheaded.

The House of Commons abolished the monarchy and declared England a republic under Cromwell, called the Commonwealth. Many new laws reflected Puritan beliefs. Cromwell did not tolerate open worship for Catholics; however, he did respect the beliefs of other Protestants and welcomed Jews back to England. Eventually people tired of the strict Puritan ways. Cromwell died in 1658. Two years later, Parliament invited Charles II to return to England as king.

Charles II's successor, James II, was forced from the English throne in 1688. Protestants feared that he planned to restore the Roman Catholic Church to power in England. Parliament offered the crown to James's Protestant daughter Mary and her husband William. However, William and Mary had to accept the English Bill of Rights. This helped establish a **limited monarchy**. This bloodless overthrow of James II was known as the Glorious Revolution.

(Continues on the next page.)

Lesson Vocabulary

dissenter Protestant whose views and opinions differed from those of the Church of England

limited monarchy government in which a constitution or legislative body limits the monarch's powers

Name _____ Class _____ Date _____

MODIFIED CORNELL NOTES

During the next century, Britain's government became a **constitutional government**, whose power was defined and limited by law. A **cabinet**, or group of parliamentary advisors who set policies, developed. In essence, British government was now an **oligarchy**—a government that was run by a powerful few.

Lesson Vocabulary

constitutional government government whose power is defined and limited by law

cabinet parliamentary advisors to the king who originally met in a small room, or cabinet

oligarchy government in which the ruling power belongs to a few people

Name _____ Class _____ Date _____

MODIFIED CORNELL NOTES

In the 1500s and 1600s, the Scientific Revolution changed the way people looked at the world. They began to use reason and science to learn how things worked. For example, they found that rules govern natural forces such as gravity. Scientists and others began to call these rules the **natural law**. They believed that natural law could be used to solve society's problems, too. In this way, the Scientific Revolution sparked another revolution in thinking known as the Enlightenment.

Two important English thinkers of the Enlightenment were Thomas Hobbes and John Locke. Hobbes argued that people were naturally cruel and selfish. They needed to be controlled by a powerful government, such as an absolute monarchy. According to Hobbes, people in a society made an agreement, or **social contract**. In this contract, people gave up their freedom in exchange for an organized society. In contrast, Locke thought that people were basically good. He believed that people had **natural rights**, or rights that belonged to all humans. These are the right to life, liberty, and property. Locke thought a government of limited power was best.

French Enlightenment thinkers, called *philosophes*, also believed that people could use reason to improve government, law, and society. These thinkers included Baron de Montesquieu, Voltaire, Denis Diderot, and Jean-Jacques Rousseau. Montesquieu, for example, developed the ideas of separation of powers and checks and balances. The Framers of the United States Constitution would later use these ideas. In a set of books called the Encyclopedia, Diderot explained the new ideas on the topics of government, philosophy, and religion. Other thinkers, including Adam Smith, focused on using natural law to reform the economy. Instead of government control, they urged the policy of **laissez faire**. This policy allowed the **free market** to regulate business.

(Continues on the next page.)

Lesson Vocabulary

natural law   unchanging principle, discovered through reason, that governs human conduct

social contract   an agreement by which people give up their freedom to a powerful government in order to avoid chaos

natural rights   rights that belongs to all humans from birth, such as life, liberty, and property

philosophe   French for *philosopher*; French thinker who desired reform in society during the Enlightenment

laissez faire   policy allowing business to operate with little or no government interference

free market   market regulated by the natural laws of supply and demand

Name _____ Class _____ Date _____

MODIFIED CORNELL NOTES

Enlightenment ideas flowed from France, across Europe and beyond. The ideas of the Enlightenment, found in books such as Diderot's Encyclopedia, challenged traditional beliefs and customs. In response, most government and church authorities waged a war of **censorship**. Censorship, however, did not stop the spread of ideas. *Philosophes* and others disguised their ideas in works of fiction.

In the 1600s and 1700s, the arts evolved to meet changing tastes and reflect new Enlightenment ideals. In visual art and in music there was a transition from the heavier splendor of the **baroque** style to the lighter, more charming style of **rococo**. Ballets and operas—plays set to music—were performed at royal courts. Opera houses sprang up in Europe. Composers later created elegant works in a style known as classical. A growing audience of middle-class readers also led to the rise of a new type of literature—a prose form called the novel.

The courts of Europe were also affected by the Enlightenment as *philosophes* tried to persuade European rulers to make reforms. A few European monarchs did accept Enlightenment ideas, but retained their absolute control. These **enlightened despots** used their power to bring about some political and social changes. In Prussia, Frederick the Great kept tight control over his subjects yet allowed a free press and religious tolerance. Catherine the Great of Russia abolished torture and criticized the institution of serfdom. In Austria, Joseph II traveled in disguise among his subjects to learn of their problems. Despite the spread of Enlightenment ideas, however, the lives of most regular Europeans changed slowly.

Lesson Vocabulary

censorship   restriction on access to ideas and information

baroque   ornate style of art and architecture popular in the 1600s and 1700s

rococo   lighter, more personal, elegant, and charming style of art and architecture popular in the mid-1700s

enlightened despot   absolute ruler who used his or her power to bring about political and social change

Lesson Summary
THE AMERICAN REVOLUTION

MODIFIED CORNELL NOTES

In the mid-1700s, Britain was a formidable global power. Key reasons for this status included its location, support of commerce, and huge gains in territory around the world. Furthermore, the new king, George III, began to assert his leadership and royal power.

Britain's growing empire included prosperous colonies on the east coast of North America. The colonists shared many values. These included an increasing sense of their own destiny separate from Britain. In some cases, Britain neglected to enforce laws dealing with colonial trade and manufacturing.

Tensions between the colonists and Britain grew as Parliament passed laws, such as the Stamp Act, that increased colonists' taxes. The colonists protested what they saw as "taxation without representation." A series of violent clashes with British soldiers intensified the colonists' anger. Finally, representatives from each colony, including George Washington of Virginia, met in the Continental Congress to decide what to do. Then in April 1775, colonists fought British soldiers at Lexington and Concord, and the American Revolution began.

On July 4, 1776, the Second Continental Congress adopted the Declaration of Independence. Written primarily by Thomas Jefferson, it reflects John Locke's ideas about the rights to "life, liberty, and property." It also details the colonists' grievances and emphasizes the Enlightenment idea of **popular sovereignty**.

At first, chances for American success looked bleak. The colonists struggled against Britain's trained soldiers, huge fleet, and greater resources. When the colonists won the Battle of Saratoga, other European nations, such as France, joined the American side. With the help of the French fleet, Washington forced the British to surrender at Yorktown, Virginia, in 1781. Two years later American, British, and French diplomats signed the Treaty of Paris, ending the war.

(Continues on the next page.)

Lesson Vocabulary

popular sovereignty   principle that asserts that the people are the source of any and all governmental power, and government can exist only with the consent of the governed

Name _____ Class _____ Date _____

MODIFIED CORNELL NOTES

   By 1789, leaders of the new United States, such as James Madison and Benjamin Franklin, had established a **federal republic** under the Constitution. The new government was based on the separation of powers, an idea borrowed directly from Montesquieu. To prevent any branch of government from becoming too powerful, the Constitution established a system of **checks and balances**. The Bill of Rights, the first ten amendments to the Constitution, protected basic rights. The United States Constitution put Enlightenment ideas into practice and has become an important symbol of freedom.

Lesson Vocabulary

federal republic   government in which power is divided between the national, or federal, government and the states

checks and balances   system in which each branch of a government has the power to monitor and limit the actions of the other two

Lesson Summary
THE FRENCH REVOLUTION BEGINS

Under France's **ancien régime**, there were three social classes, or **estates**. This social system created much friction between the upper and lower classes. At the top of this social and economic system was the First Estate, made up of the clergy. At the time, the Church exerted great influence throughout Christian Europe, specifically in France where members of the church hierarchy enjoyed enormous wealth and privilege. The Church owned about 10 percent of the land, collected tithes, and paid no direct taxes to the state.

The Second Estate consisted of the titled nobility of French society. Although its members had enjoyed numerous privileges and benefits in the past, at the time just before the French Revolution, the more ambitious nobles had to compete for royal appointments.

At the bottom of French society was the Third Estate, a diverse social class that included the **bourgeoisie**, or the middle class. Much of the Third Estate, however, consisted of rural peasants. Members of the Third Estate resented the privileges enjoyed by their social "betters." The First and Second Estates, for example, were exempt from most taxes, while peasants paid taxes on many things, including necessities.

Economic troubles added to the social unrest. **Deficit spending** had left France deeply in debt. In the 1780s, bad harvests sent food prices soaring. King Louis XVI was ineffectual and did little to reform the nation's economy. The wealthy and powerful demanded that the king do something. As a result, he summoned the Estates-General, which consisted of representatives from the three estates, before making any changes. A French king had not called the Estates-General in session for 175 years.

(Continues on the next page.)

Lesson Vocabulary

ancien régime   old order system of government in pre-revolutionary France

estate   social class

bourgeoisie   the middle class

deficit spending   situation in which the government spends more money than it takes in

Lesson Summary
THE FRENCH REVOLUTION BEGINS (continued)

MODIFIED CORNELL NOTES

It was during this meeting that members of the Third Estate called for significant reform. They were familiar with the ideals of the Enlightenment and wanted to bring change. In June 1789, claiming to represent the people of France, they declared themselves to be the National Assembly. Fearing that the king planned to dismiss them, the delegates moved to a nearby indoor tennis court and took their famous Tennis Court Oath. They swore "never to separate and to meet wherever the circumstances might require until we have established a sound and just constitution."

The growing political crisis coincided with a terrible famine. Peasants were starving and unemployed. In such desperate times, rumors ran wild. Inflamed by famine and fear, peasants unleashed their fury on the nobles. On July 14, 1789, the streets of Paris buzzed with rumors that royal troops were going to occupy the city. Then 800 Parisians assembled outside the Bastille, demanding weaponry stored there. When the commander refused, the enraged mob stormed the Bastille, sparking the French Revolution.

The storming of the Bastille and the peasant uprisings pushed the National Assembly into action. In late August, the Assembly issued the Declaration of the Rights of Man and the Citizen. It proclaimed that all male citizens were equal before the law. The National Assembly also produced the Constitution of 1791. This document reflected Enlightenment goals, set up a limited monarchy, ensured equality before the law for all male citizens, and ended Church interference in government.

Name _____ Class _____ Date _____

MODIFIED CORNELL NOTES

The events of the French Revolution stirred debate all over Europe. Some people applauded the reforms of the National Assembly. Rulers of other nations, however, denounced the French Revolution. Horror stories were told by **émigrés** who had fled France. Rulers of neighboring monarchies increased border patrols to stop the spread of the "French plague" of revolution.

In October 1791, the newly elected Legislative Assembly took office, but falling currency values, rising prices, and food shortages renewed turmoil. Working-class men and women, called **sans-culottes**, pushed the revolution in a more radical direction, and demanded a republic. The sans-culottes found support among other radicals, especially the Jacobins. The radicals soon held the upper hand in the Legislative Assembly. Eager to spread the revolution, they declared war against Austria and other European monarchies.

In 1793, the revolution entered a frightening and bloody phase. The war with Austria was not going well for France. Some felt the king was in league with France's enemies. Others wanted to restore the king's power. On August 10, 1792, a mob stormed the royal palace. Radicals then took control of the Assembly and called for the election of a new legislative body called the National Convention. **Suffrage** was to be extended to all male citizens, not just to those who owned property. The Convention that met in September 1792 was a more radical body than earlier assemblies. It voted to abolish the monarchy and establish the French Republic. Louis XVI and his queen were executed.

War with other European nations and internal rebellions concerned the government. The Convention created the Committee of Public Safety to deal with these issues. It had almost absolute power. Jacobin Maximilien Robespierre led the Committee. He was one of the chief architects of the Reign of Terror, which lasted from

(Continues on the next page.)

Lesson Vocabulary

émigré a person who flees his or her country for political reasons

sans-culottes members of the working class who made the French Revolution more radical; called such because men wore long trousers instead of the fancy knee breeches that the upper class wore

suffrage right to vote

TOPIC
12
LESSON 7

Lesson Summary
A RADICAL PHASE (continued)

September 1793 to July 1794. During that time, courts conducted hasty trials for those suspected of resisting the revolution. Many people were the victims of false accusations. About 17,000 were executed by **guillotine**.

In reaction to the Terror, the revolution entered a third stage, dominated by the bourgeoisie. It moved away from the excesses of the Convention, and moderates created the Constitution of 1795. This set up a five-man Directory to rule, and a two-house legislature. However, discontent grew because of corrupt leaders. Also, war continued with Austria and Britain. Politicians planned to use Napoleon Bonaparte, a popular military hero, to advance their goals.

By 1799, the French Revolution had dramatically changed France. It had dislodged the old social order, overthrown the monarchy, and brought the Church under state control. **Nationalism** spread throughout France. From the city of Marseilles, troops marched to a rousing new song that would become the French national anthem. Revolutionaries also made social reforms. They set up systems to help the poor and abolished slavery in France's Caribbean colonies.

Lesson Vocabulary

guillotine   device used during the Reign of Terror to execute thousands by beheading

nationalism   a strong feeling of pride and devotion to one's country

TOPIC 12
LESSON 8
Lesson Summary
THE AGE OF NAPOLEON

The last phase of the French Revolution is known as the Age of Napoleon. Napoleon Bonaparte started his rise to power as a young officer. By 1804, he had become emperor of France. At each step on his rise, Napoleon held a **plebiscite**. People voted to approve his actions, but Napoleon always kept absolute power.

Napoleon made the central government stronger. All classes of people supported his economic and social reforms. One of his most lasting reforms was the Napoleonic Code. This new code of laws embodied Enlightenment principles of equality, religious tolerance, and the end of feudalism.

From 1804 to 1812, Napoleon fought to create a vast French empire. Before each battle, he drafted a completely new plan. Because of this, opposing generals could never anticipate what he would do next. He rarely lost. Napoleon **annexed**, or added to his empire, most European nations except Russia and Britain.

He tried to wage economic warfare against Britain through the Continental System. This system closed European ports to British goods. Many Europeans did not like this blockade, and the Continental System failed. In Spain, patriots waged **guerrilla warfare**, or hit-and-run raids, against the French. In 1812, Napoleon invaded Russia. The Russians burned crops and villages. This scorched-earth policy left the French without food or shelter. The French retreated from Moscow through the Russian winter. Only about 20,000 of 600,000 soldiers made it back to France alive.

(Continues on the next page.)

Lesson Vocabulary

plebiscite a ballot in which voters have a direct say on an issue

annex add a territory to an existing state or country

guerrilla warfare fighting carried on through hit-and-run raids

Name _____ Class _____ Date _____

MODIFIED CORNELL NOTES

The Russian disaster destroyed Napoleon's reputation for success. In 1815, British and Prussian forces crushed the French at the Battle of Waterloo. Napoleon was forced to **abdicate**. After Waterloo, European leaders met at the Congress of Vienna. The Congress tried to create a lasting peace through the principle of legitimacy, or restoring monarchies that Napoleon had unseated. They also set up the Concert of Europe to try to solve conflicts.

Lesson Vocabulary

abdicate   give up or step down from power

TOPIC 12 | Review Questions
ABSOLUTISM AND REVOLUTION (1550-1850)

Answer the questions below using the information in the Lesson Summaries on the previous pages.

Lesson 1: Absolute Monarchy in Spain and France

1. How did Louis XIV strengthen the French monarchy?

_____

_____

2. Identify Main Ideas and Supporting Details What details support the main idea that the period from 1550 to 1650 was a "golden century" in Spain?

_____

_____

Lesson 2: Rise of Austria, Prussia, and Russia

3. What did Peter the Great do to modernize Russia?

_____

_____

4. Identify Supporting Details List details to support this statement: The Thirty Years' War had a terrible effect on German states.

_____

_____

Lesson 3: Triumph of Parliament in England

5. How did the English government change under Cromwell's leadership?

_____

_____

6. Identify Supporting Details Find two details in this Summary that support the statement "Parliament triumphs in England."

_____

_____

Lesson 4: The Enlightenment

7. How did the Scientific Revolution lead to the Enlightenment?

_____

_____

8. Summarize What ideas did Thomas Hobbes and John Locke have about human nature and the role of government?

_____

_____

TOPIC 12 — Review Questions
ABSOLUTISM AND REVOLUTION (1550-1850) (continued)

Lesson 5: The American Revolution

9. What first caused tensions to rise between the colonists and Britain?

_____

_____

10. Recognize Sequence Place the events leading to the American Revolution in the correct order.

_____

_____

Lesson 6: The French Revolution

11. What economic troubles did France face in the 1780s?

_____

_____

12. Recognize Multiple Causes Identify three causes of the French Revolution.

_____

_____

Lesson 7: A Radical Phase

13. Identify three changes that the French Revolution brought to France.

_____

_____

14. Recognize Sequence What occurred after the radicals took control of the Assembly in 1792?

_____

_____

Lesson 8: The Age of Napoleon

15. How did the French respond to Napoleon's economic and social reforms?

_____

_____

16. Identify Main Ideas Write a new title for this section to express the main idea in another way.

_____

_____

TOPIC 13 — Note Taking Study Guide
THE INDUSTRIAL REVOLUTION (1750–1914)

Focus Question: What was the impact of the Industrial Revolution?

As you read the Lesson Summaries on the following pages, complete the graphic organizer below to help you understand the impact of the Industrial Revolution, including the problems that were created and the proposed solutions to those problems.

Industrial Revolution	
New Manufacturing Processes	Textile Factories
Advances in Medicine	Pasteur's Germ Theory
New Transportation	Canals
Urbanization	Poor working conditions
New Ways of Thinking	Women's Suffrage

Name _____ Class _____ Date _____

MODIFIED CORNELL NOTES

The Industrial Revolution started in Britain. Production shifted from simple hand tools to complex machines, and sources of energy shifted from human and animal power to steam and, later, electricity. Like the Enlightenment, the Industrial Revolution was partially an outgrowth of the Scientific Revolution of the seventeenth century, which created a mindset of scientific and technological experimentation. In 1750, most people worked the land, using handmade tools. They made their own clothing and grew their own food. With the onset of the Industrial Revolution, the rural way of life in Britain began to disappear. By the 1850s, many country villages had grown into industrial towns and cities. New inventions and scientific "firsts" appeared each year. Between 1830 and 1855, for example, an American dentist first used an **anesthetic** during surgery and a French physicist measured the speed of light.

A series of related causes helped spark the Industrial Revolution. It was made possible, in part, by another revolution—in agriculture—that greatly improved the quality and quantity of food. Farmers mixed different kinds of soils and tried out new methods of crop rotation to get higher yields. Meanwhile, rich landowners pushed ahead with **enclosure**, the process of taking over and consolidating land formerly shared by peasant farmers. As millions of acres were enclosed, farm output and profits rose. The agricultural revolution created a surplus of food, so fewer people died from starvation. Therefore, the agricultural revolution contributed to a rapid growth in population.

Agricultural progress, however, had a human cost. Many farm laborers were thrown out of work. In time, jobless farm workers migrated to towns and cities. There, they formed a growing labor force that would soon operate the machines of the Industrial Revolution.

Another factor that helped trigger the Industrial Revolution was the development of new technology, aided by the Scientific Revolution as well as new sources of energy and new materials. In 1764, Scottish engineer James Watt improved the steam engine to make it more efficient. Watt's engine became a key power source of the Industrial Revolution. Coal powered the engine, creating steam energy. Coal was also used in the production of iron, a material needed for the construction of machines and steam engines. In 1709,

(Continues on the next page.)

Lesson Vocabulary

anesthetic   drug that prevents pain during surgery

enclosure   the process of taking over and consolidating land formerly shared by peasant farmers

TOPIC **13** LESSON 1	**Lesson Summary**
	THE INDUSTRIAL REVOLUTION BEGINS (continued)

Adam Darby used coal to **smelt** iron, or separate iron from its ore. Darby's experiments led to the production of less expensive and better-quality iron.

The start of the Industrial Revolution in Britain can be credited to many factors, including population growth and plentiful natural resources. Population was only one of the reasons that industrialization started in Britain, however. All four factors of production were available in a large supply in Britain. These factors are natural resources, labor, capital, and entrepreneurship. In addition to having resources and plenty of labor, **capital** is needed to invest in new businesses. Beginning with the slave trade, the business class accumulated capital to invest in enterprises. An **enterprise** is a business in areas such as shipping, mining, or factories. Britain had a stable government that supported economic growth. **Entrepreneurs** managed and assumed the financial risks of starting new businesses.

The Industrial Revolution first took hold in Britain's largest industry—textiles. British merchants developed the **putting-out system**, in which raw cotton was distributed to peasant families. They spun it into thread and then wove the thread into cloth, working in their own homes. Under the putting-out system, production was slow. As demand for cloth grew, inventors came up with new devices, such as the flying shuttle and the spinning jenny, which revolutionized the British textile industry. Meanwhile, in the United States, these faster spinning and weaving machines presented a challenge—how to produce enough cotton to keep up with Britain. Cleaning the raw cotton by hand was time-consuming. To solve this, Eli Whitney invented a machine called the cotton gin. This greatly increased the production of cotton. To house these machines, manufacturers built the first factories, where spinners and weavers came each day to work to produce large quantities of goods.

(Continues on the next page.)

Lesson Vocabulary

smelt melt in order to get the pure matter away from its waste matter

capital money or wealth used to invest in business or enterprise

enterprise business organization in such areas as shipping, mining, railroads, or factories

entrepreneur person who assumes financial risk in the hope of making a profit

putting-out system system developed in the 18th century in which tasks were distributed to individuals who completed the work in their own homes; also known as cottage industry

MODIFIED CORNELL NOTES

As production increased, entrepreneurs needed faster and cheaper methods of moving goods. Some capitalists invested in **turnpikes**. Goods could be moved faster on these toll roads, and turnpikes soon linked every part of Britain. Canals opened to provide a cheaper way for factories to receive coal and raw materials. The canals shortened the distance to ship goods. The great revolution in transportation, however, occurred with the invention of the steam locomotive, which made possible the growth of railroads. The world's first major rail line began operating between the British industrial cities of Liverpool and Manchester in 1830. In the following decades, railroad travel became faster and railroad building boomed. The Industrial Revolution dramatically affected the way people lived.

During the early Industrial Revolution, Britain was the world's industrial giant. Later, two new industrial powers emerged—Germany and the United States. These nations had more abundant supplies of coal, iron, and other resources than Britain. This helped them become the new industrial leaders. These nations also had the advantage of being able to follow Britain's lead, borrowing its experts and technology.

Other nations started to industrialize, although their progress was slower. Russia moved toward industrialization more than 100 years after Britain's success. In East Asia, Japan industrialized quickly after 1886, in part because of a political revolution that made modernizing a priority. The demands of an industrial society brought about many social, economic, and political changes. The living conditions in the rapidly developing **urban centers** were often difficult. However, by 1900 steps were taken to make improvements. Ordinary workers could buy goods that in earlier days only the wealthy had been able to afford. Politics changed, too, as leaders had to meet the needs of an industrial society. Globally, industrial nations competed for world trade. Western industrial powers were able to affect the world more than ever before. They had both the technological and economic advantage.

Lesson Vocabulary

turnpike   private road built by entrepreneurs who charged a toll to travelers to use it

urban center   large, crowded urban area

TOPIC 13 LESSON 2

Lesson Summary
SOCIAL IMPACT OF INDUSTRIALISM

The Industrial Revolution brought rapid **urbanization**, or the movement of people to cities. Changes in farming, soaring population growth, and a demand for workers led masses of people to migrate from farms to cities. Almost overnight, small towns that were located around coal or iron mines grew into cities. Other cities developed around the factories in once-quiet market towns.

Those who benefited most from the Industrial Revolution were the entrepreneurs who set it in motion. The Industrial Revolution created this new middle class, whose members included merchants, artisans, and inventors, as well as entrepreneurs. While the wealthy and the middle class lived in pleasant neighborhoods, vast numbers of poor struggled to survive in slums. They were packed into tiny rooms in **tenements** that had no running water and no sewage or sanitation system. Sewage rotted in the streets or was dumped into rivers, which created an overwhelming stench and contaminated drinking water. This led to the spread of diseases such as cholera.

The heart of the new industrial city was the factory. Working in a factory differed greatly from working on a farm. In rural villages, people worked hard, but the work varied according to the season. Some seasons were easier than others. The factory system imposed a harsh new way of life on workers. Working hours were long, with shifts lasting from twelve to sixteen hours, six or seven days a week. Exhausted workers were injured by machines that had no safety devices. Working conditions in the mines were even worse than in the factories. Factories and mines also hired many boys and girls. These children often started working at age seven or eight; a few were as young as five. To combat the poor conditions of children faced in factories, the Sadler Report was presented to Parliament. It brought to light children's working conditions and helped to pass the Factory Act of 1833, which provided more regulations.

The early industrial age brought terrible hardships. In time, however, reformers pressed for laws to improve working conditions. **Labor unions** won the right to bargain with employers for better wages, hours, and working conditions. Despite the social problems created by the Industrial Revolution—low pay, dismal living conditions—the industrial age did have some positive effects. Wages rose. There were more job opportunities. A variety of goods were

(Continues on the next page.)

Lesson Vocabulary

urbanization   movement of people from rural areas to cities

tenement   multistory building divided into crowded apartments

labor union   organization of workers who bargain for better pay and working conditions

MODIFIED CORNELL NOTES

available in the marketplace for prices that more people could afford. Slowly the **standard of living** rose for workers. Working-class men gained the right to vote. People had opportunities that had not been available before. The Industrial Revolution increased the chances for **social mobility**, or the ability of individuals or groups to move up the social scale.

Many thinkers tried to understand the staggering changes taking place in the early Industrial Age. These thinkers looked for natural laws that governed the world of business and economics that had first been proposed by Adam Smith, author of *The Wealth of Nations*. Middle-class business leaders embraced the laissez-faire, or "hands-off" approach, believing that a **free market** would eventually help everyone, not just the rich. However, one British laissez-faire economist, Thomas Malthus, felt that the population would grow faster than the food supply. As long as the population kept growing, the poor would suffer. He opposed any government help, including charity and vaccinations. He urged families to have fewer children.

Another British laissez-faire economist, David Ricardo, dedicated himself to economics after studying Adam Smith. Like Malthus, Ricardo suggested that poverty would be difficult to escape. In his "Iron Law of Wages," Ricardo said that wage increases would only cover the cost of basic needs. He pointed out that when families had more income, they had more children instead of increasing their standard of living.

Other thinkers sought to modify laissez-faire ideas to justify some government intervention. The British philosopher and economist Jeremy Bentham advocated **utilitarianism**, or the idea that the goal of society should be the "greatest happiness for the greatest number" of citizens. Bentham's ideas influenced the British philosopher and economist John Stuart Mill. Although he strongly believed in individual freedom, Mill wanted the government to step in to improve the hard lives of the working class.

(Continues on the next page.)

Lesson Vocabulary

standard of living   the level of material goods and services available to people in a society

social mobility   the ability of individuals or groups to move up the social scale

free market   unregulated exchange of goods and services

utilitarianism   idea that the goal of society should be to bring about the greatest happiness for the greatest number of people

MODIFIED CORNELL NOTES

To end poverty and injustice, others offered a radical solution—**socialism**. Under socialism, the people, as a whole rather than as individuals, would own and operate the **means of production**—the farms, factories, railways, and other businesses that produced and distributed goods. A number of early socialists, such as Robert Owen, established communities where all work was shared and all property was owned in common. These early socialists were called Utopians.

Karl Marx, a German philosopher, formulated a new theory. His theory predicted a struggle between social classes that would end in a classless society that he called communist. In a classless, communist society, the struggles of the **proletariat**, or working class, would end because wealth and power would be equally shared. In practice, **communism** later referred to a system in which a small elite controlled the economy and politics. In the 1860s, German socialists adapted Marx's beliefs to form the idea of **social democracy**, which called for a slow transition from capitalism to socialism.

Lesson Vocabulary

socialism   system in which the people as a whole, rather than private individuals, own all property and operate all businesses

means of production   farms, factories, railways, and other large businesses that produce and distribute goods

proletariat   working class

communism   form of socialism advocated by Karl Marx; According to Marx, class struggle was inevitable and would lead to the creation of a classless society in which all wealth and property would be owned by the community as a whole.

social democracy   political ideology in which there is a gradual transition from capitalism into socialism instead of a sudden, violent overthrow of the system

Name _____ Class _____ Date _____

MODIFIED CORNELL NOTES

Technology sparked industrial and economic growth. Henry Bessemer patented the process for making steel from iron. Steel became so important that industrialized countries measured their success in steel output. Alfred Nobel earned enough money from his invention of dynamite to fund today's Nobel prizes. Electricity replaced steam as the dominant industrial energy source. Michael Faraday created the first simple electric motor, as well as the first **dynamo**. In the 1870s, Thomas Edison made the first electric light bulb. Soon, electricity lit entire cities, the pace of city life quickened, and factories continued to operate after dark. **Interchangeable parts** and the **assembly line** made production faster and cheaper.

Technology also transformed transportation and communication. Steamships replaced sailing ships. Railroads connected cities, seaports, and industrial centers. The invention of the internal combustion engine sparked the automobile age. In the early 1900s, Henry Ford developed an assembly line to produce cars, making the United States a leader in the automobile industry. The air age began when Orville and Wilbur Wright flew their airplane for a few seconds in 1903. Communication advances included the telegraph and telephone. Guglielmo Marconi's radio became the cornerstone of today's global communication network.

New technologies needed investments of large amounts of money. To get the money, owners sold **stock** to investors, growing businesses into giant **corporations**. By the late 1800s, what we call "big business" came to dominate industry. Corporations formed **cartels** to control markets.

Between 1800 and 1900, the population of Europe more than doubled. Advances in medicine slowed death rates and caused a population explosion. In the fight against disease, scientists

(Continues on the next page.)

Lesson Vocabulary

dynamo   a machine used to generate electricity

interchangeable parts   identical components that can be used in place of one another in manufacturing

assembly line   a production method that breaks down a complex job into a series of smaller tasks

stock   shares in a company

corporation   a business owned by many investors who buy shares of stock and risk only the amount of their investment

cartel   a group of companies that join together to control the production and price of a product

TOPIC
13
LESSON 3

Lesson Summary

THE SECOND INDUSTRIAL REVOLUTION (continued)

speculated about a **germ theory**. They believed that certain germs might cause specific diseases. In 1870, French chemist Louis Pasteur showed that this link is real. Ten years later, German doctor Robert Koch identified the bacteria that causes tuberculosis, a deadly respiratory disease. As people began to understand how germs cause diseases, they practiced better hygiene. This helped decrease the number of deaths from disease. Better hygiene also led to improvements in hospital care. British nurse and reformer Florence Nightingale introduced sanitary measures in hospitals. The English surgeon Joseph Lister discovered how antiseptics prevent infection.

As industrialization progressed, city life underwent dramatic changes in Europe and the United States. The most extensive **urban renewal** took place in Paris in the 1850s. Wide boulevards, paved streets, and splendid public buildings replaced old streets full of tenement housing. Architects used steel to build soaring buildings called skyscrapers. Electric streetlights illuminated the night, increasing safety. Massive new sewage systems in London and Paris provided cleaner water and better sanitation, sharply cutting death rates from disease.

Despite these efforts, urban life remained difficult for the poor. In the worst tenements, whole families were often crammed into a single room. Slums remained a fact of city life. Still, millions of people were attracted to cities because of the promise of work, entertainment, and educational opportunities.

However, industrialization and urban improvements did not improve conditions for workers. Most experienced low wages, long hours, unsafe environments, and the constant threat of unemployment. Workers protested these terrible conditions. They formed **mutual-aid societies** and organized unions. Pressured by unions, reformers, and working-class voters, governments passed laws to regulate working conditions. Wages varied, but overall, many workers were able to buy more things because of rising wages. Worker also benefited from the move to provide public education.

Lesson Vocabulary

germ theory   the theory that infectious diseases are caused by certain microbes

urban renewal   the process of fixing up the poor areas of a city

mutual-aid society   self-help group to aid sick or injured workers

TOPIC 13 LESSON 4

Lesson Summary
CHANGING WAYS OF LIFE AND THOUGHT

In the late 1800s, the social order in the Western world slowly changed. Instead of nobles and peasants, a more complex social structure emerged, made up of three classes. The new upper class included very rich business families, as well as the old nobility. Below this tiny elite were a growing middle class and a struggling lower middle class. Workers and peasants were at the bottom of the social ladder.

The middle class developed its own values and way of life, which included a strict code of rules that dictated behavior for every occasion. A **cult of domesticity** also emerged that idealized women and the home.

Demands for women's rights also challenged the traditional social order. Across Europe and the United States, many women campaigned for fairness in marriage, divorce, and property laws. Many women's groups also supported the **temperance movement**. In the United States, reformers such as Elizabeth Cady Stanton and Sojourner Truth were dedicated to achieving **women's suffrage**.

Industrialized societies recognized the need for a literate workforce. Reformers persuaded many governments to require basic education for all children and to set up public schools. More and more children attended school, and public education improved.

At the same time, new ideas in science challenged long-held beliefs. John Dalton developed the modern atomic theory. The most controversial new idea, however, came from the British naturalist Charles Darwin. His ideas upset those who debated the validity of his conclusions. Darwin argued that all forms of life had evolved over millions of years. According to his theory of natural selection, members of each species compete to survive. Darwin's theory caused controversy, since his ideas seemed to contradict the Bible. Unfortunately, other people applied Darwin's theory of natural selection to encourage **racism**. Others applied his ideas to economic competition.

(Continues on the next page.)

Lesson Vocabulary

cult of domesticity   idealization of women and the home

temperance movement   campaign to limit or ban the use of alcoholic beverages

women's suffrage   right of women to vote

racism   belief that one racial group is superior to another

TOPIC 13 LESSON 4

Lesson Summary

CHANGING WAYS OF LIFE AND THOUGHT (continued)

Religion continued to be a major force in Western society. The grim realities of industrial life stirred feelings of compassion and charity. For example, the **social gospel** urged Christians to push for reforms in housing, healthcare, and education. The Salvation Army both spread Christian teachings and provided social services.

From about 1750 to 1850, a cultural movement called romanticism emerged in Western art and literature. The movement was a reaction against the rationality and restraint of the Enlightenment. **Romanticism** emphasized imagination, freedom, and emotion. In contrast to Enlightenment literature, the works of romantic writers included direct language, intense feelings, and a glorification of nature.

Poets William Wordsworth, William Blake, and Lord Byron were among the major figures of the Romantic Movement. Romantic novelists, such as Victor Hugo, were inspired by history, legend, and folklore. Romantic composers also tried to stir deep emotions. The passionate music of Ludwig van Beethoven conveyed universal themes that transcended his own time and place, themes such as the emotions of love, loss, death, joy, and fear. Painters, too, broke free from the formal styles of the Enlightenment. They sought to capture the beauty and power of nature with bold brush strokes and colors.

By the mid-1800s, another new artistic movement, **realism**, took hold in the West. Realists sought to represent the world as it was, without romantic sentiment. Their works made people aware of the grim conditions of the Industrial Age. Many realists wanted to improve the lives of those they depicted. Charles Dickens, for example, vividly portrayed in his novels the lives of slum dwellers and factory workers. Some of his novels shocked middle-class readers with images of poverty, mistreatment of children, and urban crime. Painters such as Gustave Courbet also portrayed the realities of the time.

(Continues on the next page.)

Lesson Vocabulary

social gospel   movement of the 1800s that urged Christians to do social service

romanticism   19th-century artistic movement that appealed to emotion rather than reason

realism   19th-century artistic movement whose aim was to represent the world as it is

Lesson Summary
CHANGING WAYS OF LIFE AND THOUGHT (continued)

By the 1840s, a new art form, photography, emerged. Louis Daguerre produced some of the first successful photographs. Some artists questioned the effectiveness of realism when a camera could make such exact images. By the 1870s, one group had started a new art movement, **impressionism**. Impressionists, such as Claude Monet, sought to capture the first fleeting impression made by a scene or object on the viewer's eye. By concentrating on visual impressions, rather than realism, artists created a fresh view of familiar subjects. Later painters, called postimpressionists, developed a variety of styles. Vincent van Gogh, for example, experimented with sharp brush lines and bright colors.

Lesson Vocabulary

impressionism   school of painting of the late 1800s and early 1900s that tried to capture fleeting visual impressions

Name _____ Class _____ Date _____

TOPIC 13 Review Questions
THE INDUSTRIAL REVOLUTION (1750–1914)

Answer the questions below using the information in the Lesson Summaries on the previous pages.

Lesson 1: The Industrial Revolution Begins

1. What factors contributed to the start of the Industrial Revolution in Britain?

_____

_____

2. **Identify Causes and Effects** Identify causes and effects of the great revolution in transportation in England.

_____

_____

Lesson 2: Social Impact of Industrialism

3. What caused rapid urbanization to occur during the Industrial Revolution?

_____

_____

4. **Understand Effects** How did the Industrial Revolution affect the lives of the working class?

_____

_____

Lesson 3: The Second Industrial Revolution

5. How did the development of electricity change life in cities?

_____

_____

6. **Identify Main Ideas** How was transportation transformed during the Industrial Revolution?

_____

_____

Lesson 4: Changing Ways of Life and Thought

7. How did the Romantic Movement differ from the Enlightenment?

_____

_____

8. **Identify Supporting Details** Identify two supporting details for the following main idea: The artists of the realism movement made people more aware of the harsh conditions of life in the Industrial Age.

_____

_____

TOPIC 14

Note Taking Study Guide

NATIONALISM AND THE SPREAD OF DEMOCRACY (1790–1914)

Focus Question: How did nationalism shape the world of the late 19th century?

As you read the Lesson Summaries on the following pages, complete the graphic organizer below to recognize the leaders and peoples that tried to encourage nationalism and those that tried to reverse it.

Against Nationalism		For Nationalism	
Action	**Result**	**Action**	**Result**
Prince Metternich of Austria opposes revolts in Spain and Italy.	French and Austrian troops smash rebellions.	Revolts in Spain and Italy	French and Austrian troops smash rebellions.

TOPIC 14 LESSON 1

Lesson Summary
REVOLUTIONS SWEEP EUROPE

After the Congress of Vienna, people with opposing **ideologies** plunged Europe into decades of turmoil. Conservatives, including monarchs, nobles, and church leaders, favored a return to the social order that had existed before 1789. They decided to work together in an agreement called the Concert of Europe.

Conservatives wanted to restore the monarchies that Napoleon had deposed. They supported a social hierarchy in which lower classes respected and obeyed their social superiors. They also backed established churches and opposed constitutional governments. Conservative leaders such as Prince Metternich of Austria sought to suppress revolutionary ideas.

Inspired by the Enlightenment and the French Revolution, liberals and nationalists challenged conservatives. Liberals included business owners, bankers, lawyers, politicians, and writers. They wanted governments based on written constitutions. They opposed established churches and divine-right monarchies. They believed that liberty, equality, and property were natural rights. They saw government's role as limited to protecting basic rights, such as freedom of thought, speech, and religion. Only later in the century did liberals come to support **universal manhood suffrage**, giving all men the right to vote. Liberals also strongly supported laissez-faire economics.

Nationalism gave people with a common heritage a sense of identity and the goal of creating their own homeland. In the 1800s, national groups within the Austrian and Ottoman empires set out to create their own states. Rebellions erupted in the Balkans, where there were people of various religions and ethnic groups. The Serbs were the first to revolt. By 1830, Russian support helped the Serbs win **autonomy**, or self-rule, within the Ottoman empire. In 1821, the Greeks revolted, and by 1830, Greece was independent from the Ottomans.

Revolts spread to Spain, Portugal, and Italy. Metternich urged conservative rulers to crush the uprisings. In response, French and Austrian troops smashed rebellions in Spain and Italy.

In the next decades, sparks of rebellion would flare anew. Added to liberal and nationalist demands were the goals of the new industrial working class. By the mid-1800s, social reformers and agitators were urging workers to support socialism or other ways of reorganizing property ownership.

(Continues on the next page.)

Lesson Vocabulary

ideology system of thought or belief

universal manhood suffrage right of all adult men to vote

autonomy self-rule

MODIFIED CORNELL NOTES

In 1824, Charles X inherited the French throne. In 1830, Charles suspended the legislature, limited the right to vote, and restricted the press. Angry citizens, led by liberals and **radicals**, rebelled and soon controlled Paris. Charles X abdicated. Radicals hoped to set up a republic, but liberals insisted on a constitutional monarchy. Louis Philippe was chosen king. As the "citizen king," Louis favored the bourgeoisie, or middle class, over the workers.

The Paris revolts inspired uprisings elsewhere in Europe. Most failed, but the revolutions frightened rulers and encouraged reforms. One notable success was in Belgium, which achieved its independence from Holland in 1831. Nationalists also revolted in Poland in 1830, but they failed to win widespread support. Russian forces crushed the rebels.

In the 1840s, discontent began to grow again in France. Radicals, socialists, and liberals denounced Louis Philippe's government. Discontent was heightened by a **recession**. People lost their jobs, and poor harvests caused bread prices to rise. When the government tried to silence critics, angry crowds took to the streets in February 1848. The turmoil spread, and Louis Philippe abdicated. A group of liberals, radicals, and socialists proclaimed the Second Republic.

By June, the upper and middle classes had won control of the government. Workers again took to the streets of Paris. At least 1,500 people were killed before the government crushed the rebellion. By the end of 1848, the National Assembly had issued a constitution for the Second Republic, giving the right to vote to all adult men. When the election for president was held, Louis Napoleon, the nephew of Napoleon Bonaparte, won. However, by 1852 he had proclaimed himself Emperor Napoleon III. This ended the Second Republic.

The revolts in Paris in 1848 again led to revolutions across Europe, especially in the Austrian empire. Revolts broke out in Vienna, and Metternich resigned. In Budapest, Hungarian nationalists led by Louis Kossuth demanded an independent government. In Prague, the Czechs made similar demands. The Italian states also revolted, and the German states demanded national unity. While the rebellions had some short-term success, most of them had failed by 1850.

Lesson Vocabulary

radical   one who favors extreme changes

recession   period of reduced economic activity

TOPIC 14
LESSON 2

Lesson Summary
LATIN AMERICAN NATIONS WIN INDEPENDENCE

By the late 1700s, revolutionary fever had spread to Latin America, where the social system had led to discontent. Spanish-born *peninsulares*, the highest social class, dominated the government and the Church. Many **creoles**—Latin Americans of European descent who owned the haciendas, ranches, and mines—resented their second-class status. **Mestizos**, people of Native American and European descent, and **mulattoes**, people of African and European descent, were angry at being denied the status, wealth, and power that the other groups enjoyed.

The Enlightenment and the French and American revolutions inspired creoles, but they were reluctant to act. However, when Napoleon invaded Spain in 1808, Latin American leaders decided to demand independence from Spain.

Revolution had already erupted in Hispaniola in 1791 when Toussaint L'Ouverture led a slave rebellion there. The fighting cost many lives, but the rebels achieved their goal of abolishing slavery and taking control of the island. Napoleon's army tried to reconquer the island but failed. In 1804, the island declared itself independent under the name Haiti.

In 1810, a creole priest, Father Miguel Hidalgo, called Mexicans to fight for independence. After some successes, he was captured and executed. Father José Morelos tried to carry the revolution forward, but he too was captured and killed. Success finally came in 1821 when revolutionaries led by Agustín de Iturbide overthrew the Spanish viceroy and declared independence. Central American colonies soon declared independence, as well.

In the early 1800s, discontent spread across South America. Simón Bolívar led an uprising in Venezuela. Conservative forces toppled his new republic, but Bolívar did not give up. In a grueling campaign, he marched his army across the Andes, swooping down into Bogotá and taking the city from the surprised Spanish. Then he moved south to free Ecuador, Peru, and Bolivia. There, he joined forces with another great leader, José de San Martín. San Martín helped Argentina and Chile win freedom from Spain.

The wars of independence ended in 1824, but power struggles among South American leaders led to destructive civil wars. In Brazil, Dom Pedro, the son of the Portuguese king, became emperor and proclaimed independence for Brazil in 1822.

Lesson Vocabulary

peninsular   member of the highest class in Spain's colonies in the Americas

creole   person in Spain's colonies in the Americas who was an American-born descendent of Spanish settlers

mestizo   person in Spain's colonies in the Americas who was of Native American and European descent

mulatto   in Spain's colonies in the Americas, person who was of African and European descent

TOPIC 14 LESSON 3

Lesson Summary
THE UNIFICATION OF GERMANY

MODIFIED CORNELL NOTES

In the early 1800s, German-speaking peoples lived in a number of German states. Many also lived in Prussia and the Austrian empire. There was no unified German nation. However, in the mid-nineteenth century events unfolded that eventually led to a united Germany.

Between 1806 and 1812, Napoleon invaded these lands. He organized a number of German states into the Rhine Confederation. After Napoleon's defeat, the Congress of Vienna created the German Confederation. This was a weak alliance of German states headed by Austria. In the 1830s, Prussia created an economic union called the *Zollverein*. This union removed tariff barriers between many German states, yet they remained politically fragmented.

Otto von Bismarck, the **chancellor** of Prussia, led the drive to unite the German states—under Prussian rule. Bismarck was a master of **Realpolitik**, or realistic politics based on the needs of the state. After creating a powerful military, he was ready to pursue an aggressive foreign policy. Over the next decade, Bismarck led Prussia into three wars. Each war increased Prussian power and paved the way for German unity.

In 1866, Bismarck created an excuse to attack Austria. The Austro-Prussian War lasted only seven weeks. Afterwards, Prussia **annexed** several north German states. In France, the Prussian victory angered Napoleon III. A growing rivalry between the two nations led to the Franco-Prussian War of 1870. Bismarck created a crisis by rewriting and releasing to the press a telegram that reported on a meeting between William I of Prussia and the French ambassador. Bismarck's editing of the telegram made it seem that William I had insulted the Frenchman. Furious, Napoleon III declared war on Prussia, as Bismarck had hoped. The Prussian army quickly defeated the French.

Delighted by the victory, German princes persuaded William I to take the title **kaiser** of Germany. In January 1871, German nationalists celebrated the birth of the Second **Reich**. Bismarck drafted a constitution that created a two-house legislature. Even so, the real power remained in the hands of the kaiser and Bismarck.

(Continues on the next page.)

Lesson Vocabulary

chancellor the highest official of a monarch, prime minister

Realpolitik realistic politics based on the needs of the state

annex add a territory to an existing state or country

kaiser emperor of Germany

Reich German empire

Name _____ Class _____ Date _____

MODIFIED CORNELL NOTES

After unification in 1871, the new German empire emerged as an industrial giant. Several factors, including ample iron and coal resources, made industrialization in Germany possible. A disciplined and educated workforce also spurred economic growth. The German middle class created a productive and efficient society that prided itself on its sense of responsibility. Additionally, a growing population provided a huge home market for goods and a large supply of industrial workers.

German industrialists recognized the value of applied science in developing new products, such as synthetic chemicals and dyes. Both industrialists and the government supported scientific research and development. The government also promoted economic development. It issued a single form of currency for Germany and reorganized the banking system. The leaders of the new empire were determined to maintain economic strength as well as military power.

Bismarck pursued several foreign-policy goals. He wanted to keep France weak and build strong links with Austria and Russia. On the domestic front, Bismarck, known as the "Iron Chancellor," targeted the Catholic Church and the Socialists. He believed these groups posed a threat to the new German state. He thought Catholics would be more loyal to the Church than to Germany. He also worried that Socialists would undermine the loyalty of workers and turn them toward revolution.

Bismarck tried to repress both groups, but his efforts failed. For example, the *Kulturkampf* was a set of laws intended to weaken the role of the Church. Instead, the faithful rallied to support the Church. When repressing the Socialists failed to work, Bismarck changed course and pioneered social reform.

In 1888, William II became the kaiser. He believed that his right to rule came from God, and he shocked Europe by asking Bismarck to resign. Not surprisingly, William II resisted efforts to introduce democratic reforms. However, his government provided many **social welfare** programs to help certain groups of people. The government also provided services such as cheap transportation and electricity.

Lesson Vocabulary

Kulturkampf Bismarck's "battle for civilization," intended to make Catholics put loyalty to the state above their allegiance to the Church

social welfare   programs provided by the state for the benefit of its citizens

MODIFIED CORNELL NOTES

TOPIC 14 LESSON 4

Lesson Summary
THE UNIFICATION OF ITALY

The peoples of the Italian peninsula had not been unified since Roman times. By the early 1800s, however, patriots were determined to build a new, united Italy. As in Germany, Napoleon's invasions had sparked dreams of nationalism.

In the 1830s, the nationalist leader Giuseppe Mazzini founded Young Italy. The goal of this secret society was "to constitute Italy, one, free, independent, republican nation." To nationalists like Mazzini, establishing a unified Italy made sense because of geography and a common language and history. It also made economic sense because it would end trade barriers among Italian states. Unification would stimulate industry, too.

Victor Emmanuel II, the constitutional monarch of Sardinia, hoped to join other states with his own and increase his power. In 1852, he made Count Camillo Cavour his prime minister. Cavour's long-term goal was to end Austrian power in Italy. Cavour provoked a war with Austria, and with the help of France, defeated Austria and annexed Lombardy.

Meanwhile, nationalist groups overthrew Austrian-backed leaders in other northern Italian states. In the south, Giuseppe Garibaldi had recruited a force of 1,000 red-shirted volunteers. He and his "Red Shirts" quickly won control of Sicily. Then they crossed to the mainland and marched triumphantly to Naples. Garibaldi turned over both regions to Victor Emmanuel. In 1861, Victor Emmanuel II was crowned king of Italy.

Only Rome and Venetia remained outside the new Italian nation. However, Italy formed an alliance with Bismarck during the Austro-Prussian War and won the province of Venetia. Then, during the Franco-Prussian War, France was forced to withdraw its troops from Rome. For the first time since the fall of the Roman Empire, Italy was a united land.

However, Italy faced many problems as **anarchists** and radicals struggled against the conservative government. Tensions grew between the north and south. The north was richer and had more cities. The south was poor and rural. Still, Italy developed economically and the population grew. For many, however, **emigration** offered a chance to improve their lives. Large numbers of Italians left for the United States, Canada, and Latin America.

Lesson Vocabulary

anarchist   a person who wants to abolish all government

emigration   movement away from one's homeland

Name _____ Class _____ Date _____

MODIFIED CORNELL NOTES

In 1815, Britain was governed by a constitutional monarchy with a Parliament and two political parties. But it was far from democratic. The House of Lords was controlled by wealthy nobles and squires. The House of Lords could veto any bill passed by the House of Commons. Catholics and non-Anglican Protestants could not vote. **Rotten boroughs** still sent members to Parliament, while new industrial cities had no seats allocated in Parliament. The Great Reform Act of 1832 redistributed seats in the House of Commons, giving representation to new cities and eliminating rotten boroughs.

From 1837 to 1901, the great symbol in British life was Queen Victoria. She set the tone for the Victorian age that was named for her. She embodied the values of duty, thrift, honesty, hard work, and respectability. Under Victoria, the middle class felt confident, and that confidence grew as the British empire expanded.

In the 1860s, a new era dawned in British politics. Benjamin Disraeli and William Gladstone alternated as prime minister and fought for important reforms. The Reform Bill of 1867 gave the vote to many working-class men, and in the 1880s, the vote was extended to farm workers and most other men. By the century's end, Britain had transformed from a constitutional monarchy to a **parliamentary democracy**. In 1911, measures were passed that restricted the power of the House of Lords, and it eventually became a largely ceremonial body.

Also during this time, Parliament passed important laws enacting economic and social reforms. The Corn Laws imposed high tariffs that benefited farmers and landowners, but made bread more expensive for consumers. In 1846, Parliament **repealed** the Corn Laws. Gradually, Parliament passed laws to regulate conditions in factories and mines. Trade unions became legal in 1825 and worked to improve the lives of their members. Both the Liberal and Conservative parties enacted reforms to benefit workers.

(Continues on the next page.)

Lesson Vocabulary

rotten borough   rural town in England that sent members to Parliament despite having few or no voters

parliamentary democracy   a form of government in which the executive leaders (usually a prime minister and cabinet) are chosen by and responsible to the legislature (parliament), and are also members of it

repeal   cancel

TOPIC 14
LESSON 5

Lesson Summary
DEMOCRATIC REFORMS IN BRITAIN (continued)

During this time, women struggled for the right to vote. When mass meetings and other peaceful efforts brought no results, Emmeline Pankhurst and other suffragists turned to more drastic, violent protest. They smashed windows, burned buildings, and went on hunger strikes. Not until 1918 did Parliament finally grant suffrage to women over 30.

Throughout the 1800s, Britain faced the "Irish Question." The Irish resented British rule. Many Irish peasants lived in poverty while paying high rents to **absentee landlords** living in England. Irish Catholics also had to pay tithes to the Church of England. The potato famine made problems worse. Under Gladstone, the government finally ended the use of Irish tithes to support the Church of England and passed laws to protect the rights of Irish tenant farmers.

Lesson Vocabulary

absentee landlord one who owns a large estate but does not live there

TOPIC 14 LESSON 6
Lesson Summary
DIVISIONS AND DEMOCRACY IN FRANCE

After the revolution of 1848, Napoleon III established the Second Empire in France. At first, he ruled like a dictator. In the 1860s, however, he lifted some censorship and gave the legislature more power. He promoted investment in industry and ventures such as railroad building. During this period, a French entrepreneur organized the building of the Suez Canal in Egypt.

However, Napoleon III had major failures in foreign affairs. He tried to put the Austrian archduke Maximilian on the throne of Mexico, but Maximilian was overthrown and killed. France and Britain won the Crimean War, but France suffered terrible losses and few gains. The Franco-Prussian War was a disaster, ending in a harsh defeat for France.

Following that defeat, republicans established a **provisional**, or temporary, government. In 1871, an uprising broke out in Paris, and rebels set up the Paris Commune. Its goal was to save the Republic from royalists. When the rebels did not disband, the government sent in troops and 20,000 rebels were killed.

The provisional government soon became the Third Republic. Although the legislature elected a president, the **premier** had the real power. There were many political parties, but none were strong enough to take control. Because of this, parties had to form **coalitions**, or alliances, to govern. Coalition governments are often unstable, and France had 50 different coalition governments in the first 10 years of the Third Republic.

A series of political scandals in the 1880s and 1890s shook public trust in the government. The most divisive scandal was the Dreyfus affair. Alfred Dreyfus was a Jewish army officer wrongly accused and convicted of spying for Germany. Author Émile Zola was convicted of **libel** when he charged the army and government with suppressing the truth. The affair revealed strong anti-Semitic feelings in France and led Theodor Herzl to launch Zionism, a movement to establish a Jewish state.

France achieved serious democratic reforms in the early 1900s. It passed labor laws regulating wages, hours, and safety conditions. Free public elementary schools were established. The French government tried to repress church involvement in their government. In 1905, the government passed a law to separate church and state. Women made some gains, but they did not win the right to vote until after World War II.

Lesson Vocabulary

provisional   temporary

premier   prime minister

coalition   temporary alliance of various political parties

libel   knowing publication of false and damaging statements

TOPIC	**Lesson Summary**
14 LESSON 7	**GROWTH OF THE UNITED STATES**

In the 1800s, the United States followed a policy of **expansionism**, or extending the nation's boundaries. In 1803, the Louisiana Purchase nearly doubled the size of the country. More territory was soon added in the West and South. Americans believed in Manifest Destiny, or the idea that their nation was destined to spread across the entire continent.

Voting, slavery, and women's rights were important issues at this time. In 1800, only white men who owned property could vote. By the 1830s, most white men had the right to vote. William Lloyd Garrison, Frederick Douglass, and other abolitionists called for an end to slavery. Lucretia Mott, Elizabeth Cady Stanton, Susan B. Anthony, and others began to seek equality for women.

Economic differences, as well as slavery, divided the country into the North and the South. When Abraham Lincoln was elected in 1860, most southern states **seceded**, or withdrew, from the Union. The American Civil War soon began. Southerners fought fiercely, but the North had more people, more industry, and more resources. The South finally surrendered in 1865.

During the war, Lincoln issued the Emancipation Proclamation, which declared that the slaves in the South were free. After the war, slavery was banned throughout the nation, and African Americans were granted some political rights. However, African Americans still faced restrictions, including **segregation**, or legal separation, in public places. Some state laws prevented African Americans from voting.

After the Civil War, the United States became the world leader in industrial and agricultural production. By 1900, giant monopolies controlled whole industries. For example, John D. Rockefeller's Standard Oil Company dominated the world's petroleum industry. Big business enjoyed huge profits, but not everyone shared in the prosperity.

Reformers tried to address this problem. Unions sought better wages and working conditions for factory workers. Farmers and city workers formed the Populist Party to seek changes. Progressives sought to ban child labor, limit working hours, regulate monopolies, and give voters more power. Progressives also worked to get women the right to vote, which they did in 1920.

Lesson Vocabulary

expansionism   policy of increasing the amount of territory a government holds

secede   withdraw

segregation   forced separation by race, sex, religion, or ethnicity

Name _____ Class _____ Date _____

MODIFIED CORNELL NOTES

In 1800, the Hapsburgs of Austria, the oldest ruling house in Europe, presided over a multinational empire. The emperor, Francis I, upheld conservative goals against growing liberal forces. He could not, however, hold back the changes that were happening throughout Europe. By the 1840s, Austria was facing the problems of industrial life, including growth of cities, worker discontent, and socialism. Nationalists were threatening the old order.

The Hapsburgs ignored these demands for change and crushed revolts. Amid the turmoil, 18-year-old Francis Joseph inherited the Hapsburg throne. He granted some limited reforms, such as adopting a constitution that set up a legislature. However, these reforms only satisfied German-speaking Austrians. The reforms did not satisfy the other national groups within the empire.

Austria's defeat in the 1866 war with Prussia brought even more pressure for change, especially from the Hungarians. Ferenc Deák helped work out a compromise known as the Dual Monarchy. Under this agreement, Austria and Hungary became separate states. Each had its own constitution, but Francis Joseph ruled both—as emperor of Austria and king of Hungary.

However, other groups within the empire resented this arrangement. Restlessness increased among various Slavic groups. Some nationalist leaders called on Slavs to unite in "fraternal solidarity." By the early 1900s, nationalist unrest left the government paralyzed in the face of pressing political and social problems.

Like the Hapsburgs, the Ottomans ruled a multinational empire. It stretched from Eastern Europe and the Balkans to the Middle East and North Africa. As in Austria, nationalist demands tore at the fabric of the Ottoman Empire. During the 1800s, various peoples revolted, hoping to set up their own independent states. With the empire weakened, European powers scrambled to divide up Ottoman lands.

A complex web of competing interests led to a series of crises and wars in the Balkans. Russia fought several wars against the Ottomans. France and Britain sometimes joined the Russians, and sometimes the Ottomans. By the early 1900s, observers were referring to the region as the "Balkan powder keg." The "explosion" came in 1914 and helped set off World War I.

By 1815, Russia was the largest, most populous nation in Europe. The Russian **colossus** had immense natural resources. Reformers hoped to free Russia from autocratic rule, economic backwardness, and social injustice. One of the obstacles to progress was the rigid social structure. Another was the absolute power that tsars had wielded for centuries, while the majority of Russians were poor serfs.

(Continues on the next page.)

Lesson Vocabulary

colossus   giant

Name _____ Class _____ Date _____

MODIFIED CORNELL NOTES

Alexander II became tsar in 1855 during the Crimean War. Events in his reign represent the pattern of reform and repression of previous tsars. The war, which ended in a Russian defeat, revealed the country's backwardness and inefficient bureaucracy. People demanded changes, so Alexander II agreed to some reforms. He ordered the **emancipation** of the serfs. He also set up a system of local, elected assemblies called **zemstvos**. Then he introduced legal reforms, such as trial by jury. These reforms, however, failed to satisfy many Russians. Radicals pressed for even greater changes and more reforms. The tsar then backed away from reform and moved toward repression.

This sparked anger among radicals. In 1881, terrorists assassinated Alexander II. In response, Alexander III revived harsh, repressive policies. He also suppressed the cultures of non-Russian peoples, which led to persecution. Official persecution encouraged **pogroms**, or violent mob attacks on Jewish people. Many left Russia and became **refugees**.

Russia began to industrialize under Alexander III and his son Nicholas II. However, this increased political and social problems. Industrialization led to poor working and living conditions. Nobles and peasants feared the changes industrialization brought. News of military losses to Japan added to the unrest.

On Sunday, January 22, 1905, a peaceful protest calling for reforms turned deadly when the tsar's troops killed and wounded hundreds of people. In the months that followed this "Bloody Sunday," discontent exploded across Russia. Nicholas was forced to make sweeping reforms. He agreed to summon a Duma. He then appointed a new prime minister, Peter Stolypin. Stolypin realized Russia needed reform, not repression. Unfortunately, the changes he introduced were too limited, and he was assassinated in 1911. By 1914, Russia was still an autocracy, but the nation was simmering with discontent.

Lesson Vocabulary

emancipation   granting of freedom to serfs or slaves

zemstvos   local elected assembly set up in Russia under Alexander II

pogrom   violent attack on a Jewish community

refugee   a person who flees from home or country to seek refuge elsewhere, often because of political upheaval or famine

Name _____ Class _____ Date _____

Answer the questions below using the information in the Lesson Summaries on the previous pages.

Lesson 1: Revolutions Sweep Europe

1. What caused the rebellion in France in 1830?

_____

_____

2. **Identify Main Ideas** What two groups generally struggled for political control during the early nineteenth century?

_____

_____

Lesson 2: Latin American Nations Win Independence

3. Why were creoles ready to revolt by 1808?

_____

_____

4. **Identify Main Ideas** In the first paragraph of the Summary, most of the sentences are supporting details. Which sentence states the main idea of that paragraph?

_____

_____

Lesson 3: The Unification of Germany

5. How did Bismarck use war to create a united Germany under Prussian rule?

_____

_____

6. **Recognize Sequence** What events led Napoleon III to declare war on Prussia?

_____

_____

Lesson 4: The Unification of Italy

7. Why did nationalists feel that a unified Italy made sense?

_____

_____

8. **Recognize Sequence** What events took place between Garibaldi's recruitment of the "Red Shirts" and Victor Emmanuel II's crowning as king of Italy?

_____

_____

TOPIC 14 Review Questions
NATIONALISM AND THE SPREAD OF DEMOCRACY (1790–1914) (continued)

Lesson 5: Democratic Reforms in Britain

9. How is a parliamentary democracy organized?

_____

_____

10. Cause and Effect What were the effects of the Great Reform Act of 1832?

_____

_____

Lesson 6: Divisions and Democracy in France

11. What failures in foreign affairs took place under Napoleon III?

_____

_____

12. Recognize Sequence List, in chronological order, the three French governments described in this section.

_____

_____

Lesson 7: Growth of the United States

13. How were African Americans deprived of equality after the Civil War?

_____

_____

14. Categorize Categorize the reforms discussed in this Summary by the group that did or would benefit from them.

_____

_____

Lesson 8: Nationalism in Eastern Europe and Russia

15. What effect did the Crimean War have on Russia?

_____

_____

16. Recognize Sequence What are two events that led to the decline of the Austrian empire in the late 1800s?

_____

_____

Name _____ Class _____ Date _____

Focus Question: How did the economic success of industrialized nations lead them on imperialist adventures in Asia, Africa, and the Pacific realm?

As you read the Lesson Summaries on the following pages, complete the graphic organizer below to identify the economic concerns that spurred imperialism and the impact imperialism had on the countries involved.

Cause (Economic Need/Want)	Effect (Imperialist Action)
Gold and diamonds in South Africa	British claimed Boer land and later moved farther north from South Africa
Oil in Iran (Persia)	
British East India Company needed money	
British needed to control India after Sepoy revolt	
	Opium War lost by China, which granted economic concessions to Britain
	China was pressured to sign treaties opening more ports and allowing Christian missionaries in China
Western powers needed Japanese ports open for trade.	
American sugar growers wanted to control Hawaii.	
U.S. invested in many Latin American countries	

Name _____ Class _____ Date _____

Lesson Summary
THE NEW IMPERIALISM

MODIFIED CORNELL NOTES

Many western countries built overseas empires in the late 1800s. This expansion, referred to as **imperialism,** is the domination by one country of the political, economic, or cultural life of another country or region. In the 1800s, Europeans embarked on a path of aggressive expansion called the "new imperialism." There were several causes. The Industrial Revolution was one. Manufacturers wanted access to natural resources and markets for their goods. Colonies were also an outlet for Europe's growing population. Leaders claimed that colonies were needed for national security. Industrial nations seized overseas islands and harbors as bases to supply their ships.

Nationalism played an important role, too. When one European country claimed an area, rival nations would move in and claim nearby areas. Europeans felt that ruling a global empire increased a nation's prestige. Missionaries, doctors, and colonial officials believed that they had a duty to spread Western civilization. Behind the idea of the West's civilizing mission was a growing sense of racial superiority. Many Westerners used the idea of social Darwinism to justify their domination of non-Western societies. As a result, millions of non-Westerners were robbed of their cultural heritage.

Europeans had the advantages of strong economies, well-organized governments, and powerful armies and navies. Superior technology, such as riverboats, the telegraph, and the Maxim machine gun, enhanced European power. Africans and Asians tried to resist Western expansion. Some people fought the invaders. Others tried to strengthen their societies by maintaining their traditions. Many organized nationalist movements to expel the imperialists.

(Continues on the next page.)

Lesson Vocabulary

imperialism   domination by one country of the political, economic, or cultural life of another country or region

TOPIC
15
LESSON 1

Lesson Summary
THE NEW IMPERIALISM (continued)

The leading imperial powers developed several systems to control colonies. The French practiced direct rule. They sent officials and soldiers from France to run the colony. Their goal was to impose French culture on the natives. The British, by contrast, often used indirect rule, governing through local rulers. In a **protectorate**, local rulers were left in place but were expected to follow the advice of European advisors on issues such as trade or missionary activity. In a **sphere of influence**, an outside power claimed exclusive investment or trading privileges but did not rule the area.

Imperialism had several consequences. Since Western powers sought to teach Christianity and their own languages to colonized people, local traditions faded. Western powers often also imposed their own political power structures without understanding the pre-existing structures. Finally, Western powers were usually interested in a specific economic resource, such as a cash crop. Colonized people were encouraged to work to produce that resource, which disrupted existing local industries.

Lesson Vocabulary

protectorate   country with its own government but under the control of an outside power

sphere of influence   area in which an outside power claims exclusive investment or trading privileges

Name _____ Class _____ Date _____

MODIFIED CORNELL NOTES

Before the scramble for colonies began in the 1800s, North Africa was under the rule of the declining Ottoman empire. West Africa experienced an Islamic revival inspired by Usman dan Fodio. In East Africa, port cities carried on a profitable trade. Zulus were a major force in southern Africa. A brilliant Zulu leader, Shaka, conquered nearby peoples. Groups driven from their homelands by the Zulus migrated north, conquering other peoples and creating powerful states. Meanwhile, European nations started to outlaw the transatlantic slave trade, but the slave trade to Asia continued.

For many years, Europeans had been trading along the African coasts. In the 1800s, contact increased as European explorers began pushing into the interior of Africa. One of the best-known was the missionary explorer Dr. David Livingstone. In 1869, the journalist Henry Stanley trekked into Africa to find Livingstone, who had not been heard from for years. Other missionaries followed explorers such as Livingstone. They built schools, churches, and medical clinics, often taking a **paternalistic** view of Africans.

About 1871, King Leopold II of Belgium hired Stanley to arrange trade treaties with African leaders. Leopold's actions prompted Britain, France, and Germany to join in a scramble for African land. Eventually, without consulting any Africans, European leaders met in Berlin to divide the continent of Africa among themselves. In the following years, Europeans expanded further into Africa, often exploiting African people and resources. In southern African, the Boer War began when Britain wanted to claim Boer land. The Boers were descendants of Dutch farmers. The British wanted the land because gold and diamonds had been discovered there.

Africans fought back against European imperialism. In West Africa, Samori Touré fought French forces. Yaa Asantewaa was an Asante queen who led the fight against the British in West Africa. Another female leader was Nehanda of the Shona in Zimbabwe. In most cases resistance was not successful. However, Ethiopia was able to keep its independence. Earlier, Ethiopia had been divided up among a number of rival princes who then ruled their own domains. Menelik II modernized his country and trained an army, successfully resisting Italian invaders.

The Age of Imperialism caused a Western-educated African **elite** to emerge. Some admired Western ways. Others sought independence through nationalist movements.

Lesson Vocabulary

paternalistic   the system of governing a country as a father would a child

elite   upper class

TOPIC 15 · LESSON 3

Lesson Summary
EUROPE AND THE MUSLIM WORLD

In the 1500s, three giant Muslim empires ruled large areas of the world—the Ottomans in the Middle East, the Safavids in Persia, and the Mughals in India. By the 1700s, all three Muslim empires were in decline, in part because of corruption and discontent. Reform movements arose, stressing religious piety and strict rules of behavior. For example, in the Sudan, Muhammad Ahmad announced that he was the **Mahdi**, the long-awaited savior of the faith. The Mahdi and his followers fiercely resisted British expansion into the region.

At its height, the Ottoman empire extended across North Africa, southeastern Europe, and parts of the Middle East. Ambitious **pashas** and economic problems added to the Ottoman decline. As ideas of nationalism spread from Western Europe, internal revolts by subject peoples weakened the empire. European states took advantage of this weakness to grab Ottoman territory. Some Ottoman leaders saw the need for reform. They looked to the West for ideas on reorganizing the government and its rigid rules. In the early 1700s, they reorganized the bureaucracy and system of tax collection. However, **sultans** usually rejected reform, adding to the tension. Tension between Ottoman Turkish nationalists and minority groups led to a brutal **genocide** of Christian Armenians. Turks accused Christian Armenians of supporting Russia against the Ottoman empire.

In the early 1800s, Egypt was a semi-independent province of the Ottoman empire. Muhammad Ali is sometimes called the "father of modern Egypt" because he introduced a number of political and economic reforms. He also conquered the neighboring lands of Arabia, Syria, and Sudan. Before he died in 1849, he had set Egypt on the road to becoming a major Middle Eastern power. His successors were less skilled, however, and in 1882 Egypt became a protectorate of Britain.

Like the Ottoman empire, Persia—now Iran—faced major challenges. The Qajar shahs exercised absolute power. Foreign nations, especially Russia and Britain, wanted to control Iran's oil fields. They were granted **concessions** and sent troops to protect their interests. These actions outraged Iranian nationalists.

Lesson Vocabulary

Mahdi   a Muslim savior of the faith

pasha   provincial ruler in the Ottoman empire

sultan   Muslim ruler

genocide   deliberate attempt to destroy an entire religious or ethnic group

concession   special economic right given to a foreign power

TOPIC 15 LESSON 4

Lesson Summary

INDIA BECOMES A BRITISH COLONY

Mughal rulers governed a powerful Muslim empire in India. The British East India Company had trading rights on the fringes of the Mughal empire. The main goal of the East India Company was to make money. As Mughal power declined, the East India Company extended its power. By the mid-1800s, it controlled three fifths of India. The British were able to conquer India by exploiting its diversity and by encouraging competition and disunity among rival princes. When necessary, the British also used force. However, British officials worked to end slavery and the caste system. They banned **sati**, a custom that called for a widow to throw herself on her husband's funeral fire. In the 1850s, the East India Company made several unpopular moves. The most serious brought about the Sepoy Rebellion. Indian soldiers, or **sepoys**, were told to bite off the tips of their rifle cartridges. This order caused a rebellion because the cartridges were greased with animal fat, violating local religious beliefs. The British crushed the revolt, killing thousands of unarmed Indians. The rebellion left a legacy of mistrust on both sides.

After the rebellion, Parliament ended the rule of the East India Company. Instead, a British **viceroy** governed India in the name of the monarch. In this way, all of Britain could benefit from trade with India as Britain incorporated India into the overall British economy. However, it remained an unequal partnership, favoring the British. Although the British built railroads and telegraph lines, they destroyed India's hand-weaving industry. Encouraging Indian farmers to grow cash crops led to massive **deforestation** and famines.

Some educated Indians urged India to follow a Western model of progress. Others felt they should keep to their own Hindu or Muslim cultures. In the early 1800s, Ram Mohun Roy combined both views. Roy condemned rigid caste distinctions, child marriage, sati, and **purdah**, or the isolation of women in separate quarters. He also set up educational societies to help revive pride in Indian culture. Most British disdained Indian culture and felt that Western-educated Indians would support British rule. Instead, Indians dreamed of ending British control. In 1885, Indian nationalists formed the Indian National Congress and began pressing for self-rule.

Lesson Vocabulary

sati   Hindu custom that called for a widow to join her husband in death by throwing herself on his funeral pyre

sepoy   Indian soldier who served in an army set up by the English trading company

viceroy   one who governed in India in the name of the British monarch

deforestation   the destruction of forest land

purdah   isolation of women in separate quarters

Lesson Summary
CHINA AND THE WEST

For centuries, China had a favorable **balance of trade** because of a **trade surplus**. Westerners had a **trade deficit** with China, buying more from the Chinese than they sold to them. This changed in the late 1700s when the British began trading opium grown in India in exchange for Chinese tea. The Chinese government outlawed opium and called on Britain to stop this drug trade. The British refused, leading to the Opium War in 1839. With outdated weapons and fighting methods, the Chinese were easily defeated. Under the Treaty of Nanjing, which ended the war, Britain received a huge **indemnity** and British citizens gained the right of **extraterritoriality**. About a decade later China lost another war. France, Russia, and the United States then each made specific demands on China. China was pressured to sign treaties stipulating the opening of more ports and allowing Christian missionaries into China.

China also faced internal problems. Peasants hated the Qing government because of corruption. The resulting Taiping Rebellion against this government led to an estimated 20 million to 30 million deaths. However, the Qing government survived. In addition, the Chinese were divided over the need to adopt Western ways. Some felt Western ideas and technology threatened Confucianism. Reformers who wanted to adopt Western ways in the "self-strengthening movement" did not have government support.

Meanwhile, China's defeat in the Sino-Japanese War of 1894 encouraged European nations to carve out spheres of influence in China. The United States feared that American merchants might be shut out. Eventually, without consulting the Chinese, the United States insisted that Chinese trade should be open to everyone on an equal basis as part of an Open Door Policy. Chinese reformers blamed conservatives for not modernizing China. In 1898, the emperor, Guang Xu, launched the Hundred Days of Reform. Conservatives opposed this reform effort and the emperor was imprisoned.

Many Chinese, including a secret society known to Westerners as the Boxers, were angry about the presence of foreigners. Anti-foreign feeling exploded in the Boxer Uprising in 1900. Although the Boxers failed, nationalism increased. Reformers called for a republic. One of them, Sun Yixian, became president of the new Chinese republic when the Qing dynasty fell in 1911.

Lesson Vocabulary

balance of trade   difference between how much a country imports and how much it exports

trade surplus   situation in which a country exports more than it imports

trade deficit   situation in which a country imports more than it exports

indemnity   payment for losses in war

extraterritoriality   right of foreigners to be protected by the laws of their own nation

Name _____ Class _____ Date _____

MODIFIED CORNELL NOTES

In 1603, the Tokugawa shoguns seized power in Japan and closed it to foreigners. For more than 200 years, Japan was isolated from other nations. Over time, unrest grew among many Japanese as they suffered financial hardship and lack of political power. The government responded by trying to revive old ways, emphasizing farming over commerce. These efforts had little success, and the shoguns' power weakened.

Then, in 1853, a fleet of well-armed U.S. ships led by Commodore Matthew Perry arrived. He demanded that Japan open its ports. Unable to defend itself, Japan was forced to sign treaties giving the United States trading and other rights. Humiliated by the terms of these unequal treaties, discontented daimyo and samurai led a revolt that unseated the shogun and placed the emperor Mutsuhito in power. Mutsuhito moved to the shogun's palace in the city of Edo, which was renamed Tokyo, and began a long reign known as the Meiji Restoration. This was a turning point in Japan's history.

The Meiji reformers wanted to create a new political and social system and build a modern industrial economy. The Meiji constitution gave all citizens equality before the law. A legislature, or Diet, was formed, but the emperor held absolute power. With government support, powerful banking and industrial families, known as **zaibatsu**, soon ruled over industrial empires. By the 1890s, industry was booming. Japan, a **homogeneous society**, modernized with amazing speed, partly due to its strong sense of identity.

As a small island nation, Japan lacked many resources essential for industry. Spurred by the need for natural resources and a strong ambition to equal the Western imperial nations, Japan sought to build an empire. In 1876, Japan forced Korea to open its ports to Japanese trade. In 1894, competition between Japan and China in Korea led to the First Sino-Japanese War, which Japan easily won. Japan gained ports in China, won control over Taiwan, and joined the West in the race for an empire. Ten years later, Japan successfully fought Russia in the Russo-Japanese War. By the early 1900s, Japan was the strong power in Asia.

Lesson Vocabulary

zaibatsu   since the late 1800s, powerful banking and industrial families in Japan

homogeneous society   society that has common culture and language

Name _____ Class _____ Date _____

MODIFIED CORNELL NOTES

In the 1700s, most of Southeast Asia was still independent. By the 1800s, however, Westerners had colonized much of Southeast Asia. The Dutch expanded to dominate the Dutch East Indies (now Indonesia). The British expanded from India into Burma and Malaya. The French invaded Vietnam, seeking more influence and trade markets. The Vietnamese fought fiercely but lost to superior European firepower. The French eventually took over all of Vietnam, Laos, and Cambodia and referred to these holdings as French Indochina. By the 1890s, Europeans controlled most of Southeast Asia.

The Philippines had been under Spanish rule since the 1500s. In 1898, the Spanish-American War broke out. Filipino rebel leaders declared independence and helped the Americans win the war against Spain, expecting independence. Instead, in the treaty that ended the war, the United States gave Spain $20 million for control of the Philippines. Bitterly disappointed, Filipinos renewed their struggle for independence, but the United States crushed the rebellion.

In the 1800s, the industrialized powers also began to take an interest in the Pacific islands. American sugar growers, for example, pressed for power in the Hawaiian Islands. When the Hawaiian queen Liliuokalani tried to reduce foreign influence, American planters overthrew her. In 1898, the United States annexed Hawaii. By 1900, the United States, Britain, France, or Germany had claimed nearly every island in the Pacific.

In 1770, Captain James Cook claimed Australia for Britain. When white settlers arrived, the **indigenous** people known as Aborigines suffered. Britain made Australia into a **penal colony** and also encouraged free citizens to emigrate to Australia. As the newcomers settled in, they thrust aside or killed the Aborigines. Like Canada, Australia was made up of separate colonies. To counter interference from other European powers and to boost development, Britain agreed to demands for self-rule. In 1901, the colonies became the Commonwealth of Australia.

Captain James Cook also claimed New Zealand for Britain. In 1840, Britain annexed New Zealand. The indigenous people of New Zealand are the Maori. As colonists poured in, they took more and more land, leading to fierce wars with the **Maori**. By the 1870s, resistance crumbled. Like settlers in Australia and Canada, white New Zealanders sought self-rule. In 1907, New Zealand won independence.

Lesson Vocabulary

indigenous   original or native to a country or region

penal colony   place where people convicted of crimes are sent

Name _____ Class _____ Date _____

MODIFIED CORNELL NOTES

Many factors undermined democracy in the newly independent nations of Latin America. Constitutions in these nations guaranteed equality before the law, but inequalities remained. With no tradition of unity, **regionalism** also weakened the new nations. Local strongmen, called *caudillos*, assembled private armies to resist the central government.

Mexico is an example of the challenges faced by many Latin American nations. Large landowners, army leaders, and the Catholic Church dominated Mexican politics. The ruling elite was divided between conservatives and liberals. Bitter battles between these two groups led to revolts and the rise of dictators. When Benito Juárez and other liberals gained power, they began an era of reform known as La Reforma. After Juárez died, however, General Porfirio Díaz ruled as a harsh dictator. Many Indians and mestizos fell into **peonage** to their employers.

Under colonial rule, Latin America was economically dependent on Spain and Portugal. After independence, the new Latin American republics adopted free trade, but Britain and the United States replaced Spain as Latin America's chief trading partners.

To discourage any new European colonization of the Americas, the United States issued the Monroe Doctrine and established "international police power" in the Western Hemisphere. U.S. companies continued to invest in the countries of Latin America. To protect these investments, the United States sent troops to many of these countries, which made the United States a target of increasing resentment. When the United States built the Panama Canal, it was an engineering marvel that boosted shipping worldwide. To people in Latin America, however, the canal was another example of "Yankee imperialism."

(Continues on the next page.)

Lesson Vocabulary

regionalism   loyalty to a local area

caudillo   military dictator in Latin America

peonage   system by which workers owe labor to pay their debts

TOPIC 15
LESSON 8
Lesson Summary
THE AMERICAS IN THE AGE OF IMPERIALISM (continued)

In Canada, Britain created two provinces: English-speaking Upper Canada and French-speaking Lower Canada. When unrest grew in both colonies, Parliament joined the two Canadas into one colony in 1840. As the country grew, Canadian leaders urged **confederation** of Britain's North American colonies. They felt that confederation would strengthen the new nation and help Canada's economic development. Britain finally agreed, and Parliament passed a law that created the Dominion of Canada. As a **dominion**, Canada had its own parliament. As the growing country expanded westward, the way of life of Native Americans was destroyed. **Métis**, people of French Canadian and Native American descent, resisted but were put down.

Lesson Vocabulary

confederation   unification

dominion   self-governing nation

métis   people of mixed Native American and French Canadian descent

Name _____ Class _____ Date _____

<table>
<tr><td>TOPIC
15</td><td>**Review Questions**
THE AGE OF IMPERIALISM (1800–1914)</td></tr>
</table>

Answer the questions below using the information in the Lesson Summaries on the previous pages.

Lesson 1: The New Imperialism

1. Which aspect of the new imperialism led to non-Westerners being robbed of their cultural heritage?

_____

_____

2. Multiple Causes List the multiple causes of imperialism mentioned in this summary.

_____

_____

Lesson 2: European Colonies in Africa

3. What set off a European scramble for African territories?

_____

_____

4. Cause and Effect What caused groups of Africans in southern Africa to migrate north? What was the effect of this?

_____

_____

Lesson 3: Europe and the Muslim World

5. Why is Muhammad Ali sometimes called the "father of modern Egypt"?

_____

_____

6. Understanding Effects What was the effect of the concessions granted to Britain and Russia in Iran?

_____

_____

Lesson 4: India Becomes a British Colony

7. How were the British able to conquer India?

_____

_____

8. Identify Causes and Effects What caused the sepoys to rebel? What were two effects of the rebellion?

_____

_____

TOPIC 15 — Review Questions
THE AGE OF IMPERIALISM (1800–1914) (CONTINUED)

Lesson 5: China and the West

9. What were the results of the Opium War?

_____

_____

10. Recognize Multiple Causes What brought about the Open Door Policy in China?

_____

_____

Lesson 6: The Modernization of Japan

11. How did the Meiji reformers try to modernize Japan?

_____

_____

12. Identify Causes and Effects What were the causes and effects of the Meiji Restoration?

_____

_____

Lesson 7: Southeast Asia and the Pacific

13. Why did Britain agree to demands for self-rule in Australia?

_____

_____

14. Identify Causes and Effects Identify the causes and effects of Liliuokalani's attempts to reduce foreign influence in Hawaii.

_____

_____

Lesson 8: The Americas in the Age of Imperialism

15. What limited democracy in the independent nations of Latin America?

_____

_____

16. Identify Causes and Effects Identify what caused the United States to issue the Monroe Doctrine and what its effects were on Latin America.

_____

_____

Name _____ Class _____ Date _____

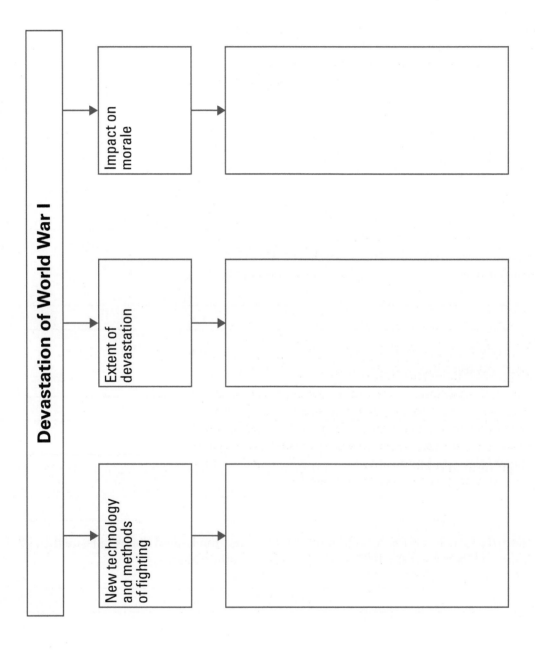

Focus Question: Why was World War I so devastating, and what was the impact of the destruction and death toll?

As you read the Lesson Summaries on the following pages, complete the graphic organizer below to help you evaluate the impact modern technology had on World War I, including the resulting devastation and the impact its destruction had on morale.

Devastation of World War I

- Impact on morale → [ ]
- Extent of devastation → [ ]
- New technology and methods of fighting → [ ]

Lesson Summary
WORLD WAR I BEGINS

MODIFIED CORNELL NOTES

Although powerful forces were pushing Europe toward war, the great powers had formed alliances, also called **ententes**, to try to keep the peace. The Triple Alliance included Germany, Austria-Hungary, and Italy. Russia, France, and Britain formed the Triple Entente. During World War I, Germany and Austria would fight together as the Central Powers, while Italy would remain neutral for a time. Russia, France, and Britain, meanwhile, would become known as the Allies.

In the decades before 1914, European powers had competed to protect their power. Overseas rivalries divided them, as they raced to acquire new colonies in Africa and elsewhere. They also began to build up their armies and navies. The rise of **militarism** helped to feed this arms race. At the same time, sensational journalism stirred the public against rival nations.

Nationalism also increased tensions. Germans were proud of their military and economic might. The French yearned for the return of Alsace and Lorraine. Russia supported a powerful form of nationalism called Pan-Slavism. This led Russia to support nationalists in Serbia. Austria-Hungary worried that nationalism might lead to rebellions within its empire, while Ottoman Turkey felt threatened by nearby new nations in the Balkans, such as Serbia and Greece. Serbia's dreams of a South Slav state could take land away from both Austria-Hungary and Turkey. Soon, unrest made the Balkans a "powder keg." Then, in 1914, a Serbian nationalist assassinated the heir to the Austrian throne at Sarajevo, Bosnia.

Some Austrian leaders saw this as an opportunity to crush Serbian nationalism. They sent Serbia an **ultimatum**, which Serbia refused to meet completely. Austria, with the full support of Germany, declared war on Serbia in July 1914.

Soon, the network of alliances drew other great powers into the conflict. Russia, in support of Serbia, began to **mobilize** its army. Germany declared war on Russia. France claimed it would honor its treaty with Russia, so Germany declared war on France, too. When the Germans violated Belgian neutrality to invade France, Britain declared war on Germany. World War I had begun.

Lesson Vocabulary

entente   nonbinding agreement to follow common policies
militarism   glorification of the military
ultimatum   final set of demands
mobilize   prepare military forces for war

Name _____ Class _____ Date _____

Lesson Summary
FIGHTING THE GREAT WAR

MODIFIED CORNELL NOTES

The Great War was the largest conflict in history up to that time. Millions of French, British, Russian, and German soldiers mobilized for battle. German forces fought their way toward France, but Belgian resistance foiled Germany's plans for a quick victory. Both sides dug deep trenches along the battlefront to protect their armies from enemy fire. The fighting on this Western Front turned into a long, deadly **stalemate**, a deadlock that neither side could break.

Technology made World War I different from earlier wars. Modern weapons caused high casualties. In 1915, first Germany then the Allies began using poison gas. Advances in technology brought about the introduction of tanks, airplanes, and modern submarines. Germany used **zeppelins** to bomb the English coast. Both sides equipped airplanes with machine guns. Pilots known as "flying aces" confronted each other in the skies, but these "dog fights" had little effect on the ground war. German submarines, called **U-boats**, did tremendous damage to the Allied ships. To defend against them, the Allies organized **convoys**, or groups of merchant ships protected by warships.

On Europe's Eastern Front, battle lines shifted back and forth, sometimes over large areas. Casualties rose higher than on the Western Front. Russia was ill prepared and suffered a disastrous defeat when pushing into eastern Germany. In 1915, Italy declared war on Austria-Hungary and Germany. In 1917, the Austrians and Germans launched a major offensive against the Italians.

Although most of the fighting took place in Europe, World War I was a global conflict. Japan used the war to seize German outposts in China and islands in the Pacific. The Ottoman empire joined the Central Powers. Its strategic location enabled it to cut off Allied supply lines to Russia through the Dardanelles, a vital strait. The Ottoman Turks were hit hard in the Middle East, however. Arab nationalists revolted against Ottoman rule. The British sent T.E. Lawrence, or "Lawrence of Arabia," to aid the Arabs. European colonies in Africa and Asia were also drawn into the war.

Lesson Vocabulary

stalemate   deadlock in which neither side is able to defeat the other

zeppelin   large, gas-filled balloon

U-boat   German submarine

convoys   group of merchant ships protected by warships

TOPIC 16 LESSON 3

Lesson Summary

WORLD WAR I ENDS

World War I was a **total war**, in which the participants channeled all their resources into the war effort. They set up systems to recruit, arm, transport, and supply their armies. Nations imposed universal military **conscription**, or "the draft," requiring all young men to be ready to fight. As millions of men left to fight, women took over their jobs and kept national economies going.

International law allowed wartime blockades to confiscate **contraband**, but the British blockaded all ships in and out of Germany. In retaliation, Germany used U-boats to impose its own blockade. In 1915, a U-boat torpedoed the British passenger liner *Lusitania*. Both sides used **propaganda** to control public opinion, circulating tales of **atrocities**, some true and others completely made up.

As time passed, war fatigue set in. High casualties, food shortages, and a stalemate caused the morale of both troops and civilians to plunge. In Russia, stories of incompetent generals and corruption eroded public confidence and led to revolution.

In 1917, the United States declared war on Germany. By 1918, about two million fresh American soldiers had joined the war-weary Allied troops on the Western Front. President Wilson issued his Fourteen Points, his terms for resolving this and future wars. Among the most important was **self-determination** for peoples in Eastern Europe.

With American troops, the Allies drove back German forces. In September 1918, the German kaiser stepped down and the new German government sought an **armistice** with the Allies. In November 1918, the Great War at last came to an end.

(Continues on the next page.)

Lesson Vocabulary

total war channeling of a nation's entire resources into a war effort

conscription "the draft," which required all young men to be ready for military or other service

contraband during wartime, military supplies and raw materials needed to make military supplies that may legally be confiscated by any belligerent

propaganda spreading of ideas to promote a cause or to damage an opposing cause

atrocities horrible act committed against innocent people

self-determination right of people to choose their own form of government

armistice agreement to end fighting in a war

Name _____ Class _____ Date _____

MODIFIED CORNELL NOTES

The human, material, and political costs of World War I were staggering. The huge loss of life was made even worse in 1918 by a deadly **pandemic** of influenza. Reconstruction costs and war debts would burden an already battered world. Governments had collapsed in Russia, Germany, Austria-Hungary, and the Ottoman empire. Out of the chaos, political **radicals** dreamed of building a new social order.

The victorious Allies met at the Paris Peace Conference to discuss the fate of Europe, the former Ottoman empire, and various colonies around the world. The Central Powers and Russia were not allowed to participate. The three main Allied leaders had conflicting goals. British Prime Minister David Lloyd George focused on rebuilding Britain. French leader Georges Clemenceau wanted to punish Germany severely. American President Wilson insisted on the creation of an international League of Nations, based on the idea of **collective security**. In this system, a group of nations acts as one to preserve the peace of all.

In June 1919, the Allies ordered representatives of the new German Republic to sign the Treaty of Versailles. The treaty forced Germany to assume full blame for the war, imposed huge **reparations** that would burden the German economy, and limited the size of Germany's military. The Allies also drew up treaties with the other Central Powers.

All these treaties left widespread dissatisfaction. New nations emerged where the German, Austrian, and Russian empires had once ruled, but many nationalities did not gain their own countries. Outside Europe, the Allies added to their overseas empires. Colonies that had hoped for an end to imperial rule were disappointed. The treaties also created a system of **mandates**, territories administered by Western powers. The one ray of hope was the establishment of the League of Nations. The failure of the United States to support the League, however, weakened the League's power.

Lesson Vocabulary

pandemic   spread of a disease across a large area, such as a country, a continent, or the entire world

radical   one who favors extreme changes

collective security   system in which a group of nations acts as one to preserve the peace of all

reparations   payment for war damage or damage caused by imprisonment

mandate   after World War I, a territory administered by a Western power

TOPIC 16 LESSON 4 — Lesson Summary
REVOLUTION IN RUSSIA

At the beginning of the 1900s, Russia had many political, economic, and social problems. Tsar Nicholas II resisted change. Marxists tried to ignite revolution among the **proletariat**. World War I quickly strained Russian resources. By March 1917, disasters on the battlefield and shortages at home brought the monarchy to collapse, and the tsar abdicated. While politicians set up a temporary government, revolutionary socialists set up soviets, or councils of workers and soldiers. These radical socialists were called Bolsheviks and were led by V. I. Lenin.

Lenin believed revolution could bring change. Leon Trotsky, another Marxist leader, helped Lenin lead the fight. To the weary Russian people, Lenin promised "Peace, Land, and Bread." In October 1917, Lenin and the Bolsheviks, renamed Communists, overthrew the government and seized power.

After the Bolshevik Revolution, events in Russia led to the nation's withdrawal from World War I. After the withdrawal, civil war raged for three years between the Communist "Reds" and the "White" armies of tsarist imperial officers. The Russians now fought only among themselves.

The Communists shot the former tsar and his family. They organized the Cheka, a brutal secret police force, to control their own people. Trotsky kept Red Army officers under the close watch of **commissars**—Communist Party officials. The Reds' position in the center of Russia gave them a strategic advantage, and they defeated the White armies.

After the civil war, Lenin had to rebuild a shattered state and economy. The new nation was called the Union of Soviet Socialist Republics (USSR), or Soviet Union. The Communist constitution set up an elected legislature. All political power, resources, and means of production would now belong to workers and peasants. In reality, however, the Communist Party, not the people, had all the power. Lenin did, however, allow some capitalist ventures that helped the Soviet economy recover. After Lenin's death, party leader Joseph Stalin took ruthless steps to win total control of the nation.

Lesson Vocabulary

proletariat   working class

commissars   Communist party official assigned to the army to teach party principles and ensure party loyalty during the Russian Revolution

TOPIC 16 — Review Questions
WORLD WAR I AND THE RUSSIAN REVOLUTION (1914–1924)

Answer the questions below using the information in the Lesson Summaries on the previous pages.

Lesson 1: World War I Begins
1. Which countries made up the Central Powers?

_____

_____

2. Summarize Describe the events that led Austria to declare war on Serbia.

_____

_____

Lesson 2: Fighting the Great War
3. What were the two battlefronts in Europe called?

_____

_____

4. Identify Supporting Details Identify important details that show the differences between the course of the war on these two battlefronts.

_____

_____

Lesson 3: World War I Ends
5. Why did women take on new jobs during the war?

_____

_____

6. Summarize Describe what made World War I a total war.

_____

_____

Lesson 4: Revolution in Russia
7. What was the name of the new Communist nation?

_____

_____

8. Summarize Describe the events that led to Communist control of Russia.

_____

_____

Name _____ Class _____ Date _____

Focus Question: How did disillusionment over war, social inequalities, and failures in political leadership give rise to authoritarian states?

As you read the Lesson Summaries on the following pages, complete the graphic organizer below to identify the events and circumstances that led to the rise of radical groups, and the ways these new groups and their leaders addressed the problems besetting these nations.

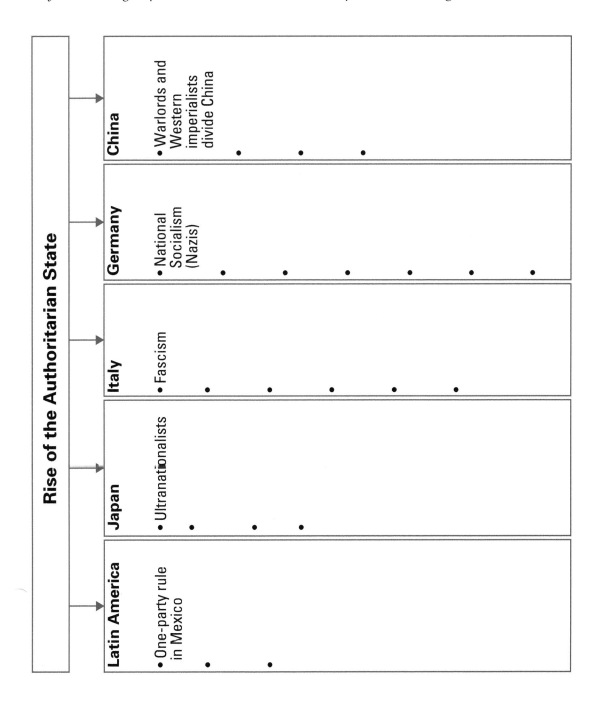

Rise of the Authoritarian State

China
- Warlords and Western imperialists divide China

Germany
- National Socialism (Nazis)

Italy
- Fascism

Japan
- Ultranationalists

Latin America
- One-party rule in Mexico

TOPIC 17 LESSON 1

Lesson Summary
REVOLUTION AND NATIONALISM IN LATIN AMERICA

MODIFIED CORNELL NOTES

In the early 1900s, exports kept Latin America's economy booming. Even though foreign investors controlled much of the natural resources, stable governments helped keep economies strong. Yet turmoil brewed because military leaders and wealthy landowners held most of the power. Workers and peasants had no say in government. These differences led to increasing unrest.

Dictator Porfirio Díaz had ruled Mexico for nearly 35 years. During this time, the nation enjoyed peace and success, but only the wealthy benefited. Peasants lived in desperate poverty while working on **haciendas**, large farms owned by the rich. A growing middle class wanted more say in government. In 1910, Francisco Madero, a reformer from a rich family, called for change. Faced with rebellion, Díaz stepped down, and a violent struggle for power—the Mexican Revolution—began.

The people fought for years before Venustiano Carranza was elected president, and a new constitution was approved. It addressed some of the issues that caused the revolution, such as land reform, religion, and labor. The Constitution of 1917 allowed **nationalization** of natural resources. In 1929, the Mexican government organized what later became the Institutional Revolutionary Party (PRI). This political party brought stability to Mexico by carrying out some reforms, but kept the real power in its hands.

During the 1920s and 1930s, the Great Depression caused Latin American exports to drop and import prices to rise. As a result, **economic nationalism** became popular. Latin Americans wanted to develop their own industries. Some Latin American nations took over foreign-owned companies. The governments became more powerful when people accepted authoritarian leaders, hoping that they could improve the economy. Along with economic nationalism, there was a growth in **cultural nationalism**. Artists such as Diego Rivera painted murals or large images of Mexico's history, culture, and the people's struggles. The United States also became more involved in Latin America, often intervening to protect U.S. interests or troops. This led to anti-American feelings. Under the Good Neighbor Policy, the United States promised less interference in Latin American affairs.

Lesson Vocabulary

hacienda   a large plantation

nationalization   takeover of property or resources by the government

economic nationalism   takeover of property or resources by the government

cultural nationalism   pride in the culture of one's country

Name _____ Class _____ Date _____

MODIFIED CORNELL NOTES

Europe ruled over most of Africa during the early 1900s. Improved farming methods meant more exports; however, this mostly benefited colonial rulers. Europeans kept the best lands, and African farmers were forced to grow cash crops instead of food. They also were forced to work in mines and then pay taxes to the colonial governments. Many Africans began criticizing imperial rule, but their freedoms only eroded further. An example was the system of **apartheid** in South Africa. Under this policy, black Africans were denied many of their previous rights, such as the right to vote.

During the 1920s, the Pan-Africanism movement called for the unity of Africans and people of African descent around the world. During the first Pan-African Congress, delegates asked world leaders at the Paris Peace Conference to approve a charter of rights for Africans. Their request was ignored. The members of the **négritude movement** in West Africa and the Caribbean protested colonial rule while expressing pride in African culture. These movements, however, brought about little real change.

In Asia Minor, Mustafa Kemal overthrew the Ottoman ruler and established the republic of Turkey. He changed his name to Atatürk (father of the Turks), and his government promoted industrial expansion by building factories and railroads. Inspired by Atatürk's successes, Reza Khan overthrew the shah of Persia. Khan sought to turn Persia into a modern country. He, too, built factories and railroads. Khan also demanded a bigger portion of profits for Persia from British-controlled oil companies. Both leaders pushed aside Islamic traditions, replacing them with Western alternatives.

Pan-Arabism was a movement based on a shared history of Arabs living from the Arabian Peninsula to North Africa. Leaders of Arab nations and territories had hoped to gain independence after World War I, but felt betrayed when the Allies signed the Treaty of Versailles, which divided Ottoman territories and turned them into mandates under the control of two Allied nations: France and Britain. Tensions in the Palestine Mandate grew due to conflicting promises made by the Allies. Arabs believed they were to be given independence, including the land known as Palestine. The Balfour Declaration stated that Britain supported the idea of a "national home for Jewish people" in the Palestine Mandate, on the historic homeland of the Jews that they called Israel. The conflicting promises led to conflict between Arabs and Jews.

Lesson Vocabulary

apartheid a policy of rigid racial segregation in the Republic of South Africa

négritude movement movement in which writers and artists of African descent expressed pride in their African heritage

MODIFIED CORNELL NOTES

TOPIC 17 LESSON 3

Lesson Summary
INDIA SEEKS SELF RULE

During World War I, more than a million Indians served in the British armed forces. Because the British were pressured by Indian nationalists, they promised more self-government for India. After the war they failed to keep their promise. The Congress Party of India had been pressing for self-rule since 1885. In 1919, it began to call for full independence. However, the party had little in common with the masses of Indian peasants. A new leader, Mohandas Gandhi, united Indians. Gandhi had a great deal of experience opposing unjust government. He had spent 20 years fighting laws in South Africa that discriminated against Indians.

In 1919, Indian protests against colonial rule led to riots and attacks on British residents. The British then banned public meetings. On April 13, 1919, a peaceful crowd of Indians gathered in an enclosed field in Amritsar. As Indian leaders spoke, British soldiers fired on the unarmed crowd. Nearly 400 people were killed, and more than 1,100 were wounded. The Amritsar massacre convinced many Indians that independence was necessary. This incident led Gandhi and many others to join the nationalist movement.

Gandhi inspired people of all religions and backgrounds. He preached **ahimsa**, a belief in nonviolence and respect for all life. For example, he fought to end the harsh treatment of **untouchables**, the lowest group of society. Henry David Thoreau's idea of **civil disobedience** influenced Gandhi. This was the idea that one should refuse to obey unfair laws. Gandhi proposed civil disobedience and nonviolent actions against the British. For example, he called for a **boycott** of British goods, especially cotton textiles.

Gandhi's Salt March was an example of civil disobedience in action. The British had a monopoly on salt. They forced Indians to buy salt from British producers even though salt was available naturally in the sea. As Gandhi walked 240 miles to the sea to collect salt, thousands joined him. He was arrested when he reached the water's edge and picked up a lump of salt. Newspapers worldwide criticized Britain for beating and arresting thousands of Indians during the Salt March. That protest forced Britain to meet some of the demands of the Congress Party. Slowly, Gandhi's nonviolent campaign forced Britain to hand over some power to Indians.

Lesson Vocabulary

ahimsa   Hindu belief in nonviolence and reverence for all life
untouchables   in India, a member of the lowest caste
civil disobedience   the refusal to obey unjust laws
boycott   refuse to buy

Lesson Summary
NEW FORCES IN CHINA AND JAPAN

MODIFIED CORNELL NOTES

Sun Yixian hoped to rebuild China when he became president of China's new republic in 1911, but he made little progress. The country fell into chaos when local warlords seized power and the economy fell apart. Sun Yixian stepped down as president in 1912. Amid the upheaval, foreign imperialism increased in China. During World War I, Japan presented Chinese leaders with the Twenty-One Demands, which were intended to give Japan control over China, and the Chinese gave in to some of those demands. This infuriated Chinese nationalists, and some students led a cultural and intellectual rebellion known as the May Fourth Movement. Leaders of this movement rejected tradition and looked to Western knowledge and learning. Other Chinese embraced Marxism as a solution instead. The Soviet Union trained Chinese students and military officers, hoping they would become the **vanguard** of a communist revolution in China.

In 1921, Sun Yixian led the Guomindang, or Nationalist party, as it established a government in south China. To defeat the warlords he joined forces with the Chinese communists. After Sun's death, Jiang Jieshi assumed leadership of the party. Jiang felt that the Communists threatened his power. He ordered his troops to slaughter Communists and their supporters. Led by Mao Zedong, the Communist army escaped north in what became known as the Long March.

While Jiang pursued the Communists across China, the Japanese invaded Manchuria, adding it to their growing empire. Then, in 1937, Japanese planes bombed Chinese cities and Japanese soldiers marched into Nanjing, killing hundreds of thousands of people. In response, Jiang and Mao formed an alliance to fight the invaders. The alliance held up until the end of the war with Japan.

The Japanese economy had grown during World War I, and in the 1920s, the Japanese government moved toward greater democracy. However, peasants and factory workers did not share in the nation's prosperity. Also, there was tension between the government and the military.

(Continues on the next page.)

Lesson Vocabulary

vanguard   group of elite leaders

MODIFIED CORNELL NOTES

The Great Depression fed the discontent of the military and the **ultranationalists**. As the economic crisis worsened, the ultranationalists set their sights on Manchuria in northern China. When the League of Nations condemned the invasion, Japan withdrew from the organization.

Militarists and ultranationalists increased their power in the 1930s. Extremists killed some politicians and business leaders who opposed expansion. To please the ultranationalists, the government suppressed most democratic freedoms. Japan planned to take advantage of China's civil war and conquer the country. In 1939, World War II broke out and the fighting quickly spread to Asia. Earlier, Japan had formed an alliance with Germany and Italy. In September 1940, Japan's leaders signed the Tripartite Pact linking the three nations. Together, the three nations formed the Axis Powers.

Lesson Vocabulary

ultranationalist   extreme nationalist

Name _____ Class _____ Date _____

TOPIC 17 LESSON 5 — Lesson Summary
THE WEST AFTER WORLD WAR I

In reaction to World War I, society and culture in the United States and elsewhere underwent rapid changes. During the 1920s, new technologies helped create a mass culture and connect people around the world. One symbol of this new age was jazz, with its original sound and improvisations, and it gave the age its name—the Jazz Age. In this new era of emancipation, women pursued careers. Not everyone approved of the freer lifestyle of the Jazz Age, however. Prohibition was meant to keep people from the negative effects of drinking. Instead, it brought about organized crime and **speakeasies**.

New literature reflected a powerful disgust with war. To some postwar writers, the war symbolized the moral breakdown of Western civilization. Writers and artists explored new ways of expressing their ideas. Some writers experimented with stream of consciousness. In the cultural movement called the Harlem Renaissance, African American artists and writers expressed pride in their culture and explored their experiences in their work. <insert>Many Western artists, such as Dada artists, rejected traditional styles that tried to reproduce the real world. New scientific discoveries challenged long-held ideas. Marie Curie and others found that atoms of certain elements spontaneously release charged particles. Albert Einstein argued that measurements of space and time are not absolute.

After World War I, Britain, France, and the United States appeared powerful. However, postwar Europe faced grave problems. The most pressing issues were finding jobs for veterans and rebuilding war-ravaged lands. The three democracies also faced international issues. Concern about a strong Germany led France to build the Maginot Line and insist on strict enforcement of the Versailles treaty. Many nations signed the Kellogg-Briand Pact, promising to "renounce war as an instrument of national policy." The great powers also pursued **disarmament**. Unfortunately, neither the Kellogg-Briand Pact nor the League of Nations had the power to stop aggression. Ambitious dictators in Europe noted this weakness.

(Continues on the next page.)

Lesson Vocabulary

speakeasy   illegal bar
disarmament   reduction of armed forces and weapons

MODIFIED CORNELL NOTES

The war affected economies all over the world. Both Britain and France owed huge war debts to the United States and relied on reparation payments from Germany to pay their loans. Britain was deeply in debt, with high unemployment and low wages. In 1926, a **general strike** lasted nine days and involved three million workers. On the other hand, the French economy recovered fairly quickly, and the United States emerged as the world's top economic power. In the affluent 1920s, middle-class Americans enjoyed the benefits of capitalism, buying cars, radios, and refrigerators.

Better technologies allowed U.S. factories to make more products faster, leading to **overproduction**. Factories then cut back, and many workers lost jobs. A crisis in **finance** led the Federal Reserve to raise interest rates. This made people even more nervous about the economy. In the autumn of 1929, financial panic set in. Stock prices crashed. The United States economy entered the Great Depression, which soon spread around the world.

Governments searched for solutions. In the United States, President Franklin D. Roosevelt introduced the programs of the New Deal. Although the New Deal failed to end the Depression, it did ease much suffering. However, as the Depression wore on, it created fertile ground for extremists.

Lesson Vocabulary

general strike   strike by workers in many different industries at the same time

overproduction   condition in which production of goods exceeds the demand for them

finance   the management of money matters, including the circulation of money, loans, investment, and banking

TOPIC 17 LESSON 6

Lesson Summary

FASCISM EMERGES IN ITALY

After World War I, Italian nationalists were outraged when Italy received just some of the territories promised by the Allies. Chaos ensued as peasants seized land, workers went on strike, veterans faced unemployment, trade declined, and taxes rose. The government could not end the crisis. Into this turmoil stepped Benito Mussolini, the organizer of the Fascist party. Mussolini's supporters, the Black Shirts, rejected democratic methods and favored violence for solving problems. In the 1922 March on Rome, tens of thousands of Fascists swarmed the capital. Fearing civil war, the king asked Mussolini to form a government as prime minister.

Mussolini soon suppressed rival parties, muzzled the press, rigged elections, and replaced elected officials with Fascists. Critics were thrown into prison, forced into exile, or murdered. Secret police and propaganda bolstered the regime. In 1929, Mussolini also received support from the pope. Mussolini brought the economy under state control, but basically preserved capitalism. His system favored the upper class and industry leaders. Workers were not allowed to strike, and their wages were kept low. In Mussolini's new system, loyalty to the state replaced conflicting individual goals. Loudspeakers blared and posters proclaimed the message "Believe! Obey! Fight!". Fascist youth groups marched in parades chanting slogans.

Mussolini built the first modern **totalitarian state**. In this form of government, a one-party dictatorship attempts to control every aspect of the lives of its citizens. Today, we usually use the term **fascism** to describe the underlying ideology of any centralized, authoritarian governmental system that is not communist. Fascism is rooted in extreme nationalism. Fascists believe in action, violence,

(Continues on the next page.)

Lesson Vocabulary

totalitarian state   government in which a one-party dictatorship regulates every aspect of citizens' lives

fascism   any centralized, authoritarian government system that is not communist, whose policies glorify the state over the individual and are destructive to basic human rights

TOPIC 17

LESSON 6

Lesson Summary

FASCISM EMERGES IN ITALY (continued)

MODIFIED CORNELL NOTES

discipline, and blind loyalty to the state. They praise warfare. They are anti-democratic, rejecting equality and liberty. Fascists oppose communists on important issues. Communists favor international action and the creation of a classless society. Fascists are nationalists who support a society with defined classes. Both base their power on blind devotion to a leader or the state. Both can become popular during economic hard times.

Fascism appealed to Italians because it restored national pride, provided stability, and ended the political feuding that had paralyzed democracy in Italy.

Name _____ Class _____ Date _____

TOPIC 17 LESSON 7

Lesson Summary
THE SOVIET UNION UNDER STALIN

MODIFIED CORNELL NOTES

Under Joseph Stalin, the Soviet Union grew into a totalitarian state, controlling all aspects of life, including agriculture, culture, art, and religion. The state also developed a **command economy**, in which it made all economic decisions. Stalin's five-year plans set high production goals. Despite great progress in some sectors, products such as clothing, cars, and refrigerators were scarce. Stalin forced changes in agriculture, too. He wanted peasants to farm on either state-owned farms or **collectives**, large farms owned and operated by groups of peasants. Some peasants balked. Stalin believed that wealthy farmers called **kulaks** were behind the resistance. He took their land and sent them to labor camps, where many died. In 1932, Stalin's policy of confiscating grain to punish protesting peasants led to a famine that caused millions to starve.

The ruling Communist party used secret police, torture, and bloody purges to force people to obey. Those who opposed Stalin were rounded up and sent to the **Gulag**, a system of brutal labor camps. Fearing that rival party leaders were plotting against him, Stalin launched the Great Purge in 1934. Among the victims of this and other purges were some of the brightest and most talented people in the country.

Stalin demanded that artists and writers create works in a style called **socialist realism**. If they refused to conform to government expectations, they faced persecution. Another way Stalin controlled cultural life was to promote **russification**. The goal was to force people of non-Russian nationalities to become more Russian. The official Communist party belief in **atheism** led to the cruel treatment of religious leaders.

(Continues on the next page.)

Lesson Vocabulary

command economy   system in which government officials make all basic economic decisions

collective   large farm owned and operated by peasants as a group

kulak   wealthy peasant in the Soviet Union in the late 1930s

Gulag   in the Soviet Union, a system of forced labor camps in which millions of criminals and political prisoners were held under Stalin

socialist realism   artistic style whose goal was to promote socialism by showing Soviet life in a positive light

russification   Stalin's policy of imposing Russian culture on the Soviet Union

atheism   belief that there is no god

Lesson Summary
THE SOVIET UNION UNDER STALIN (continued)

MODIFIED CORNELL NOTES

The Communists destroyed the old social order. Instead of creating a society of equals, Communist party members became the heads of society. Still, under communism most people enjoyed free medical care, day care for children, cheaper housing, and public recreation. Women had equal rights by law.

Soviet leaders had two foreign policy goals. They hoped to spread world revolution through the Comintern, or Communist International. At the same time, they wanted to ensure their nation's security by winning the support of other countries. These contradictory goals caused Western powers to distrust the Soviet Union.

TOPIC 17
LESSON 8

Lesson Summary
RISE OF NAZI GERMANY

After World War I, German leaders set up a democratic government known as the Weimar Republic. The Weimar constitution established a parliamentary system led by a **chancellor**. It gave women the right to vote and included a bill of rights. However, the new republic faced severe problems. When Germany could not make its war reparations, France seized the coal-rich Ruhr Valley. Government actions led to inflation and skyrocketing prices. The German mark was almost worthless. Many middle-class families lost their savings.

Many Germans believed that energetic leader Adolf Hitler would solve Germany's problems. As head of the Nazi party, Hitler promised to end reparations, create jobs, and rearm Germany. He was elected chancellor in 1933, and within a year he was dictator over the new fascist state in Germany.

To appeal to nationalism and recall Germany's glorious past, Hitler called his government the Third Reich. To combat the Depression, Hitler launched public works programs. In violation of the Versailles treaty, he rearmed Germany. Hitler relied on his secret police, the Gestapo, to root out opposition. He organized a brutal system of terror, repression, and totalitarian rule. A fanatical anti-Semite, Hitler set out to drive the Jews from Germany. In 1935, the Nazis passed the Nuremberg Laws, which deprived Jews of German citizenship and placed severe restrictions on them. The Nazis indoctrinated German youth and rewrote textbooks to reflect Nazi racial views.

Hitler also limited women's roles and encouraged "pure-blooded Aryan" women to bear many children. He sought to purge German culture of what he believed were corrupt influences. Nazis denounced modern art and jazz, but glorified German artists and myths. Hitler despised Christianity as "weak." He combined all Protestant sects into a single state church. Although many clergy either supported the new regime or remained silent, some courageously spoke out against Hitler's government.

Like Germany, most new nations in Eastern Europe slid from systems of democratic to authoritarian rule. Economic problems and ethnic tensions contributed to instability and helped fascist rulers to gain power. The new dictators promised to keep order, and won the backing of the military and the wealthy. They also supported the growth of anti-Semitism.

Lesson Vocabulary

chancellor   the highest official of a monarch, prime minister

TOPIC 17 — Review Questions
THE WORLD BETWEEN THE WARS (1910–1939)

Answer the questions below using the information in the Lesson Summaries on the previous pages.

Lesson 1: Revolution and Nationalism in Latin America

1. What was the PRI, and what was its impact on Mexico?

_____

_____

2. Identify Causes and Effects What were two effects of United States involvement in Latin America?

_____

_____

Lesson 2: Nationalist Movements in Africa and the Middle East

3. What was the négritude movement?

_____

_____

4. Identify Causes and Effects What was one effect of the Balfour Declaration?

_____

_____

Lesson 3: India Seeks Self Rule

5. What had Gandhi done before becoming a leader for Indian independence?

_____

_____

6. Identify Causes and Effects What caused the Amritsar massacre? What effect did it have on the independence movement?

_____

_____

Lesson 4: New Forces in China and Japan

7. What group of people spearheaded the May Fourth Movement?

_____

_____

8. Recognize Multiple Causes Why did Chinese peasants support the Communists?

_____

_____

TOPIC 17 — Review Questions
THE WORLD BETWEEN THE WARS (1910–1939) (continued)

Lesson 5: The West After World War I

9. What did Prohibition bring about?

_____

_____

10. Identify Supporting Details What were three aspects of postwar literature?

_____

_____

Lesson 6: Fascism Emerges in Italy

11. Who were the Black Shirts?

_____

_____

12. Identify Main Ideas How did Mussolini's Fascists take over Italy?

_____

_____

Lesson 7: The Soviet Union Under Stalin

13. What is a command economy?

_____

_____

14. Identify Main Ideas Reread the last paragraph in the Summary. Write a sentence that expresses the main idea of that paragraph.

_____

_____

Lesson 8: Rise of Nazi Germany

15. What was the purpose of the Nuremberg Laws?

_____

_____

16. Identify Main Ideas Reread the last paragraph in the Summary. Write the main idea of that paragraph on the lines below.

_____

_____

Focus Question: How did the Allies turn away from appeasement, respond to Axis aggression, and win World War II?

As you read the Lesson Summaries on the following pages, complete the graphic organizer below to understand why the Allies changed their policy of appeasement to Axis aggression to a policy of fighting back and how they won World War II.

```
┌─────────────────────────────────────────────────────┐
│                    World War II                       │
└─────────────────────────────────────────────────────┘
```

Allied appeasement	Axis aggression	Allied response
•	•	•
•	•	•
•	•	•
•	•	•
	•	•
	•	

Name _____ Class _____ Date _____

MODIFIED CORNELL NOTES

Throughout the 1930s, dictators took aggressive action. Yet they met only verbal protests and pleas for peace from Western powers. For example, when the League of Nations condemned Japan's invasion of Manchuria in 1931, Japan simply withdrew from the League. A few years later, Japanese armies invaded China, starting the Second Sino-Japanese War. Meanwhile, Mussolini invaded Ethiopia in 1935. The League of Nations voted sanctions against Italy, but the League had no power to enforce its punishment of Mussolini. Hitler, too, defied the Western democracies by building up the German military and sending troops into the "demilitarized" Rhineland. This action went against the Treaty of Versailles. The Western democracies denounced Hitler but adopted a policy of **appeasement**. Appeasement developed for a number of reasons, including widespread **pacifism**. The United States responded with a series of Neutrality Acts. The goal was to avoid involvement in a war, rather than to prevent one. While the Western democracies sought to avoid war, Germany, Italy, and Japan formed an alliance. It became known as the **Axis powers**.

In Spain, a new, more liberal government passed reforms that upset conservatives. General Francisco Franco, who was opposed to the new government, started a rebellion that led to a civil war. Hitler and Mussolini supported Franco, their fellow fascist. The Soviet Union sent troops to support the anti-Fascists, or Loyalists. The governments of Britain, France, and the United States remained neutral, although individuals from these countries fought with the Loyalists. By 1939, Franco had triumphed.

German aggression continued. In 1938, Hitler forced the Anschluss, or union with Austria. Next, Hitler set his sights on the Sudetenland. This was a part of Czechoslovakia where three million Germans lived. At the Munich Conference, which was held to discuss the situation, British and French leaders chose appeasement and allowed Hitler to annex the territory.

(Continues on the next page.)

Lesson Vocabulary

appeasement policy of giving in to an aggressor's demands in order to keep the peace

pacifism opposition to all war

Axis powers group of countries led by Germany, Italy, and Japan that fought the Allies in World War II

Name _____ Class _____ Date _____

MODIFIED CORNELL NOTES

In March 1939, Hitler took over the rest of Czechoslovakia. Months later, Hitler and Stalin signed the Nazi-Soviet Pact. They agreed not to fight each other if one of them went to war. This paved the way for Germany's invasion of Poland in September of 1939, which set off World War II.

<table>
<tr><td>

TOPIC
18
LESSON 2
</td><td>

Lesson Summary
AXIS POWERS ADVANCE
</td></tr>
</table>

In September 1939, Nazi forces launched a **blitzkrieg** against Poland. First, the Luftwaffe, the German air force, bombed. Then tanks and troops pushed their way in. At the same time, Stalin invaded from the east, grabbing land. Within a month, Poland ceased to exist.

Then, in early 1940, Hitler conquered Norway, Denmark, the Netherlands, and Belgium. By May, German forces had bypassed France's Maginot Line. British forces that had been sent to help the French were trapped. In a desperate scheme, the British rescued their troops from Dunkirk. However, in June, the French were forced to surrender. Germany occupied northern France and set up a puppet state, the Vichy government, in the south.

The British, led by Winston Churchill, remained defiant against Hitler. In response, Hitler launched bombing raids over British cities that lasted from September 1940 until June 1941. Despite this blitz, Hitler was not able to take Britain. Meanwhile, Hitler sent one of his best commanders, General Erwin Rommel, to North Africa. Rommel had a string of successes there. In the Balkans, German and Italian forces added Greece and Yugoslavia to the growing Axis territory. At the same time, the Japanese were occupying lands in Asia and the Pacific.

In June 1941, Hitler **nullified** the Soviet Union. Stalin was unprepared, and the Soviet army suffered great losses. The Germans advanced toward Moscow and Leningrad. During a lengthy siege of Leningrad, more than a million Russians died. The severe Russian winter finally slowed the German army.

As they marched across Europe, the Nazis sent millions to concentration camps to work as slave laborers. Even worse, Hitler established death camps to kill those he judged racially inferior. Among many others, some six million Jews were killed in what became known as the Holocaust.

(Continues on the next page.)

Lesson Vocabulary

Blitzkrieg   lightning war
nullify   cancel, annul

Name _____ Class _____ Date _____

MODIFIED CORNELL NOTES

The United States declared neutrality at the beginning of the war. Yet many Americans sympathized with those who fought the Axis powers. Congress passed the Lend-Lease Act of 1941, allowing the United States to sell or lend war goods to foes of the Axis. Franklin Roosevelt and Winston Churchill also agreed on the Atlantic Charter, which set goals for the defeat of Nazi Germany and for the postwar world. On December 7, 1941, under the direction of General Hideki Tojo, the Japanese bombed the U.S. fleet at Pearl Harbor. Four days later, Congress declared war on Japan.

Name _____ Class _____ Date _____

MODIFIED CORNELL NOTES

When Hitler came to power, he brought his anti-Semitic beliefs with him. Hitler's campaign against the Jews worsened over time as he expanded Nazi control over Europe. As the Nazi army marched across Europe, the German government sent millions to **concentration camps** to work as slave laborers. Further into the war, Hitler established death camps to kill those he judged racially inferior. In 1941, Hitler devised the "Final Solution," or the extermination of all European Jews. Hitler's acts of genocide led to the deaths of more than six million Jews and others and became known as the Holocaust.

In the death camps such as Auschwitz in southern Poland, Jews were stripped of their belongings, and their heads were shaved. They were sent to "showers," where they were gassed to death. Their bodies were burned in **crematoriums**. Others were worked to death or used in medical experiments, many supervised by Josef Mengele.

Jewish people resisted the Nazis even though they knew their efforts could not succeed. The Warsaw Ghetto uprising was one of the largest acts of Jewish resistance. The uprising inspired others to resist. They worked in underground networks or secretly celebrated their religion and culture to keep their faith alive. Some people helped hide or move Jewish people to safe havens. Some Jews hid in the forests and joined Soviet forces, who sabotaged the German military. Jewish resistance lasted until 1945, when the concentration camps were liberated.

Although the Allies were alerted to the horrors of concentration camps before liberation, they did little to end Hitler's actions. Many Allied countries turned down refugees or limited immigration numbers. In 1945, the Allies and Soviets liberated concentration camps, and the horrors of the Holocaust became public. Many survivors were forced to live in displaced persons camps while trying to start new lives. In 1948, the new nation of Israel was created to provide a home for Jews of every nation.

Lesson Vocabulary

concentration camps   detention center for civilians considered enemies of the state

crematorium   a place used to burn corpses

Name _____ Class _____ Date _____

Lesson Summary
THE ALLIES TURN THE TIDE

MODIFIED CORNELL NOTES

To defeat the Axis powers in World War II, the Allies devoted all their resources to the war effort. Governments took a greater role in the economy. For example, governments ordered factories to make tanks instead of cars. Consumer goods were rationed, and wages and prices were regulated. A positive result was that the increase in production ended the Great Depression. However, governments also limited citizens' rights, censored the press, and resorted to propaganda. In the United States and Canada, racial prejudice and concerns about security led to the **internment,** or confinement during wartime, of citizens of Japanese descent. At the same time, women, symbolized by "Rosie the Riveter," replaced men in factories. Women also played a more direct role in some military operations.

The years 1942 and 1943 marked the turning point of the war. In the Pacific, Allied forces won the battles of the Coral Sea and Midway. In both battles, attacks were launched from enormous **aircraft carriers**. In North Africa, British and American forces, led by General Dwight Eisenhower, soon trapped Rommel's army, and he surrendered in May 1943. With North Africa under their control, the Allies crossed the Mediterranean and landed in Sicily. Allied victories in Italy led to the overthrow of Mussolini, but fighting continued in Italy for another 18 months. On the Eastern front, a key turning point was the Battle of Stalingrad. After a German advance on the city and brutal house-to-house fighting, the Soviet army encircled the German troops. Without food or ammunition, the Germans surrendered.

(Continues on the next page.)

Lesson Vocabulary

internment   confinement during wartime

aircraft carrier   ship that accommodates the taking off and landing of airplanes, and transports aircraft

Name _____ Class _____ Date _____

MODIFIED CORNELL NOTES

On June 6, 1944, the Allies launched the D-Day invasion of France. Allied troops faced many obstacles, but the Germans finally retreated. As the Allies advanced, Germany reeled from incessant, around-the-clock bombing. A German counterattack, the Battle of the Bulge, resulted in terrible losses on both sides. However, with Germany's defeat seeming inevitable, the "Big Three"—Franklin Roosevelt, Winston Churchill, and Joseph Stalin—met to plan for the end of the war. Key features of this Yalta Conference were the Soviet agreement to enter the war against Japan and the division of Germany into four zones of occupation. However, growing mistrust at Yalta foreshadowed a split among the Allies.

Name _____ Class _____ Date _____

MODIFIED CORNELL NOTES

In Europe, World War II officially ended on May 8, 1945, or V-E Day. The Allies were able to defeat the Axis powers for many reasons. Because of their location, the Axis powers had to fight on several fronts at the same time. Hitler also made some poor military decisions. For example, he underestimated the Soviet Union's ability to fight. The huge productive capacity of the United States was another factor. At the same time, Allied bombing hindered German production and caused oil to become scarce. This nearly grounded the Luftwaffe.

Although Germany was defeated, the Allies still had to defeat the Japanese in the Pacific. By May 1942, the Japanese had gained control of the Philippines, killing thousands during the Bataan Death March. However, after the battles of Midway and the Coral Sea, the United States took the offensive. General Douglas MacArthur began an **"island-hopping"** campaign to recapture islands from the Japanese. The captured islands served as steppingstones to the next objective—Japan. The Americans gradually moved north and were able to blockade Japan. Bombers pounded Japanese cities and industries. At the same time, the British pushed Japanese forces back into the jungles of Burma and Malaya.

In early 1945, bloody battles on Iwo Jima and Okinawa showed that the Japanese would fight to the death rather than surrender. Some young Japanese became **kamikaze** pilots who flew their planes purposefully into U.S. ships. While Allied military leaders planned to invade, scientists offered another way to end the war. They had conducted research, code-named the Manhattan Project,

(Continues on the next page.)

Lesson Vocabulary

"island-hopping"   during World War II, Allied strategy of recapturing some Japanese-held islands while bypassing others

kamikaze   Japanese pilot who undertook a suicide mission

TOPIC 18 LESSON 5

Lesson Summary
VICTORIES FOR THE ALLIES (continued)

that led to the building of an atomic bomb for the United States. The new U.S. president, Harry Truman, decided that dropping the bomb would save American lives. The Allies first issued a warning to the Japanese to surrender or face "utter and complete destruction," but the warning was ignored. On August 6, 1945, a U.S. plane dropped an atomic bomb on the city of Hiroshima, instantly killing more than 70,000 people. Many more died from radiation sickness. When the Japanese did not surrender, another bomb was dropped on Nagasaki on August 9. The next day, Japan finally surrendered, ending World War II.

While the Allies enjoyed their victory, the huge costs of World War II began to emerge. As many as 50 million people had been killed. The Allies also learned the full extent of the horrors of the Holocaust. War crimes trials, such as the Nuremberg Trials in Germany, held leaders accountable for their wartime actions. To ensure tolerance and peace, the Western Allies set up democratic governments in Japan and Germany.

In 1945, delegates from 50 nations convened to form the United Nations. Under the UN Charter, each member nation has one vote in the General Assembly. A smaller Security Council has greater power. It has five permanent members: the United States, the Soviet Union (today Russia), Britain, France, and China. UN agencies have tackled many world problems, from disease to helping refugees.

Name _____ Class _____ Date _____

Answer the questions below using the information in the Lesson Summaries on the previous pages.

Lesson 1: Aggression, Appeasement, and War

1. Who were the members of the Axis powers?

_____

_____

2. Recognize Sequence What happened in Spain before Francisco Franco started a civil war there?

_____

_____

Lesson 2: Axis Powers Advance

3. What was the name of the German government in southern France?

_____

_____

4. Sequence Events When did the United States declare neutrality?

_____

_____

Lesson 3: The Holocaust

5. Which new country was created to provide a home for Jews of every nation?

_____

_____

6. Identify Supporting Details What were some of the atrocities the Nazis committed against Jews at death camps such as Auschwitz?

_____

_____

Lesson 4: The Allies Turn the Tide

7. Who were the "Big Three"?

_____

_____

8. Recognize Sequence List the sequence of events in 1942–1943 that gave the Allies control of North Africa.

_____

_____

TOPIC 18

Review Questions

WORLD WAR II (1930–1945) (continued)

Lesson 5: Victories for the Allies

9. What was the "island-hopping" campaign?

_____

_____

10. **Recognize Sequence** Create a timeline of the events that took place in Japan from August 6 to August 10, 1945.

_____

_____

TOPIC 19

Note Taking Study Guide
THE COLD WAR ERA (1945–1991)

Focus Question: What were the circumstances that led to the East-West tensions known as the Cold War, and what events brought about its end?

As you read the Lesson Summaries on the following pages, complete the graphic organizer below to identify events or circumstances that led to the escalation and decline of the Cold War.

Escalation of the Cold War	Decline of the Cold War
•	•
•	•
•	•
•	•

TOPIC 19 LESSON 1 — Lesson Summary

A NEW GLOBAL CONFLICT

Disagreements began to grow between the Allies not long after World War II ended. Conflicting ideologies soon led to a Cold War. This refers to the state of tension and hostility between the United States and the Soviet Union from 1946 to 1990. Soviet leader Stalin wanted to spread communism into Eastern Europe. He also wanted to create a buffer zone of friendly countries as a defense against Germany. By 1948, pro-Soviet communist governments were in place throughout Eastern Europe, behind what Winston Churchill referred to as the "Iron Curtain."

When Stalin began to threaten Greece and Turkey, the United States outlined a policy called the Truman Doctrine. This policy meant that the United States would resist the spread of communism throughout the world. To strengthen democracies in Europe, the United States offered a massive aid package, called the Marshall Plan. Western attempts to rebuild Germany triggered a crisis over the city of Berlin. The Soviets controlled East Germany, which surrounded Berlin. To force the Western Allies out of Berlin, the Soviets blockaded West Berlin, but a year-long airlift forced them to end the blockade.

However, tensions continued to mount. In 1949, the United States and nine other nations formed a new military alliance called the North Atlantic Treaty Organization (NATO). The Soviets responded by forming the Warsaw Pact, which included the Soviet Union and seven Eastern European nations.

After World War II, the United States and the Soviet Union emerged as **superpowers**. They each created military alliances made up of nations they protected or occupied. The United States helped form the North Atlantic Treaty Organization (NATO), an alliance of Western European allies. The Soviet Union signed the Warsaw Pact with Eastern European countries. The line between the democratic West and communist East was called the Iron Curtain. Many revolts challenging Soviet domination were suppressed with military force.

(Continues on the next page.)

Lesson Vocabulary

superpower   a nation stronger than other powerful nations

Name _____ Class _____ Date _____

MODIFIED CORNELL NOTES

The superpowers also engaged in a weapons race—both developed nuclear weapons. To reduce the threat of war, the two sides held several disarmament talks. Agreements limited the number of nuclear weapons that nations could maintain, which eased Cold War tensions. This period was called the era of **détente**. It ended, however, when the Soviet Union invaded Afghanistan in 1979.

During the 1950s, Fidel Castro led a revolution in Cuba and became its leader. To bring down Castro's communist regime, U.S. President John F. Kennedy supported an invasion of Cuba, but the attempt failed. One year later, the Soviets sent nuclear missiles to Cuba. Many feared a nuclear war. After the United States blockaded Cuba, Soviet leader Nikita Khrushchev agreed to remove the missiles.

The Soviets wanted to spread communist **ideology** around the globe. When Khrushchev came to power, he eased censorship and increased tolerance. However, repression returned under Leonid Brezhnev. American leaders followed a policy of **containment**. This was a strategy of keeping communism from spreading to other nations. In addition, a "red scare" in the United States resulted in Senator Joseph McCarthy leading an internal hunt for communists in the government and military. The House Un-American Activities Committee (HUAC) also sought out communist sympathizers.

Lesson Vocabulary

détente   the relaxation of Cold War tensions during the 1970s

ideology   system of thought and belief

containment   the U.S. strategy of limiting communism to the areas already under Soviet control

Name _____ Class _____ Date _____

MODIFIED CORNELL NOTES

During the postwar period, U.S. businesses expanded into the global marketplace, and **interdependence** increased. Other nations needed goods and services to rebuild. This led to a period of economic success that changed life in the United States. During the 1950s and 1960s, **recessions** were brief and mild. As Americans prospered, they left the cities to live in the suburbs. This trend is called **suburbanization**. Also, job opportunities in the Sunbelt attracted many people to that region. By the 1970s, however, a political crisis in the Middle East made Americans aware of their dependence on imported oil. The price of oil and gas rose substantially, which meant that people had less money to buy other products. The decades of prosperity ended in 1974 with a serious recession.

During the period of prosperity, African Americans and other minorities faced **segregation** in housing and education. They suffered from **discrimination** in jobs and voting. Dr. Martin Luther King, Jr., emerged as the main civil rights leader in the 1960s. The U.S. Congress passed some civil rights legislation. Other minority groups were inspired by the movement's successes. For example, the women's rights movement helped to end much gender-based discrimination.

Western Europe rebuilt after World War II. The Marshall Plan helped restore European economies by providing U.S. aid. After the war, Germany was divided between the communist East and the democratic West, but reunited at the end of the Cold War in 1990. Under Konrad Adenauer, West Germany's chancellor from 1949 to 1963, Germany built modern cities and re-established trade. European governments also developed programs that increased

(Continues on the next page.)

Lesson Vocabulary

interdependence   mutual dependence of countries on goods, resources, labor, and knowledge from other parts of the world

recession   period of reduced economic activity

suburbanization   the movement to build up areas outside of central cities

segregation   forced separation by race, sex, religion, or ethnicity

discrimination   unequal treatment or barriers

MODIFIED CORNELL NOTES

government responsibility for the needs of people. These **welfare states** required high taxes to pay for their programs. During the 1980s, some leaders, such as Britain's Margaret Thatcher, reduced the role of the government in the economy. Western Europe also moved closer to economic unity with the European Union, an organization dedicated to establishing free trade among its members.

Japan also prospered after World War II. Its **gross domestic product** (GDP) soared. Like Germany, Japan built factories. The government protected industries by raising tariffs on imported goods. This helped create a trade surplus for Japan.

Lesson Vocabulary

welfare state   a country with a market economy but with increased government responsibility for the social and economic needs of its people

gross domestic product   the total value of all goods and services produced in a nation within a particular year

TOPIC
19
LESSON 3

Lesson Summary
COMMUNISM IN EAST ASIA

MODIFIED CORNELL NOTES

After World War II, Mao Zedong led communist forces to victory over Jiang Jieshi's Nationalists, who fled to Taiwan. Then Mao began to reshape China's economy. First, he gave land to peasants, but then called for **collectivization**. Under this system, Mao moved people from their small villages and individual farms into communes of thousands of people on thousands of acres. Known as the Great Leap Forward, the program was intended to increase farm and industrial production. Instead, it produced low-quality, useless goods and less food. Bad weather also affected crops, and many people starved.

To remove **bourgeois** tendencies from China, Mao began the Cultural Revolution. Skilled workers and managers were removed from factories and forced to work on farms or in labor camps. This resulted in a slowed economy and a threat of civil war.

At first, the United States supported the Nationalist government in Taiwan. The West was concerned that the Soviet Union and China would become allies, but border clashes led the Soviets to withdraw aid and advisors from China. U.S. leaders thought that by "playing the China card," or improving relations with the Chinese, they would further isolate the Soviets. In 1979, the United States established diplomatic relations with China.

Korea was an independent nation until Japan invaded it in World War II. After the war, American and Soviet forces agreed to divide the Korean peninsula at the 38th parallel. Kim Il Sung, a communist, ruled the North; and Syngman Rhee, allied with the United States, controlled the South. In 1950, North Korean troops attacked South Korea. The United Nations forces stopped them along a line known as the Pusan Perimeter, then began advancing north. Mao sent troops to help the North Koreans. UN forces were pushed back south of the 38th parallel.

In 1953, both sides signed an armistice to end the fighting, but troops remained on both sides of the **demilitarized zone (DMZ)**. Over time, South Korea enjoyed an economic boom and a rise in living standards, while communist North Korea's economy declined. Kim Il Sung's emphasis on self-reliance kept North Korea isolated and poor.

Lesson Vocabulary

collectivization   the forced joining together of workers and property into collectives, such as rural collectives that absorb peasants and their land

bourgeois   characteristic of the middle class

demilitarized zone (DMZ)   a thin band of territory across the Korean peninsula separating North Korean forces from South Korean forces; established by the armistice of 1953

MODIFIED CORNELL NOTES

In the 1800s, the French ruled the area in Southeast Asia called French Indochina. During World War II, Japan invaded that region, but faced resistance from **guerrillas**. After the war, the French tried to reestablish authority in Vietnam. However, forces led by communist leader Ho Chi Minh fought the colonialists. The French left Vietnam in 1954, after a Vietnamese victory at Dienbienphu. After that, Ho controlled the northern part of Vietnam while the United States supported the noncommunist government in the south.

Ho wanted to unite Vietnam. He provided aid to the National Liberation Front, or Viet Cong, a communist guerrilla organization in the south. American leaders saw Vietnam as an extension of the Cold War and developed the **domino theory**. This was the belief that if communists won in South Vietnam, then communism could spread to other governments in Southeast Asia. After a North Vietnamese attack on a U.S. Navy destroyer, Congress authorized the president to take military measures to prevent further communist aggression in Southeast Asia.

Despite massive American support, the South Vietnamese failed to defeat the Viet Cong and their North Vietnamese allies. During the Tet Offensive, the North Vietnamese attacked cities all over the south. Even though the communists were not able to hold any cities, it marked a turning point in U.S. public opinion. Upset by civilian deaths from the U.S. bombing of North Vietnam, as well as growing American casualties, many Americans began to oppose the war. President Nixon came under increasing pressure to terminate the conflict. The Paris Peace Accord of 1973 established a ceasefire, and American troops began to withdraw. Two years later, communist North Vietnam conquered South Vietnam.

Neighboring Cambodia and Laos also ended up with communist governments. In Cambodia, guerrillas called the Khmer Rouge came to power. Led by the brutal dictator Pol Pot, their policies led to a genocide that killed about one third of the population. When Vietnam invaded Cambodia, the genocide ended. Pol Pot and the Khmer Rouge were forced to retreat. Communism did not spread any farther in Southeast Asia.

Lesson Vocabulary

guerrilla   a soldier in a loosely organized force making surprise raids

domino theory   the belief that a communist victory in South Vietnam would cause noncommunist governments across Southeast Asia to fall to communism, like a row of dominoes

Name _____ Class _____ Date _____

MODIFIED CORNELL NOTES

The Soviet Union emerged from World War II as a superpower, with control over many Eastern European countries. For many people, the country's superpower status brought few rewards. Consumer goods were inferior and workers were poorly paid. Because workers had lifetime job security, there was little incentive to produce high-quality goods. Still, there were some important technological successes. One example was Sputnik I, the first artificial satellite. Keeping up with the United States in an arms race also strained the economy. Then, in 1979, Soviet forces invaded Afghanistan and became involved in a long war. The Soviets had few successes battling the **mujahedin**, or Muslim religious warriors, creating a crisis in morale in the USSR.

New Soviet leader Mikhail Gorbachev urged reforms. He called for **glasnost**. He ended censorship and encouraged people to discuss the country's problems. Gorbachev also called for **perestroika**, or a restructuring of the government and economy. His policies, however, fed unrest across the Soviet empire.

Eastern Europeans demanded an end to Soviet rule. Previous attempts to defy the Soviets had failed. When Hungarians and Czechs challenged the communist rulers, military force subdued them. By the end of the 1980s, a powerful democracy movement was sweeping the region. In Poland, Lech Walesa led Solidarity, an independent, unlawful labor union demanding economic and political changes. When Gorbachev declared he would not interfere in Eastern European reforms, Solidarity was legalized. A year later, Walesa was elected president of Poland.

Meanwhile, East German leaders resisted reform, and thousands of East Germans fled to the West. In Czechoslovakia, Václav Havel, a dissident writer, was elected president. One by one, communist governments fell. Most changes happened peacefully, but Romanian dictator Nicolae Ceausescu refused to step down and he was executed. The Baltic States regained independence. By the end of 1991, the remaining Soviet republics had all formed independent nations. The Soviet Union ceased to exist after 69 years of communist rule.

In 1992, Czechoslovakia was divided into Slovakia and the Czech Republic. Additionally, some communist governments in Asia, such as China, instituted economic reforms.

Lesson Vocabulary

mujahedin   Muslim religious warriors

glasnost   "openness" in Russian; a Soviet policy of greater freedom of expression introduced by Mikhail Gorbachev in the late 1980s

perestroika   a Soviet policy of democratic and free-market reforms introduced by Mikhail Gorbachev in the late 1980s

TOPIC 19 — Review Questions
THE COLD WAR ERA (1945–1991)

Answer the questions below using the information in the Lesson Summaries on the previous pages.

Lesson 1: A New Global Conflict
1. Who were the two superpowers during the Cold War?

_____

_____

2. Summarize What was the United States policy known as containment?

_____

_____

Lesson 2: The Western Democracies and Japan
3. What is suburbanization?

_____

_____

4. Categorize In what ways were minorities denied equality and opportunity?

_____

_____

Lesson 3: Communism in East Asia
5. What is the significance of the 38th parallel?

_____

_____

6. Summarize Summarize the effects of the Great Leap Forward on the Chinese people.

_____

_____

Lesson 4: War in Southeast Asia
7. What was significant about the Tet Offensive?

_____

_____

8. Summarize Summarize U.S. involvement in Vietnam.

_____

_____

Lesson 5: The Cold War Ends

9. How did the arms race affect the Soviet economy?

_____

_____

10. **Categorize** Which leaders mentioned in the summary supported reform and which leaders opposed reform?

_____

_____

Name _____ Class _____ Date _____

Focus Question: What events followed independence in the former European colonies of Africa, the Indian subcontinent, and the Middle East?

As you read the Lesson Summaries on the following pages, complete the graphic organizer to identify the divisions between rival groups in the Indian subcontinent, Africa, and the Middle East and the impact of these divisions.

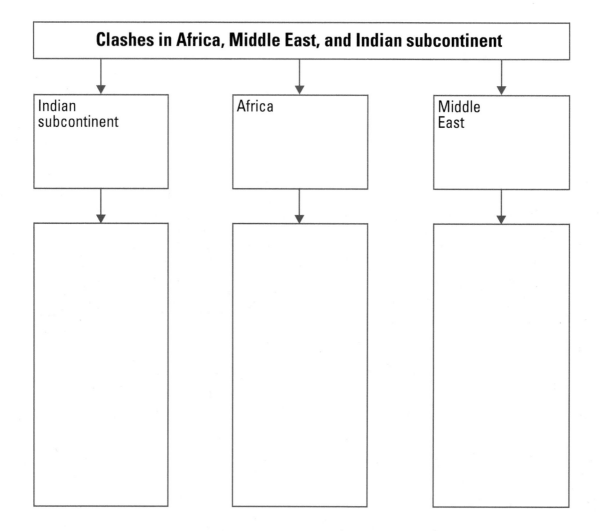

Clashes in Africa, Middle East, and Indian subcontinent

Indian subcontinent	Africa	Middle East

TOPIC 20 LESSON 1 — Lesson Summary
NEW NATIONS IN SOUTH ASIA AND SOUTHEAST ASIA

MODIFIED CORNELL NOTES

In the 1940s, tensions between Hindus and Muslims in India led to violence. The ruling British decided that the only solution was a **partition**, or division, into a Muslim-majority Pakistan and a Hindu-majority India. After Pakistan and India gained their independence in 1947, Hindus in Pakistan fled to India, while Muslims in India fled to Pakistan. As they fled, Muslims, Hindus, and another religious group called Sikhs slaughtered one another.

In 1947, Jawaharlal Nehru became India's first prime minister. He tried to improve living conditions and end discrimination against **dalits**, or outcasts. Nehru's daughter, Indira Gandhi, became prime minister in 1966. While she was in office, Sikhs pressed for independence for the state of Punjab. In 1984, Sikh separatists occupied the Golden Temple, the holiest Sikh shrine. Gandhi sent troops to the temple, and thousands of Sikhs were killed. A few months later, Gandhi's Sikh bodyguards assassinated her.

In 1947, Pakistan was a divided country. A thousand miles separated West Pakistan from East Pakistan. West Pakistan dominated the nation's government. Most people in East Pakistan were Bengalis. They felt their government neglected their region. In 1971, Bengalis declared independence for East Pakistan under the name of Bangladesh. Pakistan tried to crush the rebels, but was eventually compelled to recognize the independence of Bangladesh.

Despite their differences, India and Pakistan helped organize a conference of newly independent states in 1955. This marked the birth of **nonalignment**, or political and diplomatic independence from the United States or the Soviet Union.

Mainland Southeast Asia is a region of contrasts. Thailand and Malaysia have prospered as market economies. In Malaysia, people of Chinese and Indian descent have made the nation a leader in profitable industries. However, the government has also tried to include the Malay majority in the country's prosperity. By contrast, Myanmar, or Burma, has suffered under an **autocratic** government—a government that has unlimited power. The government has limited foreign trade, and living standards remain low. In 1990, elections were held in Myanmar, and a party that opposed military rule won. It was led by Aung San Suu Kyi. However, the military rejected the election results, and Suu Kyi was put under house arrest. She was not released until November 2010.

(Continues on the next page.)

Lesson Vocabulary

partition   a division into pieces

dalits   outcast or member of India's lowest caste

nonalignment   political and diplomatic independence from both Cold War powers

autocratic   having unlimited power

Name _____ Class _____ Date _____

TOPIC 20 LESSON 1 — Lesson Summary

NEW NATIONS IN SOUTH ASIA AND SOUTHEAST ASIA (continued)

MODIFIED CORNELL NOTES

After World War II, Indonesia, formerly the Dutch East Indies, achieved its independence. Indonesia faced many obstacles to its unity. It consists of more than 13,000 islands. Javanese make up almost half of the population, but there are hundreds of ethnic groups. After independence, Indonesia formed a democratic, parliamentary government under its first president, Sukarno. In 1966, an army general, Suharto, seized power and ruled as a dictator until 1998.

In the Philippines, Catholics are the predominant religious group, but there is a Muslim minority in the south. In 1946, the Philippines gained freedom from United States control. Although the Filipino constitution established a democratic government, a wealthy elite controlled politics and the economy. Ferdinand Marcos, elected president in 1965, became a dictator and cracked down on basic freedoms. He even had Benigno Aquino, a popular rival, murdered. When Corazon Aquino was elected in 1986, Marcos tried to deny the results, but the people forced him to resign. Since then, democracy has struggled to survive in the Philippines. Communist and Muslim rebels continue to fight across the country.

Lesson Summary
AFRICAN NATIONS WIN INDEPENDENCE

Africa is a diverse continent. Vast savannas, or tree-dotted grasslands, cover much of it, but there are also rain forests and deserts. The continent also has diverse peoples, languages, and traditions. After World War II, many Africans demanded freedom from European powers. European powers had drawn colonial boundaries without regard for Africa's ethnic groups. This led to ethnic conflict in many new nations once colonial powers withdrew.

In 1957, Gold Coast gained its freedom from Britain and took the name Ghana. The government of its first president, Kwame Nkrumah, became corrupt, and Nkrumah was overthrown in a military **coup d'état**. In Kenya, rebels turned to guerrilla warfare, but the British crushed the rebellion. Kenya finally gained its independence in 1963. Jomo Kenyatta, a prominent independence leader, became the first president of the new country.

Algeria achieved independence from France in 1962. A coup in 1965 began a long period of military rule. When the government held free elections in 1992, an Islamist party won. The military rejected the results, and seven years of civil war followed. After Congo became independent from Belgium, Joseph Mobutu ruled as a harsh military dictator from 1965 to 1997. Civil war then raged, as rivals fought to control mineral resources.

Nigeria won its independence in 1960. However, Nigeria faced ethnic, religious, and regional conflict, including a war to end a rebellion in oil-rich Biafra. A series of military dictators then ruled the country, but Nigeria returned to democracy in 1999. Angola and Mozambique fought Portugal until granted independence in 1975. In Rwanda, one of Africa's deadliest ethnic conflicts occurred. There, the extremist Hutu slaughtered about 800,000 Tutsis and moderate Hutus. Millions of Rwandans lost their homes.

In Sudan, non-Muslim peoples in the south fought Arab Muslims from the north. This, along with drought and famine, killed millions. By 2005, there was peace in the south. However, a new ethnic conflict had emerged. In Darfur, in western Sudan, government-backed Arabs attacked non-Arab Muslim villagers and drove them off their land. Deprived of the land that fed them, the villagers faced possible starvation in refugee camps. Signs of war crimes and genocide brought calls for UN peacekeepers.

Lesson Vocabulary

coup d'état   the forcible overthrow of a government

Name _____ Class _____ Date _____

TOPIC 20 LESSON 3	Lesson Summary
	THE MODERN MIDDLE EAST TAKES SHAPE

MODIFIED CORNELL NOTES

Most of the people in the Middle East are Muslims, but there are also Christian communities and the predominantly Jewish nation of Israel. Most countries also have many ethnic groups. Arabs are a majority in some countries, such as Egypt. Non-Arab Muslims are the majority in others, such as Turkey.

After World War I, Britain and France were given **mandates** over large parts of the Middle East. Under the mandate system, territories taken from the defeated Ottoman empire were administered, or run, by Europeans. Arabs resisted the mandate system. By the late 1940s, the mandates had been divided up into independent countries.

The Holocaust created support for a Jewish state after World War II. In 1947, the UN drew up a plan to divide Palestine into an Arab and a Jewish state. In 1948, Jews proclaimed the independent state of Israel. Arab rejection of the state of Israel led to war. Despite the conflicts, Israel has developed rapidly. Kibbutzim work on what is called a **kibbutz**, or collective farm, and produce crops for export. An early Israeli leader was Golda Meir, who became Israel's first woman prime minister in 1969.

After achieving independence, Middle Eastern nations set out to build strong modern economies. Only a handful of nations in the region had rich oil reserves. Most Middle Eastern nations were poor. In some countries, authoritarian military leaders seized power. In others, such as Jordan and Saudi Arabia, hereditary monarchs controlled the government. Only Israel and Turkey had stable multiparty systems.

Egypt, the most populous Arab country, controls the Suez Canal. Under Gamal Abdel Nasser, Egypt fought two unsuccessful wars against Israel. Nasser's successor, Anwar Sadat, made peace with Israel. Islamists were angry about government corruption and the failure to end poverty. In 1981, Sadat was assassinated by Muslim fundamentalists.

In 2011, popular unrest swept across the Middle East, launching pro-democracy movements, known as the "Arab Spring." Frustration with corrupt and dictatorial governments along with high unemployment fed demands for change. The "Arab Spring," which started in Tunisia, spread to Egypt and other nations.

(Continues on the next page.)

Lesson Vocabulary

mandate   after World War I, a territory administered by a Western power

kibbutz   a collective farm in Israel

Name _____ Class _____ Date _____

MODIFIED CORNELL NOTES

In Iran, Shah Mohammad Reza Pahlavi ruled with the support of the United States, which helped oust one of his opponents, Mohammad Mosaddeq. In the 1970s, the shah's enemies rallied behind Ayatollah Ruhollah Khomeini. Protests forced the shah out of power, and Khomeini established an Islamic theocracy, or government ruled by religious leaders.

Turkey became a republic in the 1920s under Ataturk. Although it is a Muslim country, most of its people are Turks, not Arabs. Turkey has served as a link between Europe and the Middle East and has also sought closer ties with its Middle Eastern neighbors. Today, Turkey is a multiparty democracy with a market economy. Clashes erupted in 2013, however, that pitted the moderate Islamist government against protesters who opposed Islamic reforms.

The Middle East has the world's largest oil and gas reserves. In 1960, the oil-producing nations of the Middle East, along with Venezuela, set up the Organization of the Petroleum Exporting Countries (OPEC). Middle Eastern members of OPEC have used oil as a political weapon. Other countries have tried to develop other sources of oil as a result. Saudi Arabia has the world's largest oil reserves. Oil wealth allowed Saudi Arabia to modernize.

Some Middle Eastern countries have adopted **secular**, or nonreligious, government and laws. However, many Muslim leaders argue that a renewed commitment to Islamic doctrine is needed. Some reformers are fundamentalist extremists who believe in using violence to achieve their goals.

Conditions for women vary greatly across the Middle East. Some have greater rights, but many still face legal and social hurdles. In Iran and Saudi Arabia, women are required to wear **hejab**, the traditional Muslim garments. In others, women have given up the traditional dress. With the "Arab Spring," more women are demanding reform and opportunity.

Lesson Vocabulary

secular   having to do with worldly, rather than religious, matters; nonreligious

hejab   headscarves and loose-fitting, ankle-length garments meant to conceal the body; traditionally worn by many Muslim women

MODIFIED CORNELL NOTES

Lesson Summary
CONFLICTS IN THE MIDDLE EAST

The Middle East has seen many conflicts. Modern Israel was created in 1948. Palestinian Arabs claimed the same land. Arab countries attacked Israel in 1967. Israel fought for its right to exist, and in the process of turning back Arab forces, it gained control of the West Bank, East Jerusalem, the Gaza Strip, and the Sinai Peninsula.

The Palestine Liberation Organization, led by Yasir Arafat, fought against the Israelis. Some Palestinians took part in uprisings called **intifadas**, and suicide bombers spread terror inside Israel. The Israelis responded with armed force, and Palestinian bitterness increased. Israeli Prime Minister Yitzhak Rabin and Yasir Arafat signed a peace accord in 1993. There were many stumbling blocks, however, such as disagreements over Jerusalem, a city sacred to Jews, Christians, and Muslims. In recent years, new conflicts flared between Israel and the Palestinians that set back hopes for peace.

Lebanon is home to diverse ethnic and religious groups. There is a delicate balance among Arab Christians, Sunni Muslims, Shiite Muslims, and Druze. Tensions among the diverse groups erupted into civil war that lasted from 1975 to 1990. Christian and Muslim **militias**, or armed groups of citizen soldiers, battled each other. Later, Israel and Syria were drawn into the fighting. Sectarian divisions remained even after a fragile peace was restored. By 2012, the civil war in neighboring Syria threatened renewed violence among rival militias in Lebanon. In addition, a huge number of refugees fled the civil war in Syria, straining Lebanon's resources.

Conflicts also plagued Iraq. Iraq's Sunni Arab minority had long dominated the country. Iraq's Kurdish minority and Shiite Arab majority were excluded from power. In 1980, Iraq's dictator Saddam Hussein fought a prolonged war against neighboring Iran. In 1990, Iraq invaded Kuwait. In response, the United States led a UN coalition that liberated Kuwait and crushed Iraqi forces in 1991. Saddam Hussein remained in power. The UN set up **no-fly zones** to protect the Kurds and Shiites.

In 2003, the United States led a coalition that invaded Iraq and overthrew Saddam Hussein because U.S. leaders believed Hussein to be building biological, nuclear, or chemical weapons, called **weapons of mass destruction (WMDs)**, though no WMDs were ultimately found. In 2005, national elections were held for the first time. However, **insurgents** and ethnic division were still obstacles. In 2011, the last American troops withdrew, leaving a Shiite-led government in control, but ongoing violence remained a problem.

Lesson Vocabulary

intifada Palestinian Arab uprising against Israel
militia armed group of citizen soldiers
no-fly zone in Iraq, area where the United States and its allies banned flights by Iraqi aircraft after the 1991 Gulf War
weapon of mass destruction (WMDs) nuclear, biological, or chemical weapon
insurgent rebel

TOPIC 20 — Review Questions
NEW NATIONS EMERGE (1945–PRESENT)

Answer the questions below using the information in the Lesson Summaries on the previous pages.

Lesson 1: New Nations in South Asia and Southeast Asia

1. What is nonalignment?

_____

_____

2. Identify Causes and Effects What caused the British to partition India? What were some of the effects the partition had on Muslims and Hindus?

_____

_____

Lesson 2: African Nations Win Independence

3. What is a coup d'état?

_____

_____

4. Identify Causes and Effects How did past decisions made by European powers cause ethnic conflict in many new African nations?

_____

_____

Lesson 3: The Modern Middle East Takes Shape

5. What is a secular government?

_____

_____

6. Identify Causes and Effects What effect did the Holocaust have on support for a Jewish state?

_____

_____

Lesson 4: Conflicts in the Middle East

7. What are the four major groups of people in Lebanon?

_____

_____

8. Summarize Summarize the events that happened in Iraq in 1990 and 1991.

_____

_____

TOPIC 21

Note Taking Study Guide

THE WORLD TODAY (1980–PRESENT)

Focus Question: How have developing nations attempted to solve the economic problems of their regions?

As you read the Lesson Summaries on the following pages, complete the graphic organizer below. Choose a difficult economic problem faced by developing nations in a particular region (Africa, Asia, or Latin America). Identify the problem and describe why it exists. Then note attempted solutions and the results of those attempts. Finally, describe the end or current result of efforts to overcome that economic problem.

Problem	What
	Why

Solution	Attempted Solutions	Results
	1.	1.
	2.	2.

End Result		

TOPIC 21 LESSON 1

Lesson Summary
CHALLENGES OF DEVELOPMENT

After World War II, a central goal in Africa, Asia, and Latin America was **development**, or creating a more advanced economy and higher living standards. Nations that are working toward this are referred to as the **developing world**. They are also called the global South, because most of these nations are south of the Tropic of Cancer. Most industrialized nations are north of the Tropic of Cancer, so they are sometimes called the global North. Nations of the global South have tried to develop economically by improving their agriculture and industry. They have also built schools to increase **literacy**.

To pay for development, many countries in the global South procured large loans from industrialized nations. For centuries, most people in the global South had lived and worked in **traditional economies**. After gaining independence from European colonists, some of these countries experimented with government-led command economies. However, when these countries had trouble paying off their loans, lenders from the global North required many of them to change to market economies. Now many developing nations depend on the global North for investment and exports.

Beginning in the 1950s, improved seeds, pesticides, and mechanical equipment led to a Green Revolution in many parts of the developing world. This increased agricultural production, feeding many more people. It also benefited large landowners at the expense of small farmers. These farmers sold their land and moved to cities.

The global South still faces many challenges. Some developing nations produce only one export product. If prices for that product drop, their economies suffer. Also, the population in many of these countries has grown rapidly. Many people are caught in a cycle of poverty. When families are forced to move to cities, they often find only low-paying jobs. As a result, many children must work to help support their families. With so many moving to cities, many people are forced to live in crowded and dangerous **shantytowns**.

(Continues on the next page.)

Lesson Vocabulary

development   the process of building stable governments, improving agriculture and industry, and raising the standard of living

developing world   nations working toward development in Africa, Asia, and Latin America

literacy   the ability to read and write

traditional economy   economy that relies on habit, custom, or ritual and tends not to change over time

shantytown   slum of flimsy shacks

Name _____ Class _____ Date _____

Lesson Summary
CHALLENGES OF DEVELOPMENT (continued)

MODIFIED CORNELL NOTES

Economic development has brought great changes to the developing world. In many countries, women have greater equality. However, some religious **fundamentalists** oppose these changes and have called for a return to the basic values of their faiths.

Lesson Vocabulary

fundamentalist   religious leader who calls for a return to what he or she sees as the fundamental, or basic, values of his or her faith

TOPIC 21 LESSON 2

Lesson Summary

CHALLENGES FOR AFRICAN NATIONS

A close look at South Africa reveals the problems that many African countries have faced with building national unity. After South Africa achieved self-rule in 1910, the white minority controlled the government and the economy. During the period of **apartheid**, the white-minority government passed laws that severely restricted the black majority. The African National Congress (ANC), with Nelson Mandela as one of its leaders, opposed apartheid and led the struggle for majority rule. A massacre by government troops at Sharpeville in 1960 brought world condemnation, and the work of Anglican bishop Desmond Tutu helped rally opposition. After sanctions by many world countries, South African president F.W. deKlerk ended apartheid in 1990 and released Nelson Mandela from prison. Mandela was then elected president in the country's first multiracial elections.

After World War II, African nations had little capital to invest, so they had to make difficult economic choices. Some nations chose **socialism**, a system in which the government controls parts of the economy. The leaders of these governments hoped to end foreign influence in their countries and to close the gap between the rich and the poor. However, socialism sometimes led to large, inefficient bureaucracies. Other nations relied on capitalism, or market economies. These economies were often more efficient, but foreign owners of businesses took profits out of the country. Some governments tried to fund development by growing crops for export, rather than food crops. However, this forced them to import food to replace the food crops. Governments then had to subsidize part of the cost of importing food from overseas.

African nations faced many obstacles to development. Droughts led to famine in parts of Africa. This was especially true in the Sahel, where overgrazing and farming led to **desertification**. People in African nations also faced the devastating disease AIDS. Since the 1980s, millions of children in Africa have been orphaned by AIDS. **Urbanization** has also created problems in Africa. This shift from rural areas to cities has meant hardship for many and has weakened traditional cultures and ethnic ties. However, in West Africa, the growth of urban markets has increased opportunities for women.

(Continues on the next page.)

Lesson Vocabulary

apartheid   a policy of rigid segregation of nonwhite people in the Republic of South Africa

socialism   system in which people as a whole, rather than private individuals, own all property and operate all businesses

desertification   process by which fertile or semidesert land becomes desert

urbanization   movement of people from rural areas to cities

TOPIC 21 LESSON 2

Lesson Summary

CHALLENGES FOR AFRICAN NATIONS (continued)

Another concern in Africa is environmental threats. Many of Africa's animal habitats have been destroyed, causing many animals to become **endangered species**. Other animal species are being killed for their tusks or fur. One environmental activist, Wangari Maathai, has fought back by starting the Green Belt Movement. This organization promotes reforestation. It also helps local women with projects of **sustainable development** that aim to provide lasting benefits for future generations.

Lesson Vocabulary

endangered species   species threatened with extinction

sustainable development   development that meets the needs of the present without compromising the ability of future generations to meet their own needs

Name _____ Class _____ Date _____

TOPIC **21** LESSON 3	**Lesson Summary**
	RAPID DEVELOPMENT IN CHINA AND INDIA

MODIFIED CORNELL NOTES

After Mao Zedong died, moderate leaders took control of China. Deng Xiaoping began a program called the Four Modernizations, which allowed some features of a free-market economy. Some private ownership of property was permitted, and entrepreneurs could set up businesses. Farmers were allowed to sell surplus produce and keep the profits. Foreign investment was also welcomed. These reforms brought a surge of economic growth, although a gap developed between poor farmers and wealthy city dwellers. After 30 years of reforms, China's economic output quadrupled.

Despite these economic reforms, however, Communist leaders refused to allow more political freedom. Demonstrators seeking democratic reforms occupied Tiananmen Square in Beijing in May 1989. When the demonstrators refused to disperse, the government sent in troops and tanks. Thousands were killed or wounded.

China continues to face many challenges. Its population is the largest in the world. Many rural workers have moved to cities, but they often live in poverty there. Pollution and HIV/AIDS are also problems. Critics of the government are jailed, and human rights abuses continue. The government started the **one-child policy** to prevent population growth from hurting economic development. Population growth slowed.

By contrast, India has a democratic government. After gaining independence, India's government adopted a socialist model, but development was uneven. The Green Revolution in the 1960s improved crop output, but most farmers continued to use traditional methods. Since the 1980s, India has shifted to a free-market system. Despite setbacks, it has grown greatly in industry and technology.

Despite these improvements, India's population growth has hurt efforts to improve living conditions. The Indian government backed family planning, but it had limited success. More than one third of Indians live below the poverty line. Many rural families moved to overcrowded cities like Kolkata and Mumbai. To help the urban poor, Mother Teresa founded the Missionaries of Charity.

Changes in India have brought improvements for India's lowest social castes and women. India's constitution bans discrimination against **dalits**, people in the lowest caste, but prejudice persists. The constitution also grants equal rights to women.

Lesson Vocabulary

one-child policy   a Chinese government policy limiting urban families to a single child

dalits   member of India's lowest caste

Name _____ Class _____ Date _____

MODIFIED CORNELL NOTES

In the 1950s and 1960s, many governments in Latin America encouraged industries to manufacture goods that had previously been imported. This is called **import substitution**. More recently, government policies have focused on producing goods for export. Governments have also tried to open more land to farming, but much of the best land belongs to large **agribusinesses**. In many countries, a few people control the land and businesses, and wealth is distributed unevenly. Another problem is population growth, which has contributed to poverty. Many religious leaders have worked for justice and an end to poverty in a movement known as liberation theology. One reformer, Archbishop Oscar Romero of El Salvador, preached **liberation theology** until he was assassinated in 1980.

Because of poverty and inequality, democracy has been difficult to achieve in Latin America. Between the 1950s and 1970s, military leaders seized power in Argentina, Brazil, Chile, and other countries. From the 1960s to the 1990s, civil wars shook parts of Central America. In Guatemala, the military targeted the **indigenous** population and slaughtered thousands of Native Americans. When socialist rebels called Sandinistas came to power in Nicaragua, the United States supported the **contras**, guerrillas who fought the Sandinistas.

By the 1990s, democratic reforms led to free elections in many countries. In Mexico, the Institutional Revolutionary Party (PRI) had dominated the government since the 1920s. In 2000, an opposition candidate was elected president. However, PRI candidate Enrique Peña Nieto was elected in 2012, and his administration pledged numerous reforms and promised to improve the economy and fight organized crime.

(Continues on the next page.)

Lesson Vocabulary

import substitution   manufacturing goods locally to replace imports

agribusiness   giant commercial farm, often owned by a multinational corporation

liberation theology   movement within the Catholic Church that urged the church to become a force for reform and social justice and to put an end to poverty

indigenous   original or native to a country or region

contra   guerrilla who fought the Sandinistas in Nicaragua

Name _____ Class _____ Date _____

MODIFIED CORNELL NOTES

The United States has had a powerful influence in Latin America. It has dominated the Organization of American States (OAS). During the Cold War, the United States backed dictators who were anti-communist. The United States has also pressed Latin American governments to help stop the drug trade. Many Latin Americans alleged that the problem was not in Latin America but was based on the demand for drugs in the United States.

Argentina experienced years of political upheavals beginning in the 1930s. Juan Perón, Argentina's president from 1946 to 1955, enjoyed great support from workers but was ousted in a military coup. The military seized control again in 1976 and murdered or kidnapped thousands. Mothers whose sons and daughters were missing protested and became known as the Mothers of the Plaza de Mayo. By 1983, the military was forced to allow elections.

Name _____ Class _____ Date _____

MODIFIED CORNELL NOTES

The end of the Cold War brought major changes to the world economy and balance of power. The division between communist Eastern and democratic Western Europe crumbled. At the same time, new challenges emerged, including a rise in unemployment and in immigration from the developing world. One exciting change was the reunification of Germany. However, East Germany's economy was weak and had to be modernized. Another change was that NATO became more of a peacekeeping organization with an emphasis on protecting human rights.

In the 1990s, the European Economic Community became the European Union (EU). The **euro** soon became the common currency for most of Western Europe. More than a dozen new countries have joined the EU, including some Eastern European nations. The expanded EU allowed Europe to compete economically with the United States and Japan. However, older members of the EU worried that the weak economies of Eastern European nations might harm the EU. Northern Ireland and Ireland also became politically linked when Protestants and Catholics in different parts of the country agreed to a power-sharing agreement.

One long-standing conflict in Europe has been mostly resolved. Britain kept control of Northern Ireland. After violence that lasted for three decades, both sides signed a peace accord, known as the Good Friday Agreement in 1998. There is now a power-sharing government.

After the breakup of the Soviet Union, Russia struggled to forge a market economy. In 1998, Russia **defaulted** on much of its foreign debt. High inflation and the collapse of the Russian currency forced banks and businesses to close. When Vladimir Putin became president in 2000, he promised to end corruption and strengthen Russia's economy. However, he also increased government power at the expense of civil liberties. In 2008, Putin stepped down as president, but in 2012 he was elected to another six-year term.

(Continues on the next page.)

Lesson Vocabulary

euro   common currency used by most member nations of the European Union

default   fail to make payments

TOPIC 21 LESSON 5

Lesson Summary
THE INDUSTRIALIZED WORLD (continued)

After the Cold War, the United States became the world's only superpower. It waged wars in Afghanistan and Iraq. An economic boom in the 1990s produced a budget **surplus** in the United States. Within a decade, however, slow economic growth and soaring military expenses led to huge budget **deficits**. In 2008, a financial crisis shook the American economy, sparking a global recession. President Obama responded with a multi-billion-dollar economic stimulus package to revive the economy. In addition, the federal government provided financial support for banks and car manufacturers. By 2013, the stock market had recovered, but unemployment remained high.

The former Soviet republics have struggled to find their way after independence. Ethnic and religious tensions have fueled tensions both internally and with Russia. In 1994, separatists in Chechnya tried to break away from Russian rule, but the revolt was crushed. Azerbaijan, Armenia, and Georgia all had difficulties during their struggles for independence.

Yugoslavia had been a **multi-ethnic** country, made up of Serbs, Montenegrins, and Macedonians. Ethnic, nationalist, and religious tensions tore Yugoslavia apart during the 1990s. Yugoslavia was made up of six republics, but the fall of communism fed nationalist unrest. Republics broke away and declared independence. Civil war erupted in Bosnia when it declared independence. Serbian president Slobodan Milosevic supported Bosnian Serbs in their attempt to set up their own government. War broke out in Kosovo as well. **Ethnic cleansing** was carried out during these wars.

The Pacific Rim nations have become a rising force in the global economy. Following World War II, Japan became an economic powerhouse and dominated this region. However, by the 1990s, Japan's economy began to suffer, while China's economy boomed. Other powerhouses include the "Asian tigers"—Taiwan, Hong Kong, Singapore, and South Korea—which are known for their electronics exports. All of these economies suffered during the global recession that began in 2008, but all have recovered and continue to grow.

Lesson Vocabulary

surplus an amount that is more than needed; excess

deficit gap between what a government spends and what it takes in through taxes and other sources

multi-ethnic made up of several ethnic groups

ethnic cleansing the killing or forcible removal of people of different ethnicities from an area by aggressors so that only the ethnic group of the aggressors remains

TOPIC 21 LESSON 6

Lesson Summary
GLOBALIZATION AND TRADE

MODIFIED CORNELL NOTES

Globalization defines the post–Cold War world. It is the process by which national economies, politics, and cultures become integrated with those of other nations. One effect of globalization is economic **interdependence**. This means that countries depend on one another for goods, resources, knowledge, and labor.

Improvements in transportation and communication, the spread of democracy, and the rise of free trade have made the world more interdependent. Developed nations control much of the world's capital, trade, and technology. Yet they rely on workers in developing countries, to which they **outsource** jobs to save money or increase efficiency. Globalization has also encouraged the rise of **multinational corporations** that have branches and assets in many countries.

One effect of interdependence is that an economic crisis in one region can have a worldwide impact. For example, any change to the global oil supply affects economies all around the world. Another example is debt. Poor nations need to borrow capital from rich nations in order to modernize. When poor nations cannot repay their debts, both poor nations and rich nations are hurt.

Many international organizations and treaties make global trade possible. The United Nations deals with a broad range of issues. The World Bank gives loans and advice to developing nations. The International Monetary Fund promotes global economic growth. The World Trade Organization (WTO) tries to ensure that trade flows smoothly and freely. It opposes **protectionism**—the use of tariffs to protect a country's industries from competition. Regional trade **blocs**, such as the EU in Europe, NAFTA in North America, and APEC in Asia, promote trade within regions.

(Continues on the next page.)

Lesson Vocabulary

globalization   the process by which national economies, politics, cultures, and societies become integrated with those of other nations around the world

interdependence   mutual dependence of countries on goods, resources, labor, and knowledge from other parts of the world

outsource   the practice of sending work to companies in the developing world in order to save money or increase efficiency

multinational corporation   company with branches in many countries

protectionism   the use of tariffs and other restrictions to protect a country's home industries against competition

bloc   a group of nations acting together in support of one another

Name _____ Class _____ Date _____

<table>
<tr><td>TOPIC
21
LESSON 6</td><td>## Lesson Summary
GLOBALIZATION AND TRADE (continued)</td></tr>
</table>

MODIFIED CORNELL NOTES

Global trade has many benefits. It brings consumers a greater variety of goods and services. It generally keeps prices lower. It also exposes people to new ideas and technology. However, some people oppose globalization of trade. They claim that rich countries exploit poor countries and that the emphasis on profits encourages too-rapid development. This endangers **sustainability**, thereby threatening future generations.

Lesson Vocabulary

sustainability   balances people's needs today with the need to preserve the environment for future generations

Name _____ Class _____ Date _____

TOPIC 21 LESSON 7

Lesson Summary

SOCIAL AND ENVIRONMENTAL ISSUES

MODIFIED CORNELL NOTES

Poverty, disasters, and disease are still challenges today. The gap between rich and poor nations is growing. Half the world's population earns less than $2 a day. Poverty is a complex issue with many causes. Many poor nations owe billions in debt and have little money to spend to improve living conditions. Political upheavals, civil war, corruption and poor planning inhibit efforts to reduce poverty. Rapid population growth and urbanization also contribute to poverty.

Natural disasters cause death and destruction around the world. One example is the **tsunami** in the Indian Ocean in 2004. Other natural disasters include earthquakes, floods, avalanches, droughts, fires, hurricanes, and volcanic eruptions. Natural disasters can cause unsanitary conditions that lead to disease. Global travel makes it possible for diseases to spread quickly. When a disease spreads rapidly, it is called an **epidemic**. HIV/AIDS is an epidemic that has killed millions. Natural disasters can also cause **famine**. Wars and problems with food distribution also contribute to famine. Poverty, disasters, and wars have forced many people to become **refugees**.

International agreements, such as the Universal Declaration of Human Rights and the Helsinki Accords, have tried to guarantee basic human rights around the world. However, human rights abuses continue. Women in both the developed and developing world often lack equal rights. Worldwide, children suffer terrible abuses. In some nations, they are forced to serve as soldiers or slaves. **Indigenous people** around the world also face discrimination and exploitation.

(Continues on the next page.)

Lesson Vocabulary

tsunami very large, damaging wave caused by an earthquake or very strong wind

epidemic outbreak of a rapidly spreading disease

famine a severe shortage of food in which large numbers of people starve

refugee a person who flees from home or country to seek refuge elsewhere, often because of political upheaval or famine

indigenous peoples term generally used to describe the descendants of the earliest inhabitants of a region

TOPIC 21 LESSON 7

Lesson Summary

SOCIAL AND ENVIRONMENTAL ISSUES (continued)

Industrialization and the world population explosion have caused damage to the environment. Strip mining, chemical pesticides and fertilizers, and oil spills are all environmental threats. Gases from power plants and factories produce **acid rain**. Pollution from nuclear power plants is another threat. Desertification and **deforestation** are major problems in certain parts of the world. Deforestation can lead to **erosion** and is a special threat to the rain forests. One hotly debated issue is **global warming**. Many scientists believe that Earth's temperature has risen because of gases released during the burning of fossil fuels. Others argue that global warming is due to natural fluctuations in Earth's climate.

Lesson Vocabulary

acid rain   a form of pollution in which toxic chemicals in the air come back to Earth in the form of rain, snow, or hail

deforestation   the destruction of forest land

erosion   the wearing away of land

global warming   the increase in Earth's average surface temperature over time

Name _____ Class _____ Date _____

MODIFIED CORNELL NOTES

During the Cold War, the United States and the Soviet Union built up arsenals of nuclear weapons. To ensure that nuclear weapons did not **proliferate**, or spread rapidly, many nations signed the Nuclear Nonproliferation Treaty (NPT) in 1968. However, the treaty does not guarantee that nuclear weapons will not be used. Some nations have not signed the treaty. Others are suspected of violating it. Nuclear weapons, along with chemical and biological weapons, make up a category of weapons called weapons of mass destruction (WMD).

Recently, terrorist groups and **rogue states** have begun to use WMDs for their own purposes. **Terrorism** is the use of violence, especially against civilians, to achieve political goals. Terrorist groups use headline-grabbing tactics to draw attention to their demands. Regional terrorist groups, such as the Irish Republican Army (IRA), have operated for decades. Increasingly, the Middle East has become a training ground and source for terrorism. Islamic fundamentalism motivates many of these groups. One important Islamic fundamentalist group is al Qaeda, whose leader was Osama bin Laden. Al Qaeda terrorists were responsible for the attacks on the United States on September 11, 2001.

In response to these attacks, the United States and other nations made fighting terrorism a priority. In 2001, Osama bin Laden and other al Qaeda leaders were living in Afghanistan. Afghanistan's government was controlled by the Taliban, an Islamic fundamentalist group. When the Taliban would not surrender the terrorists, the United States and its allies overthrew the Taliban and supported the creation of a new government. Because President Bush claimed that Iraq had WMDs, the United States later declared war on Iraq.

During the early 2000s, concerns grew that North Korea was developing nuclear weapons. In 2006, North Korea actually tested such a weapon. Meanwhile, Iran announced plans to develop nuclear power plants. The United States and other nations, however, believed that Iran aimed to build nuclear weapons, too. The United States and other countries worked to stop this nuclear proliferation.

Lesson Vocabulary

proliferate   to multiply rapidly

rogue state   nation that ignores international law and threatens other nations

terrorism   deliberate use of random violence, especially against civilians, to achieve political goals

Lesson Summary
ADVANCES IN SCIENCE AND TECHNOLOGY

MODIFIED CORNELL NOTES

Since 1945, scientific research and technological developments have transformed human existence. One example is the exploration of space. During the Cold War, the United States and the Soviet Union competed in a "space race." This began in 1957 when the Soviet Union launched Sputnik, the first **artificial satellite**. By 1969, the United States had landed the first human on the moon. Both super-powers explored military uses of space and sent spy satellites to orbit Earth.

Since the end of the Cold War, however, nations have worked in space together. For example, several countries are involved in the International Space Station (ISS). Thousands of artificial satellites belonging to many countries now orbit Earth. They are used for communication, observation, and navigation.

Another important technological development is the invention of the computer. It has led to the "Information Age." Personal computers, or PCs, have replaced typewriters and account books in homes and businesses. Factories now use computerized robots, and computers remotely control satellites and probes in space. The **Internet** links computer systems worldwide and allows people to communicate instantly around the globe. It also allows people to access vast storehouses of information that were unavailable before.

(Continues on the next page.)

Lesson Vocabulary

artificial satellite   manmade object that orbits a larger body in space

Internet   a huge international computer network linking millions of users around the world

Lesson Summary
ADVANCES IN SCIENCE AND TECHNOLOGY (continued)

MODIFIED CORNELL NOTES

Other important developments have occurred in medicine and **biotechnology**—the application of biological research to industry, engineering, and technology. Vaccines have been developed that help prevent the spread of diseases. In the 1970s, surgeons learned to transplant human organs. **Lasers** have made many types of surgery safer and more precise. Computers and other technologies have helped doctors diagnose and treat diseases. The fields of genetics and genetic engineering have made dramatic advances. **Genetics** is the study of genes and heredity. **Genetic engineering** is the manipulation of genetic material to produce specific results. Genetic research has produced new drug therapies to fight human diseases and has created new strains of disease-resistant fruits and vegetables. Genetic cloning has many practical applications in raising livestock and in research. However, cloning raises ethical questions about the role of science in creating and changing life.

Lesson Vocabulary

biotechnology   the application of biological research to industry, engineering, and technology

lasers   a high-energy light beam that can be used for many purposes, including surgery, engineering, and scientific research

genetics   a branch of biology dealing with heredity and variations among plants and animals

genetic engineering   manipulation of living organism's chemical code in order to produce specific results

Lesson 9: Advances in Science and Technology

17. What are the three uses of artificial satellites?

_____

_____

18. **Compare** How have people benefited from advances in science and technology since the space race began?

_____

_____